Enigmatic North-East

Attention Authors

'We Convert Fighters into Writers'. That's the motto of Manas Publications since more than four decades. Our message to the world is that India can win the battle not only by the bullet but also by the pen. There is no dearth of intellectuals in our country, but their knowledge is confined to them only. No sincere effort has been made by any other publisher to channelise their knowledge in national interest. That is why the talent of a large number of intellectuals remains latent. An author transforms his knowledge into a manuscript, and it is our job to spread his/her knowledge by converting it into a beautiful book. For over four decades, Manas has been motivating the intellectuals by publishing their manuscripts and would like to publish your manuscript too. If you or your colleagues have any manuscript ready for publication or are working on it, kindly contact us with detailed synopsis and list of contents. We will transform your work into a valuable publication. If you wish, we can also suggest you the suitable subjects for writing the books related to your area of expertise. Manas is known for its publishing quality and commitments. We take utmost care in production and give wide publicity to the book as well as its author through our national and international distribution network.

Enigmatic North-East

A Novel by

Lt Col (Dr) Mohit Nayal

Manas Publications
(We Convert Fighters into Writers)
New Delhi-110002 (INDIA)

MANAS PUBLICATIONS
(We convert Fighters into Writers)
(Publishers, Library Suppliers, Importers & Exporters)
4402/5-A, Ansari Road (Opp. HDFC Bank)
Darya Ganj, New Delhi-110 002 (India)
Off: ✆ 011-23260783, 23265523, Res: 011-23842660
Fax: 011-23272766
E-mail: manaspublications@gmail.com
manaspublications@yahoo.com
Website: www. manaspublications.in

ISBN 978-81-7049-479-9
₹ 595/-

Designed at
Manas Publications

Printed in India at
H S Offsets, Delhi
and published by Mrs Suman Lata for
Manas Publications, 4402/5-A,
Ansari Road, (Opp HDFC Bank),
Darya Ganj, New Delhi-110 002 (INDIA)

PREFACE

The region of Northeast India, especially the state of Manipur, is perceived to be fairly backward and volatile. Such perception has overshadowed the beautiful region and its people. This work is dedicated to the people of Manipur who even today find the larger majority of country's population insensitive towards them. There is a need for better understanding of the situation within Manipur and the lives of the people. Above all, the book is an attempt to highlight the goodness and upright character of the common people of the state. To elaborate this aspect regarding people of Northeast, there is an old saying in this region that once God visited our great country and wanted to distribute some important attributes of human personality to its people. He gave more beauty to the people from the Northern region. To the people from the South, He gave a sharper mind. To the people of Western region, He gave blessings for more materialistic riches. When it came to the people of the Northeast region, He gave emotions in abundance. An insight of God gifts to the people reflects that He parted the best human attribute to the people here. As a matter of fact, without human emotions one cannot appreciate the power of mind, the beauty of body and soul and riches of this world. The book will also subtly unfold the culture of Manipur and provide information about various places of interest.

Arun, Rajiv, Rashid, Max, Dhayan Singh Hashnam and Esha are friends who are studying together in a management institute in South India. They share no commonality in their backgrounds but still they develop a unique bonding amongst themselves. Max and Dhayan Singh are both from the state of Manipur. During the term break, the group decides to visit Manipur for attending the marriage of Hashnam's twin sister. Apart from attending a Meitei marriage in which various culture and traditions of Manipur are highlighted, the group also visits various places of interest in and around Imphal. This is also an opportunity for this group of students to closely interact with the people of Manipur at close quarters. Within the group, the trip further facilitates the development of interpersonal relations amongst them. Friends become closer friends. The relation of love between Arun and Esha mature to a commitment for marriage.

However when all seems to be going good, a situation develops. Rashid is abducted by a militant outfit. Initially, motives for such actions are beyond the understanding of all those who are absolved in the crisis. Some questions arise which are difficult to answer. Somewhere the clues indicate that Max has a role in the abduction. The motive for such treachery stays unknown till Max's past gets disclosed. which he had never disclosed to anyone. What is Max's past? Will Rashid return safe? Will the goodwill developed in the heart of the visitors get tarnished? Will friends become enemy? Will the image of Manipur and its people stay volatile in the larger perception? The story will go through the roller coaster ride finding answers to all these issues.

I wish to thank my wife Smita who whole heartedly encouraged me to write this book. Without her support it would never have been possible to develop the sensitivity about the region and its people. Abhiraj, my son who never complained regarding my self -imposed isolation for completion of this work. My parents, whose blessings have always motivated me to put in my sincere efforts.

Lt Col (Dr) Mohit Nayal
email: mohitnayal16@gmail.com

Ruskin Bond Speaks

Good wishes to Mohit Nayal
for the success of his book,
"The Enigmatic Northeast".
May it find many readers!

Ruskin Bond
14/12/13

ENIGMATIC NORTH-EAST

Doesn't fair and equal opportunity in itself reflect the scope of progress and growth? Although, this may be accepted without contention in the intellectual fraternity but on the other side the common man may spend his entire life marvelling the genesis of the norms which are popularly been encouraged in all civilized societies across the world. The criticality arises with regards to redefining and deliberating upon the concept of fairness and equal opportunity. Are all human beings under competitiveness availing this brand equity in parity with others? If not, then the words like fairness and equal opportunity seem so pretentious. This is the way Rashid felt.

The loud bang on the door startled Rashid, who was on his solo philosophical journey in the dream land, so badly, that he almost felt as if his heart had missed a beat. Before he could recover and react, Lalu lurched inside the room with the cups and the tea kettle.

Rashid gasped and shouted, "Next time, you enter my room like this I will hammer your head off."

Lalu mechanically filled the cup with tea as if he was all alone in the room and hurriedly moved towards the door. Before exit, he looked at Rashid who was still staring at him and smiled. His missing canines between the incisors and the premolars gave him weird look. Through the gaps of his teeth he said, "Bhaiya ji, you have still not cleared your dues for the last two months. Seth is not happy." Rashid's blazing eyes stared at the boy and it was enough for him to vaporize. He felt so incensed that had the boy stayed a moment longer, he would have instigated a violent reaction.

Sipping the tea, Rashid tried to recall his thoughts before the ugly intruder had arrived. Suddenly, it struck him that the clock on the study table showed ten minutes past four o'clock. There was an evening guest lecture scheduled to start in next twenty minutes. He had to be real fast to make it on time. Post lunch, his friends had decided to stay at the library whereas he had excused himself claiming to catch up some sleep. Now, there was no possibility of a hitch ride as the hostel corridors were near empty. The Dean, Mr R R Vankatash will be in attendance and his absence, if registered, would prove to be disastrous. Rashid was out of his room in next three minutes and ran towards the South Block where the lecture was due. His legs and lungs were put to extreme test limits. Last time he probably ran was five months prior that too four hundred meters to catch a fleeing bus. He cursed the scheduled lecture, its guest speaker Mr Mathew from HBC Bank, the distance from hostel location to the South Block and his own physical and mental state. There was a door at the rear entrance of the hall and Rashid sneaked in. Mr R R Vankatash had just started with the welcome note for the guest speaker. Somehow, Rashid managed to get a seat. He was still shaking with the trauma of the Olympic sprint of last fifteen minutes and was profoundly sweating.

By now, Mr Mathew had taken charge of the dais and beamed a confident smile. He said that twenty years ago he had almost joined this institute but an opportunity to study abroad lead to the loss of not becoming the alumni of this great management institution. The Dean was possibly unaware of this fact, as one could see him turning over his notes. Whether it was a compliment or a matter of relief to Mathew stayed unknown. Mr Mathew said, "Friends, we all are very fortunate to be living in such challenging times where the country has opened the window of equal opportunity to all". Rashid was reminded of his solo philosophical debate in the afternoon. The world economic recession and its implications for India were to be covered in the next two hours.

Mathew filled his lungs with what was left of the fresh air in the jam-packed hall of two hundred fifty students and staff members. He blurted, "A number of developed economies such as Greece, Italy, Turkey and Spain have reeled under the impact of debt crisis. The American economy is slowly moving on a down slide. Even the Indian markets are feeling the heat, with Nifty falling twenty six percent from 6,177 to 4,888 between January 1 and October 7."

The start was good and a large number of dirigible book worms had already started noting down the gospel facts which were being decimated. Amongst the numerous scalps that Rashid saw from the rear, he could not locate his friends. He was sure that the rascals would be sitting together as usual somewhere. By the time he zoomed at the near distance, his face lost all colour. He was sitting in the row that was occupied by the faculty members of the institution. On his left was Prof P K Das, who had yesterday caught him, sleeping during the statistics lecture. Rashid felt so cautious that he could almost feel Das breathe through his broad nostrils. The only saving grace was that the lights on top, at the rear were dim and probably if the faculty members were listening to the speaker attentively then his presence would go unnoticed. Now, he truly prayed that Mathew delivers a good lecture.

With surgical precision Mathew was doing the post-mortem of the world economic crisis of the past three years. "In 2008, when the world faced an economic recession, central banks of all leading economies had extended emergency credit, cumulated with higher government spending and reduced rate of interest. This policy took almost two years to stabilize the economies of various countries. However, in present situation the scope of such drastic measures will fail to accomplish any worthwhile dividends. This was primarily due to two outcomes. Firstly, the interest rates across United States and Europe were already close to zero. Secondly, many governments did not hold enough financial resources to undertake any further spending. As far as India is concerned, in spite of stock market sharply declining by 60 percent, the Indian financial institutions remained strong," said Mathew

Rashid was hardly listening to the speaker as his mind was more absorbed in somehow making himself invisible. He internally continued cursing his bad luck as usual and was tempted a number of times to get up and disappear. Knowing the risk involved Rashid sat. Mathew was now moving from one end of the central platform to the other. In the background of his PowerPoint presentation, he rattled down data which ensured that students got profoundly busy in making notes. To a neutral observer he would have looked more like alienated Hitler before the Barbarossa campaign. The Indian economy and its achievements were elaborated and the future of the finance world was assured to be a promising one. The market analysis of investments in all sectors was covered. As far as Rashid was concerned, he felt that he was a man for marketing and not suited for the world of finance. His close friends strongly felt that his decision was a big mistake and he would not survive in the marketing arena for long. This was the main reason to opt for marketing and prove the bastards wrong.

It was Arun in their group who was keen to join some financial institute once the course was over. After all, as a banker's son it seemed to be quite a natural choice. Arun's father was a senior manager with the State Bank of India in Delhi and his family affluence at times perturbed Rashid. He always wondered as to why some people had all the luck? Initially, when Arun joined the institute, his popularity amongst the opposite sex led to a natural envy among his peers. Rashid was no different. Arun was a tall, fair, well-built, intelligent Punjabi boy who was well-groomed and had best of the education and family background. However, over the last two years both these young men had become friends even though there was hardly anything common in their backgrounds. Rather in one way, none of the others in their group had anything in common. That is what had made their group so different and unique.

Rashid had lost his father when he was seven years old. At the time of his father's death, the family included his mother and two sisters aged ten and four. Rashid's father Mohammad Rashool Khan was a foreman in the textile factory in Surat. His own father had migrated as a young boy from Jalalabad which became part of Pakistan. There was no further family links of theirs in Pakistan. Mohammad's father died as a poor labourer and left behind four kids. Rashid's father was the youngest, who completed his elementary education and became a foreman in a factory. In 1979, when Mohammad also died, his wife along with her children went to live at her brother's house in Muzaffarnagar. From then on, Rashid had no contact with his remaining paternal relatives. He did not have much memories of his own father. All that he remembered was a man who used to wear a blue uniform and came back home late after a long day's work. They all used to call him 'Abba' who never scolded them and on holidays he took Rashid to the Masjid. On their way back from Masjid, as a routine, Abba apart from buying Gajra for Ammi, also purchased *Jalebees* for the whole family. Sometimes, in his lonely moments he used to miss his father who he barely knew. Rashid's mother did not want to tax her brother for long who had his own family to fend. Thus, she stitched clothes of the neighbours and did other menial jobs to survive. With the assistance of her brother, soon she managed a small house of her own. For this illiterate woman, her biggest achievement was Rashid, her son. Rashid from the very beginning was a brilliant student and today he was part of this premium management institution. The flash back of Rashid came to an abrupt end when he heard the standing ovation being given to Mr Mathew.

Rashid quickly moved out of the hall avoiding any attention from the faculty members. He checked his watch. It was about to be 6.30 in the evening and still there was adequate sunlight in this part of the country. As compared to the regions of North India, South had more moderate temperature. He thought of sending an SMS to his friends but as an after thought decided to rather wait for them to come out of the hall. The examination dates had been put on the notice board and the first paper of this semester was to start in another two weeks. The coming two weeks were going to be really very busy. From tonight he would plan his schedule to cover the syllabus well in time. If Max, Hashnam, Rajiv and Arun were serious, then they could pull up the common subjects with joint studies. The big question was why these guys were not moving out? Rashid went and stood near the parking. From here, he would be able to keep an eye on the hordes leaving the hall. Within next ten minutes, huge crowd of students moved out of the hall. Now, it was all the more difficult for Rashid to trace his friends. So finally, he called Rajiv on his mobile and confirmed his location. Almost all of them assumed that Rashid had missed the lecture.

"Lazy bump! You missed the lecture and the beautiful chick of the HBC Bank," said Max.

"Bloody chap; don't try to throw that smart one. All along I sat next to that horrible P K Das and watched that finance wizard rape you. And yes! There was no chick, only chickens like you. Where is Arun?"

"He said he will drop Esha home. Oh! By the way, I forgot to tell you guys that tonight the Tintin movie is on at Inox. Anyone interested?" said Hashnam.

Rashid couldn't resist himself and took out the folded sheet of paper which he started unwrapping. Hashnam was excited, "Hey great guy! You already purchased the tickets?"

"No moron, this is the schedule of the third semester finals that Ramchander had put on notice board after the class. I got a copy from the hostel notice board," said Rashid. Ramchander was the coordinator of the institute who loved to throw surprises and screw the happiness of others around. The exams had been scheduled a month in advance. This was planned so as the month of December would be for the projects and on-job-training.

Hashnam could not hide his disappointment. Max put his hand around his shoulder, "You'll miss Tintin, huh."

"No yaar! But my sister's marriage is scheduled for next month. I hope Ramchander and his likes don't mess up the plan."

Rashid put the piece of paper under his nose and adjusted his glasses. "As per the schedule, once the exams are over we get a break of two weeks and then it will be time for one month on-job-training. That means Hashnam, that, Ramchander has rather worked it quite well for you and us," Rashid said.

It was 15 October and the exams were to start from Ist November. All of them decided to get together anyhow at the cafeteria by eight.

Max and Hashnam were the first to reach the cafeteria and selected their usual place. Although, the ragging was out of tradition within the campus still the juniors did not occupy the seats usually reserved for their seniors. Max and Hashnam were roommates and incidentally both belonged to the state of Manipur. They used to hang around together and had become at ease to be addressed as 'Chinks'. Max was a good guitarist and sang English numbers which were liked by all. He claimed having a girlfriend in Delhi but nobody had even seen this 'ghost girlfriend' or even her photograph. The latest rumour was that Max was a gay in relationship with Hashnam. Max could still smile on such stupid ones but not Hashnam. This Manipuri state level boxer kept his 'Don't Mess with Me' title. Hashnam in spite of his sports background was academically quite good. In fact, in the last semester he had the fourth highest score in the class. Within their group, he was just marginally behind Arun. As far as Max was concerned, his making up to this institute was in itself a miracle and further passing in all three semesters was god's own doing. And for him, his academic god was Hashnam. Max ordered for noodles whereas Hashnam preferred just a cup of coffee.

By the time waiter took their order, Arun, Rashid and Rajiv also came over. The trio had come on Arun's bike. Their hostel rooms were adjoining each others and Arun's bike had become their official transport. Rashid was carrying a side bag which seemed to be full of some papers. He looked like someone who was on a crusade to file an RTI with all the government departments running within the country. Rashid was a slogger and was meticulous in his work. The only thing that held him back was the shade of negativity and aggression in his basic nature. But maybe, these attributes of his personality assisted him to progress in life in spite of a modest background.

Rashid summarized the problem in terms of the syllabus and things that were to be covered for the exams. Now they were to distribute the topics and follow the practice of last two semesters. The ritual was that the common subjects and topics between the finance and marketing streams were sub-distributed amongst them and then it was the responsibility of the topic in charge to empower the others. For this, each would undertake solo study and would daily get together in the evening for about two hours to update. In the next one hour, the topics were distributed and each ordered for their dinner. The cafeteria was a big saving grace considering the blended food served at the hostel mess.

"Let's have tomorrow's session at my room and guys come adequately dressed. I have also called Esha," Arun said.

"So the lover boy wants to have his free family ride on our expense. We slog and the Lady Macbeth gets to rule Rome. I object for our friend mixing work with leisure," said Rajiv.

"Rajiv just shut up. Don't forget you were the one who was begging her last week to manage a date for you for the movie," said Arun, who was now trying to start his bike on which one of the pillion riders, Rashid, had already occupied the seat.

"That is precisely all the more reason to protest. I paid the entire expense for the movie and dinner of the buffalo that she tied me along for that entire evening".

"If Esha hears your comments she will kill you. Sit behind if you don't intent to take a post-dinner stroll. Bye guys! See you tomorrow at six."

Esha was Arun's girlfriend for the last eight months and studied in the same semester. Her parents were from Mumbai. Her mother was a Parsee and her father, Mr Deshpande, from Maharashtra. Having seen her father at the reception of the institute on her first day there was no doubt in the mind of the onlookers that she was lucky not to inherit any of her father's physical attributes. The 'Black Polar Bear' was hairy and scary. Whereas, Esha was beautiful and her right curves with heavy bosom made her a perfect fantasy of the entire desperate lobby of male management aspirants. Her entry into the classroom changed the complete body language of the male counterparts. Even the biggest book-worm Ankit, got distracted by her looks. Ankit was the topper of their class whose reflection was poorer than his self-perception. Chemistry between Arun and Esha was so very natural. The good looking couple with brains and strong family background was envy for many. The day Rashid got to know about their relationship, he was thunder-struck as if love of his life had betrayed him. The pain was not due to the breakdown of his self-illusion, but, with how Arun had managed Esha's friendship?

As for their group; they had readily accepted Esha who was now treated as part of the group. Esha stayed as a paying guest in the house of one of her distant relatives who had their house close to the institute. The Parsee family of Mr Wadley who was Esha's maternal uncle was good to her and she found comfort in their house. After Esha joined the institute, her father got a job in Singapore. Thus, her parents had moved out of the country along with her fourteen years old brother. This left Mr Wadley as the relative-cum-guardian of Esha. The family had on number of occasions hosted dinner for Esha's friends and had some clue of her relationship with Arun.

Rajiv was the last one to enter and quietly sat in the corner realizing that Max had already started covering his topic. The rest of the gang did not notice his quiet entry into the room or rather ignored it for obvious reasons. Max was covering the International Marketing Principles for which he made full use of the black roll board on the wall to explain the mechanics and equations in play. The occasional nods of Hashnam were quite reassuring for him. For the next hour, barring his own laughter at times, which came so naturally to Max, he continued undisturbed to pour out his knowledge. By the time he ended, all seem to be well exhausted.

"Ladies and gentlemen, it will be ten minutes tea break and then we all can clarify our doubts," said Arun. He partially opened the window and shouted for Lalu to get six cups of tea. Ramji's tea stall was just at the entrance of the hostel complex and he and his boys were quite used to of receiving orders in this fashion.

"You guys continue with tea. I'll better leave. Wadley uncle and aunty have to attend a party and I need to be back at home on time. And yes, thanks Max for covering the topic so well," said Esha who had already collected her bag to leave. She was wearing a yellow colour top over black jeans and looked stunning as ever.

"Should I drop you back? Give me five minutes to change," said Arun. Without waiting for Esha's response Arun moved to the adjoining room to change. At least after Esha leaves, Rajiv and Hashnam would be free to light a smoke. From the time Esha had joined their group she had requested Rajiv and Hashnam not to smoke in front of her. The smoke made her feel nauseous. Rajiv would have still tried to talk her out and fagged. But Hashnam would not do such a thing. He was very polite and off late had become almost like a second guardian to Esha. In fact, last week the two of them had gone out together for shopping and Esha was the one who had selected all the items that Hashnam had purchased for his twin sister who was getting married.

"Esha, will you come along for the marriage? Now the exams are also not overlapping with the marriage date. Shilpa has yet again asked me to confirm your presence during marriage," said Hashnam. He had been persistently convincing Esha to come to Imphal to attend his sister's wedding. His sister Shilpa was getting married to a software engineer who was running an Imphal based software security company along with his father. In May this year, Shilpa had come over to meet Hashnam and had spent a week along with his friends. Now that her marriage was scheduled, she wanted Hashnam to get all his friends. The others in the group had already confirmed except Esha.

"Hey, only condition, if my parents do not schedule their visit to Mumbai during the same time. Can I confirm to you by tomorrow? You know how much I want to be part of this trip."

"All right, by tomorrow positively or else it will be difficult to get the air tickets," said Hashnam. Lalu entered with the cups and the steaming kettle. His electric speed of delivery could put the Dominos pizza employees to shame. Rajiv offered a cup of tea to Esha who after a bit of hesitation took it. By now Arun was also ready. For the next few minutes, Rashid slotted the topic for the subsequent session which Rajiv was to deliver. Arun and Esha were the first to leave. The rest would disperse after a smoke. Arun requested Rashid to latch his room before leaving. Arun and Esha were going around for quite sometime and their equation was near perfect. As love couples they restrained from expressing their feelings openly and were taken to be quite matured. Their friends found it much easier to interact with both of them without any inhibition. Esha was a girl who was not only beautiful and intelligent but also knew how to find her own space. That is the reason she had adjusted so well amongst Arun's friends. Apart from Arun's close friends of the campus, Esha also had some other girl friends in the campus as well as outside, with whom she interacted on regular basis. Initially, Rajiv was far too keen to acquaint with Esha's friends but probably his last few encounters had deeply discouraged his pursuit. It was now becoming clear to him that his love story will either have to wait or else take its own independent course.

Esha noticed that Arun had changed his T-shirt and was wearing the yellow one that she had purchased for him last week from the mall. The colour looked brighter on his fair skin even when the light outside was so dim. She was walking closely along his left side and a brisk touch of Arun on her fingers almost tempted her to hold his hand. She checked herself. As a rule between the two, there was no room for public display, especially within the campus. However, when they were in their moments of privacy it seemed that Esha was someone entirely different. She was aware what effect it left on Arun. Her occasional wildness left him bewildered and his control mechanism was tested to its utmost peak. He wished for more but then clearly knew Esha's mind. At times, he felt that she had more self-control then he probably could develop. It did hurt his male ego sometimes.

"You look so good in this yellow colour, my devil!" Esha said. He looked into her eyes and tried to say something but stopped. It seemed to Esha that his mind was somewhere else. Probably still over the topic Max had covered.

"What?" she said. This time she looked at him more closely.

"Well, what have you decided?" His face was still grim.

"Decided what?"

"Oh! Come on Esha. You very well know what I mean. Are you coming for Shilpa's marriage or not?"

"Mr Banker, I guess you must clear your priorities first and be more concerned about the forthcoming exams."

"Sweetheart, my priorities in life are far too clear. If you don't come along with us to Imphal then I will also cancel my trip," said Arun. Esha knew that he genuinely meant what he just said.

"Don't be silly. You can't do that. Hashnam will feel very bad. He has been planning it for so long."

"Precisely, then I take it that you are coming to Imphal."

"Arun, I will feel quite out of place and then it is far too away," Esha said, but her voice betrayed her own true feelings.

"Esha! Please. Come along, it will mean a lot to me. In the middle of this mad house we hardly get time enough for ourselves. Please".

"OK. I'll come. But till then, let's focus on the forthcoming exams," she said with her voice cracking into sweet laughter.

"Esha, I love you," said Arun without noticing the guard at the gate who was looking at them with extra curiosity. It was Esha's blazing eyes which brought him back to his normal self.

On his way back after he left Esha, Arun went to the shopping complex. He had to get his mobile recharged. His mind was running wild from the time Esha had confirmed her trip. It would be for good about ten odd days that they would plan for. Max and Hashnam had already said that any time less than that would not be adequate to see the area in and around Manipur. And of course, then it was also the occasion for Shilpa's marriage. Arun had known all along that this year Esha's parents were not likely to come to India. His only inhibition was regarding Esha going to Singapore for the holidays. Now, things were finally in place. He would have to hold up the temptation of breaking this news of Esha's plan to his pals. Let her do it herself.

By the time Arun returned to his room it was almost 8 o'clock. Henceforth, till exams he would ask Esha to commute on her scooty and focus more towards studies. Rashid knocked on the door while Arun was still changing into his track pants.

"Are you coming for the dinner?" asked Rashid.

"No thanks!"

The first lecture of the day for the finance students was of 'Security Analysis and Portfolio Management'. Professor Tripathi had almost covered the entire syllabus and only last portion of the syllabus was underway. Hashnam and Arun from within the group had opted for finance stream. Both had done well in the last semester and this time also the faculty expected higher results from them. The finance companies visiting the campus by December end of the year were likely to interview the top five within the class of fourth semester finance students. Both Arun and Hashnam were a sound bet. In terms of their personal relation, both shared a good equation. Arun was a meticulous worker who had the ability to clearly define his objective of focus. On the other hand, Hashnam was a reserve person and was selective about his friends. But 'Once a friend always a friend' was what he followed. One more angle was attached to their relationship off late. Hashnam had become close to Esha and felt that Arun was surely a right choice for her.

By the time Professor Tripathi ended the lecture, it was time for the tea break. As per the revised schedule, the students were to attend the classes from 9.30 onwards till 5.30 in the evening. This excluded the half hour break for tea and an hour off for lunch. The marketing classes were conducted in the north block which was diagonally opposite from the classroom of the finance students. This actually left no time for common interaction, especially during the tea break. By the time Arun came out of the classroom, Hashnam had already purchased tea for both of them from the counter of the local cafeteria.

"So, have the two of you finally decided your programme?" said Hashnam while handing over the cup of tea to Arun.

"Well, she told you that she would confirm you by evening," Arun said. He almost had the temptation to tell Hashnam that Esha was coming along with them and that he had been dreaming on and off about the forthcoming trip. He knew that Esha would not like it. She had always kept her individual identity which he had learnt to respect. Hashnam nodded in agreement and as if thinking loud, said, "Well, I have already worked out the programme for you guys. Obviously, apart from attending the marriage you would also like to see the area in and around Imphal. As such, we have a very small state and you can cover the maximum of it within the period of your stay. Max will show you the hill regions of Manipur during the time I prepare for the ceremonies."

"Well, sounds great! I am sure it will be a great experience and lot of fun....to...." The buzzer for the next class was far too loud for Arun to be heard any more. The institute had lately installed these horrible buzzers all along the premises to instill consciousness of ineluctable timings amongst students. This was one of the fads of Mr R R Vankatash, the dean, who had tasked Ramchander the coordinator, to do the needful. Such tasks which could possibly irritate the students were fairly orgasmic for the twice divorced, attention seeking Ramchander.

For the next two weeks, the life in the campus was fairly busy for all students who had to focus on the forth-coming exams. Rashid ensured that the evening discussions within the group continued almost two days prior the exams. The earliest dropout from the group was Esha who stopped coming for the evening sessions a week before the commencement of the first paper. However, she had confirmed her trip to Manipur as promised. Hashnam had booked tickets for everyone through the internet. It was Rashid whose entire cost of fare, Hashnam had insisted to pay. Knowing the financial constrains of his friend, Hashnam was touched when Rashid had offered to come by train on his own. On 15 November, the last paper was over. This time, the exams were more analytical and each felt that they had preformed reasonably well.

On the last day of exam, Hashnam boarded the first available flight to Imphal. Max went to drop his friend to the airport with the promise to get others, just after two days. All passenger reaching Imphal are routed through Guwahati or Kolkata. Hashnam had got the flight reservations for all through Guwahati. Before moving in the airport for check in, Hashnam and Max went over the entire programme of their friends. In addition, to their presence in Shilpa's marriage, the group was very excited to visit the state of Manipur and Hashnam felt morally responsible to make their two weeks trip a memorable one.

"Why do I get a feeling that you are already leaving for the airport?" Rashid said. He was peeping in through window of Rajiv's room, holding a cup of tea.

"Very funny. I am going to the market along with Arun and Esha for some shopping. You want to come?"

"Well, nobody asked me," said Rashid still sipping his tea.

"Yes or No?" he said. As such Rajiv was almost ready and sure won't ask again.

"OK! Give me five minutes and I'll be ready."

At 5.30, Rajiv and Rashid reached the mall where they were to meet Arun and Esha. Rashid's pink shirt with floral design, black trouser and canvas shoes made them an easy landmark to be identified. Rajiv, seeing the amused look on the faces of by passers was almost tempted to rip apart this pink garment off Rashid's body and soul but knew too well the emotional cords attached. Rashid's mother had gifted him this shirt last year. And, he actually thought that he looked real cool wearing this one. Apart from their own personal purchases, they all mutually decided to buy a common gift for Shilpa. The power of attorney was vested upon Esha who after two hours of market survey finally homed on to an Italian tea set. By now, the boys were exhausted from shop to shop running and the purchase went uncontested. Arun still managed to paste a smile on his face, assuring Esha that she had not only selected a right gift but also a right derby for a long race. While the others were at the cash counter, Rashid actively involved himself in guiding the salesman as to how he should go about packing the gift to give it extra safety.

Arun had brought along with him a list of items that he wanted to carry for the forthcoming trip. Most of the items in the list were purchased and he hoped Esha too would be able to timely finish off her shopping. However, it seemed that her shopping agenda would even continue the next day. As far as Rajiv and Rashid were concerned, they had nothing to purchase. Thus, both of them decided to go back to the hostel. Rashid volunteered to carry back Shilpa's gift.

There were very few people at the dining hall. Most of the students had already left for the midterm break. The majority of the occupants in the hall were the first term students whose exams were yet to be scheduled. As an exception, Max was sitting along with the fresher's and outpouring wisdom like an overflowing syntax tank without the cut off mechanism valve. Seeing Rajiv and Rashid enter the hall, Max finally uprooted and joined his friends.

"Hey guys! How did your shopping go?" said Max, as he pulled a chair for himself. Rashid gave a thumps up, indicating that he had a fabulous evening. Rajiv seemed to be a little cheesed off, as on their return Rashid had insisted for having dinner only at the hostel mess. He was amongst the rare species in the campus that had an appetite for the hostel food. Or maybe, he just wanted to cut upon the cost.

"Hashnam had called to confirm that his flight landed in time. During this part of the year, the weather in Manipur is actually very pleasant. I am sure you guys are going to enjoy this trip," said Max.

"Due to the exams, one was so busy that we did not even ask you and Hashnam much about Manipur. So tell us, how is the place? Is it as bad as they say it is in the newspapers? Do you guys actually eat dogs? Is there human right abuse at your place?" Rajiv suddenly seemed to have so many queries.

Max burst of laughter filled the hall. This was typical of Max when he had to convey how stupid he felt the questions were. Rashid had by now started stuffing his mouth with Chapatis as if he had been hungry for days. A few photos of his having meal could make India a strong contender for food aid through the United Nations Malnutrition Support Fund. Rajiv tried not to look annoyed and patiently waited for Max to stop laughing and Rashid to stop making those animal sounds.

After sometime Max said, "Rajiv have you ever been to the Northeast before?"

"I never crossed ahead of Patna. That too, I went as a small kid to attend a marriage of one of our distant relative."

"Even I have not gone to east beyond Delhi," said Rashid with his mouthful.

"Delhi is not towards the east". Protested Max with both arms in the air.

"Well, whatever."

"And how much have you read about Northeast?" asked Max, already amazed with the ignorance of his friends.

"Not much. Only, that it is a disturbed area which is backward and economically poor. Off late, it has been in news due to the economic blockade. People there have tribal culture and majority of them have converted to Christianity in the last fifty years. In addition, there is large scale deployment of security forces in the area to fight the militancy," assisted Rajiv.

Max stared at Rajiv and the quietness in his eyes made Rajiv quite uncomfortable. He hoped he hadn't said anything which would offend his friend. As such, people from this region seemed too emotionally charged-up. By now, even Rashid had also finished his dinner.

"Are you really interested to know about Northeast and its people?" Max finally said.

Both Rajiv and Rashid nodded with full sincerity. Max recommended that they would walk back to the hostel and en route he will try to answer their queries. It was a moonlit night with pleasant weather. Max told them that he would just talk of Manipur per say as he himself belonged from there and also that is where they will be spending the next two weeks. Manipur is on the extreme east of India and shares common border with Myanmar. The state has a large number of tribes primarily belonging to the Kuki and Naga clan. Although, both the set of clans have been living in close proximity of each other, but still, they have managed to keep their cultural and traditional entity intact. Even within own clan, there are large number of sub-clans which have variance in culture and traditions. This leads to complex diversity of populace. The Naga and the Kukis mainly live in the hill regions. In 1962, the Nagas residing in Assam managed to get a statehood which came to be known as Nagaland. The Union of Government of India at the time recognizing this new state also agreed on the clause that if other Nagas settled outside the state wanted to form part of Nagaland, this could be considered. This later led to problems in the state of Manipur as a segment of Nagas want to be part of Nagaland. Such a thing is not practical as these Nagas are occupying areas in various pockets in Manipur itself. However, they demand to establish Nagalim with fresh review of Government of India by allocating them more territory. Then, there is another segment of Nagas who do not want to merge with Nagaland but want more autonomy within the state. On ground, there are large numbers of Naga groups which are supporting either of the theories. Due to their continued protest the state stays volatile.

"Wow! So this is the reason as to why Manipur is so unstable?" asked Rashid.

"No. This is the tip of the iceberg. And I am sure you guys would have already lost interest in my talks and the problem of Manipur and its people," Max said with a smile.

"Rubbish. Rather, Max, you are actually increasing our interest in the whole thing and we want to know more."

"Really?"

"Yeah."

"If that be so, then let's go to my room and we can talk about it further," said Max who was fairly excited to talk more about his state.

Max and Hashnam used to stay in the hostel block right behind the one where the others were allotted rooms. Max had placed poster size photo of number of English singers in his room. One look and one could make out that the occupant of the room was crazy for music. Max's guitar hung on the side wall. He was really very good with it.

"Care for some coffee?" asked Max who went around to the adjoining room to get an extra chair.

Rashid was eager to have coffee and loudly acknowledged the call. As far as eating and drinking was concerned, Rashid was vulnerable to be lured as long as he was not shelling the extra bucks. This at times irritated his friends.

Max poured water in the electric kettle and took out the coffee mugs. He also continued talking about Manipur. In addition, to the demands of the Nagas, the Kukis have also been demanding

Kukiland for themselves. As per them, the area will also cover some portions of Myanmar. Even in the case of Kukis, there are many fractions that have a different set of demands. If you look at the intent of the central government, the actions if not all, were positive. Both the Nagas and the Kukis are covered under the minority groups and enjoy the privileges attached with this status. However, the aspirations of the people are far more and most of the time they are misguided by the political representatives to meet their own selfish interests. It seems that the differences between the Kukis and the Nagas are great and both will not be able to accept each others existence. But this is not true at all. In fact, both these clans have been living together from centuries. The Nagas used to encourage Kuki settlement next to their own villages. This was because the Kuki were known to be better fighters and their presence in the neighbourhood was an assurance of safety. The Kukis kept changing their settlement and did not restrict to single locations. Now, with changing times this practice has also stopped. Even the Kukis want a more secure and stable life for their future generations.

In addition to the Kuki and the Nagas, the plain areas or the valley portion is occupied by the Meitei's who are primarily the Hindus. The kingdom under the Meitei had ruled Manipur state for centuries. Even when the British involvement in this region increased after 1848, the Meiteis still continued to hold influential positions. Even today, most of the top government officials and people in power in Manipur are from the Meitei community. Over the last few years, especially after the Naga and the Kuki have been given the status of backward communities, this status of Meitei domination is also slowly undergoing a change. Today, Kuki and Naga representation in the government and political arena is quietly increasing. With the aim to connect the Kuki and the Naga with the mainstream of the state they are allowed to procure land for settlement in the plains. However, the same is not applicable for the Meiteis. They have restrictions for settlement in the hilly region of the state.

"What about the militant outfits and their agenda?" asked Rashid who was very seriously listening to Max.

"Well, there are a large number of militant outfits that are present in the state. They claim to represent the general aspirations of the people. But the fact is that most of them have made militancy a business to earn easy money. Today, a huge extortion racket is run in the state in the name of 'fight for people's cause". As for the people of Manipur, they are sick of such circumstances. They also want development in their region and a life as normal as that of any other citizen of India in any other state. Those who are now exposed to a better life in other parts of the country are slowly opting to settle there."

It was almost 12 o'clock but still Max found his audience keen and alert. Maybe his coffee or his talks had got them in active mode.

"By the way, all is not so bad in Manipur. There is better side of life in Manipur also. I guess the younger generation has learnt to enjoy the diversity than to find common grounds for conflict. As far as the place is concerned, it is closer to nature and I am sure that you all will enjoy your trip to our state," said Max.

Max went further talking about Manipur and its people for next few hours and it was quite late by the time Rajiv and Rashid came back to their respective rooms.

There were not many occasions when the management students in the institute got the opportunity to sleep late in the day. Today was an exception. By the time Rajiv and Rashid finally got up, the water supply in the bathroom was over. Actually, from last few months the plastic overhead tanks in the hostel were leaking and nobody had bothered much as their requirements were catered for by the fresh water supply coming twice in the day. Even the Sundays and holidays were not much of an exception. Rajiv agreed to pay Lalu ten rupees a bucket to freshen up. Rashid met his requirement by using half the bucket left over by Rajiv. As such, bathing was not much of a priority in Rashid's life. By the time they made it to the dining hall it was lunch time. The strength at the hall had further pruned due to the mid-term break. Post lunch Rashid decided to spend time in the library, where as Rajiv went out probably to watch a movie.

One person who had left the hostel early was Arun. He had promised Esha that they would spend the day together. As such, Esha's shopping for the forthcoming trip was still due. Today, they had decided to go to the City Centre mall which had lately been opened. Come to think of it, some years prior the malls were unheard of in India. Now, they had mushroomed in all small and major cities of the country. Most of the shops became optimally functional by 11 o'clock. Esha went into one of the shops to purchase cosmetics whereas Arun preferred to wait for her outside. From the glass window of the shop he saw her at the counter with the salesgirl. She was looking stunning in the blue colour sleeveless salwar suit. The peacock colour dupatta added elegance to her dress. Her long hair were falling on to one side. Esha was 5' 7" ft tall and when she wore heels, she made people all around her look so short. Arun who himself was reasonably tall as per Indian standards, had to maintain an erect posture to match up. Arun had noticed in the morning, the new shade of nail polish that Esha had applied to match with her dress. The fragrance of her perfume made him all the more aware of her presence. Even though, she stood so far away he could still see the dimple on her right cheek. Initially, when heads used to turn for Esha, naturally, Arun felt quite uneasy. However, now he had more or less got use to this aspect of their lives together. Rather he enjoyed the startling impact this girl had on others, especially the opposite sex.

In the growing years of his life, Arun did have some casual flings with girls. But nothing was as close to what he experienced with Esha. She had actually swapped him off his feet from the time he had laid eyes on her. Initially, Esha had resisted committing for any relationship with Arun but then his persistency had made her give in. He counted himself lucky to have Esha in his life. He really loved her and accepted her the way she was. At times, Esha was very stubborn, sensitive and closely guarded her viewpoint till the end. She also lacked the patience which came so naturally to Arun. But in spite of all such shades in her personality, Arun just loved her.

It took Esha more than forty minutes in the shop. By the time she came out she had two shopping bags in hand. Arun took the bags from her.

"Thanks. I hope I didn't take too long," she said.

"No".

"You should have come inside."

"Well, there was far too much of girly stuff inside you know. So what's next?"

"I am feeling hungry. Let's first eat something and then we will continue with some more shopping," said Esha.

They took the escalator for the third floor as food court was on the top floor. Even though it was just noon time, still, there seem to be far too many people standing at the counters. Esha managed to find a place to sit in the huge hall while Arun went to one of the counters to join the long waiting queue. He wondered as to how many changes had taken place in the lifestyle of people living in big cities across the country. Such places in India were beyond thinking, some years back. The younger generation had transformed and adjusted to such changes so fast. In spite that he was still in his mid-twenties, he felt as if he belonged to an entirely different time zone. The kids along with whom he stood in the queue today shared nothing in common with him or his so-called generation. He would still for instance let an older gentleman or a lady take priority at the counter. But here, he found a complete air of indifference. Most of them were either on a phone call or were glued up to the music through the ear plugs. Even their dress sense seemed so weird to Arun. Jeans wore in common, were hanging far below the waist line and the shirts seems so short. Striking colour contrast of the footwear gave them the so called 'cool dude' look. A large number of them were contributing to the figures of obese index of emerging India. And yet they stood at such counters for more! Arun felt that he was much fitter than most of them. He was regular with his early morning runs and managed to be at the college gym frequently regardless of the gruelling schedule. During his school days, he had been a good sportsman and played almost all outdoor games. As far as tennis was concerned, he had represented his state at the junior national level.

Still, each younger generation seems to be smarter than their previous one. And rightly that's what is called the 'generation gap'. At the counter, Arun paid for the lunch and soon joined Esha who seemed to have covered her appetite by drinking water. From day one Arun found it quite amazing the way Esha took small bites of her meal. She seemed to be so elegant even while she ate quietly. Arun had ordered for Rava Masala Dosa which was her all time favourite. Arun really didn't like it much but then, love makes you do a lot many things.

"After this, I want to have an ice-cream," declared Esha. She had a sweet tooth. However, she kept her urge for sweets under check and very few knew that it was one of her weaknesses. The graph of such consumption was in equivalence to her good mood. This meant without saying that today Esha was really happy. By the time they came to the second floor, Esha had convinced Arun to let her purchase a pair of trousers for him. Initially, he protested but later relented as he wanted her to stay happy. In the men's changing room Arun kept trying all varieties and with each disapproval of Esha, who forced him to come out each time, he tried some more. Women can be really finicky, especially, when it comes to their men. As for men under target, options at times are very limited. By now, two salesmen at the counter had also formed part of the delegation headed by Esha and were extending their free advices. After half an hour of ramp walking by Arun in the narrow ally, finally Esha selected a light cream colour trouser. She thought Arun looked really cool in it. Her newly acquired advisers were also of the same opinion. Arun felt that the fabric of the trouser was quite translucent. Anyways, not many would have cared for his opinion in the present situation. He wanted to protest but seeing Esha's enthusiasm realized it would be dangerous. The occasion where he would wear his latest gift was also declared.

"Of course, you will wear it on the day of Shilpa's marriage function," said Esha, who was making the payment at the counter.

When they came out of the shop, Arun was still thinking if the tucked in shirt could at least cover the translucent portion of the trousers from the top. He usually preferred to wear jeans and in formal attire it was always the conventional pattern. With Esha around, he was learning to live with these changes. At times, he wondered what will become of him in next ten years with Esha.

"Thanks."

"You're welcome," Esha smiled. She was well aware that Arun didn't like to venture out for shopping unless it was a diehard requirement. He had just come for her. As such, Arun was not very vocal about his feelings.

As soon as they got on to the lift, Arun was busy on his mobile. His head was tilted to hold on the phone while his hands held the shopping bags. Another few seconds on the phone and he dropped the bags on the floor of the lift. Now, holding the phone in his right hand he was rapidly asking the 'when, where and what' details. By now, even Esha was also attentively trying to listen the conversation on the phone. It seemed that someone was not too well and she hoped it was not as bad as it looked. The lift stopped at the ground floor and Arun while still on the phone moved out. Esha quickly picked up the shopping bags and followed Arun. She held Arun's left arm while he confirmed to the person on the other side of the phone that he will shortly be at the medical room. The moment the call was disconnected, Esha enquired, "What happened?"

"Rashid just had a slip in the bathroom. Rajiv has taken him to the college medical room. He says that Rashid has hurt his back and cannot stand without support. He wants me to immediately come to the medical room," said Arun.

"I'll also come along with you. Poor guy, I hope he is not too badly hurt."

"Let's go," said Arun taking the bags from Esha's hand and started towards the exit door.

They soon found an auto and headed straight for the college. There was a medical room in the institute which catered for basic medical facilities to the students. For critical cases, the patient was shifted to the nearby hospital. Arun hoped that Rashid would not avail that option. In twenty odd minutes, they reached the college and were soon at the medical room. They saw Rashid lying on his stomach on the side table of the medical examiner. The doctor was trying to move his legs and each movement led to the animal cry which amused Rajiv who stood in close attendance. Rashid was wailing and was half way through cursing the world when he saw Esha present in the room. For a second it seemed that the pain had just vanished and the wounded warrior lay in the glory of his battle deeds.

"Hey! What are you doing here?" was what Rashid could manage. Then there was panic on his face as he realized that the resident doctor had half ripped his clothes as if he was a birthday present.

"You go…please go".

Even Esha realized and quickly moved out of the room. She could hear Rashid yell "Why did you have to call her?" Rajiv laughed uncontrolled and sprang out of the room.

Although Esha didn't find it humorous but didn't know what to do. Even Rajiv came to her a little sobered and showed some prudence.

"Hey, Esha! Don't you worry; the doctor says he will be just fine. You know how Rashid is. He was getting difficult to handle so I called Arun. I didn't know that you two were together."

"What happened?" said Esha, still looking concerned.

"Oh! Nothing great. He just slipped in the bathroom. Then he refused to sit on the bike. It took almost an hour to get him here. Doctor says no major injuries. He should be walking soon."

Arun also came out of the room. "Esha, I guess Rashid will be fine. The doctor has given him an injection for pain relief. Rajiv and I will take him back."

"OK. Then I must leave. Tell him to get well soon. Bye," said Esha.

Rashid had spent an hour in the library and had finally decided to be back in his room. When he entered the room, the sound of the water tap made it evident that he had forgotten to close it tightly in the morning. Once in the bathroom, he finally decided to finish off the ritual of bathing. The slippery floor and hurry as usual worked in combination and led to the fall of the tiger. Luckily, he managed to get through to Rajiv on phone, who came back to nurse his friend. In spite, his dramatized description of the fall, Rashid failed to impress the doctor. It was a minor bruise on the elbow and a little sprain near the hip bone. To put matter to rest, the doctor gave him a shot of the painkiller and a day's medicine. The war hero was taken back to the hostel by his comrades to take some rest.

"Arun, I guess we need to tell Hashnam that Rashid will not be able to undertake the trip. Let's get his ticket cancelled," said Rajiv.

"Are you nuts? Why the hell will you do that? I will be OK by tomorrow," said Rashid. He realized that it was a catch 22 situation. If he played his health card far too much, then a trip to Manipur was out. Now, for the next few minutes Rashid did the reverse engineering of convincing his friends that he was fit and they really need not bother. After sometime, Rajiv and Arun fairly amused left Rashid in peace.

"You got the better of him," said Arun.

"Well you know him. His sympathy campaign was driving me crazy. Only the chance of free trip to Manipur getting cancelled got him back to his senses. However, we will check on him in the evening."

By evening, Rashid seemed to be much better and even Max joined in to check up the condition of their friend. They assisted Rashid to get his things packed for the trip. Early the next day at 8.30, they all had to catch a flight to Guwahati. Max had already tied up the transport to the airport, which was about an hour away from their institute location. Arun had told Esha to be ready accordingly. On their way to the airport they would pick her up. Therefore, to reach the airport in time they planned to start from the hostel by 6 o'clock.

There was excitement in the air. Each had made a check-list of the items that they needed to carry for the trip. Rajiv was taking his high resolution digital camera with attached lens. It was gifted to him by his brother on his previous birthday. Rajiv was a keen photographer. He had told his friends that photography had been his hobby since the age of twelve. His group of friends had accepted him to be their official photographer. Rajiv took pride in his talent and had converted hard copy of a number of photographs. One of his hostel trunks was full of them. The best ones were of the outdoor activities which again was another passion of Rajiv. He loved going out on jungle safari, rock climbing and tracking activities. This was all the more reason for Rajiv to be excited regarding this trip. Hashnam had promised him a large share of outdoor activities in Imphal and its neighbouring areas.

As far as Arun was concerned, he was on cloud nine. For the first time he and Esha were going out. He hoped and planned to spend a lot of time together. In his excitement, he had called her a number of times in the last few hours. Rather, the frequencies of his calls were annoying his friends. Especially, Rashid who felt that no censorship was exercised while explaining details of his tragic moments. As such it was embarrassing to see Esha at the medical room. Initially, when he fell there was panic but then he reconciled that the damage was not much. However, when Rajiv came, he did like getting so much attention. But, rest he did not foresee. He had spoken to his mother before the fall. She was very happy but equally concerned. The concern was for two reasons.

Firstly, Rashid would be travelling for the first time by air. In his entire family, only one of Rashid's uncles had travelled by air. He was a carpenter who was working in Dubai and sometimes came over to visit his native village. One of his stories regarding the air turbulence during flight was fresh in Ammi's mind. Secondly, someone yet again had told Ammi that Manipur was only a jungle area which had tribes who could eat humans. Last night she had some bad dreams. Although, she knew that Rashid was excited about going on this trip but then her fears seems so natural. The way she described the tribal eating pattern, Rashid could easily imagine a part of his leg on somebody's rice plate. At times, he felt that his mother was fooled by other people's opinion. But her innocence and love made him feel so overwhelmed.

Max was also no less excited regarding going home. He will be meeting his people after a very long time. In addition, his friends will be coming to his native place. Max's father was a teacher in an intermediate school near Jaribam. Although, their native village was in the interiors, his father had settled the family closer to Imphal. The aim had been to give better education and future to his children. On the weekends he visited his family. In addition to Max, his parents had three other children. He was the youngest amongst his siblings. His eldest sister was a nurse who worked in a private hospital in Guwahati. The second one was a teacher in a primary school in Imphal and stayed along with their mother. The next sister was a housewife whose husband worked in a factory in Noida. She was settled in Delhi with her family for the last three years. Apart from the younger sister, both the elder ones were not yet married. Although, his responsibility towards his home sometimes bothered Max but most of the time he stayed cheerful. In fact, Rashid always felt that Max was far too lucky and surely without much personal problems in life.

Before coming to see Rashid, Max had spend time packing his stuff and tightening the chords of his guitar. It was one of the few prized possessions of Max. Very few even in his close circle knew that the Baptist priest of his village had gifted him this guitar when he was fifteen years old. Since then, Max had carried this guitar to all places. In fact, this time he seriously thought of taking the guitar along during this short leave. However, in the last he changed his mind. As compensation, he spent much of the afternoon playing guitar in his room.

"Rashid I hope you will be able to cope up with the journey tomorrow. Are you sure you want to come along?" asked Max vacillating over the options with concern.

But before even Rashid could reply, Rajiv said, "Don't worry, couple of injections up his butts will keep him going."

"Very funny." Rashid managed to say. However, he seemed to be much better and knew quite well that even the slightest of his sympathy tactics will ruin his chance to go to Manipur. He was dealing with very ruthless and heartless management wizards.

Arun had paid Lalu to get dinner for them from the dhaba. Rajiv would have loved to take a drink before dinner but knew that the proposal will be shot down by the majority considering the busy schedule of next day. The tandoori roti had become cold and seemed like rubber pieces on chewing. Max, whose staple diet did not cover such food bonanza, gulped each piece with a lot of water. Arun felt that by the time Max will finish eating there will be no water left in the water camper. As far as Rashid was concerned, his quota of complaints for the day was as such over.

After dinner, a call was made to Hashnam who confirmed that he will be coming in the afternoon tomorrow to get them picked up at the airport. He also advised them to get few warm clothes, as in Manipur it was a little nippy.

Rashid got up in panic not due to the bang on the door but more so with the fear of getting late for the flight.

"Hey! Rashid get up or you'll get late. Are you feeling OK?" said Rajiv with a little concern in his voice.

"Can't be better. Will catch up with you in next twenty minutes," said Rashid as he tried to get out of the bed. Rajiv gave a thumps up and left.

The pain was still there. The painkillers had assisted him to have a peaceful night. If the pain stayed he will gulp one more pill later. He found that the movement of his back had got slightly restricted, but then he will sail through this trip. The only problem was in using the toilet. In their block, the work of repairs had not started. Under the repair works, the college had sanctioned the replacement of Indian seat with the western ones. Their block happened to be oldest building of the hostel. Once again, Rashid cursed Ramchander for the slow progress of the repair work and slowly tried to settle down.

By the time Rashid was combing his hair he heard the sound of the horn. Max shouted for them to move out quickly. It was 6.05 o'clock and he was all set to leave. Rashid yelled for Lalu to carry his bag to the taxi. The others had already settled in the cab. Considering Rashid's fresh physical status, his friends had left the front seat vacant for him.

"Why on earth are you carrying this water bottle?" said Rajiv who helped Rashid to settle down in the front seat.

"Oh! I will require it during the journey."

Rajiv explained that this won't be required. The bottle was handed back to Lalu to keep it safely till Rashid returns. The moment they started, Lalu waved at them with the full swing of his right hand. He looked so much young and shared the excitement of their trip without actually being part of it. Rajiv felt a little sad for the boy and decided to purchase something for him on return.

The next destination was Esha's place. All was as per plan but none of them had anticipated an early morning encounter with the Wadley family. Esha's landlord-cum-guardian-cum-relative, Mr Wadley, seemed to have a look of concern on his face, although he was well acquainted with each of them. Before Esha left, he repeated his list of do's and don'ts for the trip. It is only during such moments that one realized how people are attached to one another in spite not being too verbose about their inner feelings.

Finally, the group said goodbye to the Wadley's and were off to the airport.

The drive to the airport entailed covering twenty odd kilometres from the main city. The morning breeze through the rolled down window of the car looked so refreshing. The wide road along the countryside had been constructed a few years ago. There was hardly much traffic on the road. Although, area en route was partially inhabited but still the crop fields were prominently visible. Such things in a way are not seen in the big cities. Arun was sitting next to Esha and her slight touch made him feel so warm. She wore a red top over the blue jeans and looked stunningly beautiful. Apart from asking Rashid about his health she otherwise stayed generally quite.

At 7.30 sharp they reached the airport. Rajiv paid for the cab. It had been unanimously decided that all the payments during the trip will be made by Rajiv and the spending will be equally shared. Esha had insisted to be treated at par and it was agreed to. Max and Arun got the trolley to get the luggage unloaded. Rashid preferred to maintain the status of a patient and stayed invisible during the loading of the trolleys. The only time his eyes looked curious was when his own stuff was being loaded. After the initial verification at the entrance they moved into the hall. Even at this hour of the day, the airport seemed so busy. A number of airlines were operating their domestic and international flights through this airport. The entry of international passengers had been lately separated from the domestic traffic. Inside the hall, there were a number of shops with all variety of stores. The group moved for the luggage screening. All this was new for Rashid who was travelling by air for the first time. He therefore, moved around a little more slow and deliberate. The pain seemed to be much less. In fact, he avoided taking the painkiller in the morning.

The flight schedule displayed on the LCD screen confirmed that the flight was well in time. It took the group a while to get the check-in procedures completed. Their flight was routed through Guwahati where the stoppage was for about twenty odd minutes.

The landing time at Imphal was 11.30. The inner waiting lounge had passengers of the flight which were to take off shortly. A majority of the people present seemed to belong to the region of North-East. Max had found someone known and was busy talking to him in his native language. After a while, he got his friend to be introduced to the group.

"Hey! Everybody, meet my friend Daniel. He is a lead guitarist and hails from Imphal. We two went to school together. Daniel is going to Imphal to perform in the rock concert organized by his home band during the Sangai festival. He otherwise works with a company in Mumbai," said Max who was radiating a lot of warmth.

Each one shook hands with Daniel. His body frame was almost like Max and from a distance it would be difficult to differentiate the two. On the closer look Daniel had a moustache which was almost drooping down his chin. He had coloured his hair and wore a large number of accessories on his wrist and neck. But, the most appealing thing about Daniel was his disarming smile which impressed everyone. Daniel said that during Sangai festival there were huge entertainment and cultural programmes lined up. He extended the invitation to all to attend the events. Max promised that his friends would surely be present to witness the festival.

"Let's go for a fag," said Rajiv. As such during the journey there was no scope to smoke. Amongst the volunteers were Rajiv and Daniel. Max just accompanied them.

"Don't get late for the flight," said Esha. Rajiv did a thumbs-up. His typical trademark.

Esha found it really funny as to how someone could be so desperate for a smoke. Thank god! Arun was a non-smoker. She just detested the smell. Had Arun smoked, she would not have even got in relationship with him. Most of the smokers have such bad breath. They keep coughing like old men and above all, such a waste of money and health. During this loud thinking she blankly looked at Arun. Arun was cautious with each passing minute and couldn't avoid her gaze while he chatted with Rashid. Rashid had parked himself on the nearest chair.

Even though with so much noise around, the announcement for boarding was clearly heard. Rashid took out the boarding pass from his side pocket and tallied the correctness of the flight number that was announced. The speed of his action reflected his distrust on the airport authorities, who may let the flight go without him. He almost pulled Arun to hurry up. The announcements also called for Esha's attention, especially to Arun's relief, she dropped her gaze.

The last to join in was the smokers club. Soon after the boarding procedures were over they mounted the bus to the plane.

"Thank god they catered for the bus. My back is still paining," said Rashid.

"Oh! This they placed only because they came to know you were coming and were not too well," said Rajiv taking a dig at Rashid.

"Very funny."

In the plane Arun and Esha sat close together. The third seat next to them was taken by Rajiv. Esha took the window seat. In fact, the others were also in the same row. Daniel had successfully managed to get his seat interchanged and was busy yapping with Max. Rashid seemed to be self amused. He was checking out the air hostesses. Especially the one who had welcomed him on board. Her smile had made his heart skip a beat. He had not seen someone as beautiful and welcoming for such a long time. He hoped she was single. He could almost feel the fragrance of her perfume. She was all that a man could ask for. The only problem was that she wore the western attire. He could in his mind see his mother looking disapprovingly at his choice. Although such visual scared him, still he reassured himself that he will somehow make it work. Her name was Shruti. He read her nameplate when she came to assist him in placing his hand bag on the side shelf. Yet again, he saw his mother from his third eye. A girl from a different community! His mother was veiling and hitting her chest. There was lump in his throat when he told himself yet again that he will somehow make it work.

Rajiv was a prophylactic reader and carried a book even during travel. After a little chit-chat with Arun and Esha, he thought it better to put his head down in the latest novel of Jeffrey Archer. As such, he did not want to look like a surveillance boy hired by Mr Wardley.

Arun finally whispered, "Why were you staring at me in the lounge? Woman, you really have some piercing eyes."

"And these eyes can read minds, Mr Arun," said Esha teasing him.

"Well, tell me what they read?"

"Oh! Nothing."

"Nothing."

"Yes. Nothing."

"Now you are lying."

"Am I."

"Yes."

"Well! I caught you eying the girls passing by," said Esha who now had a smile on her face.

Poor Arun got on the defensive. "Hey! I did not look at anyone."

"Yes you did."

"No".

"Now you are lying," said Esha who burst out in laughter. Sometimes she felt that Arun was really so innocent. He took her very seriously and his love for her was so much visible in his eyes.

Arun realized that he could not win this one and thus held Esha's hand that she had subtly extended towards him. Both were smiling when Esha drew Arun's attention towards Rashid.

"Don't you feel that he is acting a bit awkward from the time we have boarded the flight. I hope he is OK. Although, I feel he is the one out of you all who seems to be drawn towards that air hostess," said Esha.

"Really," said Arun a bit surprised.

"Yeah. Just watch him and don't make it so obvious."

The young girl this time came forward to demonstrate the safety measures that were to be adhered during the flight. She stood few feet away from their row. Rashid it seemed was shortly going to put all his newly acquired knowledge to test. The plane had started rolling on the runway. Within minutes they were airborne. The female voice on the speaker in addition to other instructions informed that the time of flight to Guwahati was a little over two hours.

In the last few years, a number of domestic airlines had started operating across the country. The competition between them was tough which gave the consumer a number of options to choose from. To reduce the fare, most of the airlines serve beverages only on order. On this plane also, the passengers had the option of ordering beverages as per their taste buds.

The view outside was quite mesmerizing and both Arun and Esha were looking at the magnificent clouds which seem to be all around. They were still holding hands. Rajiv's reading lamp was on but his drooping neck confirmed that he had long gone off to sleep. Arun switched off his reading light. The frequency of chit-chat between Max and his friend had also slowed down. By the time the air hostesses came with the beverages, only Rashid was the one who seemed to be eager to take a bite. When he was asked for his choice of drink, the newly turned health freak ordered for a diet coke. Rajiv even in his half sleep overheard Rashid ordering his menu and couldn't avoid a smirk on his face. He had to give his famous thumbs-up sign.

After sometime, a male voice on the speaker identified himself to be of the pilot and announced that they will now prepare for landing at Guwahati. Outside temperature was eighteen degrees as per the pilot. The entire countryside seemed to be lush green and there were number of water bodies which were quite visible. Then there was the full view of the Brahmaputra.

"You know what? My father says that there is a local belief that if you cross Brahmaputra once then you will invariably cross it a minimum of seven times," said Arun.

"I am ready to cross it any number of times as long my lovely banker is besides me."

The plane got aligned to the runway and soon the wheels touched the ground. There seemed to be military and air force station closer to the Guwahati civil airport. The building seemed to be uniformly painted and gave a very clean look. At the near distance one could also see military planes. Once the plane finally came to a halt, the passengers due for Guwahati got down. The others were requested to remain seated. Rashid was moving his head at almost 360 degrees. Probably, he was inspired by the wild turkey to locate objects in the close vicinity. By now, his object of interest was quite well known to all his friends.

"Rashid comfortable?" asked Rajiv who got up to stretch himself.

"Yes. Very comfortable. Can we go outside?"

"I guess the answer is no. The halt is just for twenty minutes and then you have much more here than outside," said Rajiv with a smile.

Rashid pretended as if he did not make much of what Rajiv said. Soon the airport staff was identifying the luggage on board along with the ticket and also the plane was being pumped with steam fog for fragrance and cleaning. The empty seats were being filled up by the passengers who were boarding for Imphal. The general crowd around seemed to be quite young and most of them were quite fashionably dressed up. The western style of dressing was predominant amongst most of the people. However, there were some women who were dressed in their traditional dress. Arun and Esha had been quite observant of such details.

"Those wrap around seemed so colourful," said Arun who was quite impressed with the dress sense of some of the female co-passengers.

"Well, these are called Mekhla which are the traditional outfit of the women of this region. Even I want to pick one for myself."

"With your height it may actually look like a short skirt." Arun laughed at his own joke. But quickly sobered down, thereby, avoiding the inevitable trouble. "Actually, I mean that the people from this region are not too tall."

Rajiv was in conversation with Daniel and Max on the other side. Daniel was explaining him about the Sangai festival. Even Rashid who was mostly day-dreaming was attentively listening to Daniel.

"You see, Sangai is a type of a deer of the local area which reflects peace and tranquility. So firstly, the festival is named on it to depict the same emotions. During the festival, a number of cultural programmes which have representation from almost all the districts of Manipur are performed. The event is for about seven days," said Daniel.

"Wow! That must be awesome. And what else is there?" said Rajiv who was already visualizing the great opportunity of clicking some memorable photographs.

"Well, there are number of rock bands that will be performing. Even my band has a programme scheduled for three days during the festival," said Daniel

"Can I also join in the band to play something?" Max said with all earnestness.

"Why not? You are as such a good guitarist," said Daniel.

"Even I can sing a song or two," volunteered Rashid.

"Really?" said Rajiv who almost knew Rashid in and out. And also his shrieking voice, which he had actually inherited from his mother.

"You see. With good music around it will not be much of a problem," said Rashid who was now glued to the poor air hostess. Rajiv smiled when he saw what Rashid was up to. Had the girl known Rashid's mind, she would have happily preferred to jump out of the plane in mid-air. She was a pretty girl and surely seemed attuned to handle the likes of Rashid. Rajiv just hoped that Rashid didn't make a fool of himself.

The plane was once again ready for takeoff. The pilot announced that the flight time to Imphal will be thirty minutes. The routine drill of safety precaution was yet again executed by the staff. The plane was soon airborne. This time, the flying time seemed to be far too less and Max's subsequent move for toilet was withheld by the cabin crew in want of the landing procedures. The wheels touched the runway and the airlines thanked its passengers with hope to serve them soon. The outside temperature was seventeen degrees. Imphal has a small airport but then meets the general requirements. A large number of passengers were busy on their mobile phones. Probably either confirming the news of their arrival or arranging for commutation to their final destination. Seeing so much dependency on mobile phones, sometimes Arun wondered how their life will be without them. Even Esha and Max were busy on the phone. Max was probably checking if Hashnam had come to receive them. In the meantime, Rashid was still turning around to get the last glimpse of the girl who almost stole his heart. Life was not something on the silver screen. He probably will never see her again. She was not even at the exit door to say a final bye to him. Although, he felt a sense of loss but still tried to find solace that ammi would not have approved of this girl.

"Did you ever have a girlfriend Rashid?" asked Rajiv who had put his arm around Rashid's shoulder to give him support or maybe just to console his friend. Rashid was a bit surprised. He realized that his friend had read his mind. He almost looked blankly at Rajiv.

"Don't worry, such things keep happening. Now cheer up a little. Hashnam must be waiting. It's a new world outside," said Rajiv.

Arun and Esha were the first to reach for their luggage collection. In the way, they saw a counter which displayed a request for foreigners to take a valid permit to move inside Manipur.

"I never knew the entry in this state was restricted," said Esha.

"Yeah! In some states of North-East, even the Indian citizen due to inner line permit policy, is suppose to take permission for visiting certain areas. This law is in place to ensure that the culture and the traditions of the locals are not threatened," said Arun.

The group soon got together and collected their luggage. At the entrance of the airport, Hashnam and his look alike younger brother was waiting for them. There was so much resemblance amongst the brothers. The younger one was Gopal and was in the final year of school. They all had seen his photograph with Hashnam but were meeting him for the first time. The boy was lean and was not very muscular, unlike his elder brother. He was a good football player and was in the state junior team. Max was the first to jump and hug Hashnam as if they had last met during the 'French Revolution'. It seemed that everybody was speaking to everyone. Hashnam was especially happy to see Esha.

"Thanks for making it. Shilpa is really very excited on your arrival. In fact, she even wanted to come to receive you but then there was work at home," said Hashnam.

"Oh! I am so happy that I could actually make it."

"Hashnam, you must also thank Rashid for falling, sprawling, wailing, galling and still sailing till Imphal," said Arun.

"Arun don't be cheap. It is creditable for Rashid to travel so far in spite of all the pain," said Esha rescuing him from the vultures. Rashid still was under the jet lag of the air hostess. He felt cheated. But then, apart from himself he had no one to blame. He did not muster enough guts to even speak a single word with the girl he liked so much. It was not that he couldn't speak with girls. But then not really with one whom he was drawn to. Hell why not? This he had asked himself a thousand times. Still, there was no reason. Apart from the fact, that when it came to the issue of his love life he was stupid. Stupid is what he had been all his life. Maybe, that is the reason he never had a girlfriend. He envied Arun and his likes who could openly express their inner feelings. Somewhere, he felt that he was not born with the same privilege. Things will have to change, he told himself. He will not toddle behind his mother like a small child all his life but rather grow to be a man. A man every woman desires. The thought almost expanded his chest. But then, the pain in his back put his wishful urge under control. Daniel extended his hand to say goodbye to Rashid which finally brought him back from the fallacy world.

The luggage was rechecked and loaded on to the van which Hashnam had brought. There was also a car with a driver. Max, Rajiv and Hashnam got into the van while the others along with Gopal used the car. Yet again Rashid took the co-driver seat. Unlike his elder brother, Gopal was quite talkative. He sat next to Esha and started acquainting them with the town. He informed them that Hashnam had made arrangements for their visit to places in and around Imphal.

"I hope your family will be comfortable regarding my coming along with these guys to attend Shilpa's marriage?" said Esha who found Gopal quite interactive.

"Come on didi, you are more than welcome. Bhaiya and Shilpa didi keep talking about you. In fact, Shilpa didi has made arrangements for your stay along with her."

Arun felt electrocuted. During the entire trip he wanted to be just close to Esha. And here they had already made arrangements for her. What about him? And what about them? He felt a strong urge to elope with Esha to some place where nobody would separate them. He thought of Hashnam and wondered if he had been tricked. However, he tried to maintain his composure. After all, he didn't want to look too desperate in front of the kid.

"So where are the rest of us staying?" Arun said sounding casual.

"Oh! You all will be staying in Irom uncle's house. Bhaiya has already prepared the rooms there for all of you," said Gopal who was very seriously playing the role of a good guide.

Well, Arun looked a little bewildered. Esha could read his mind and quickly intervened, "How far is your house from Irom uncle's house?"

"It's adjacent to our house. Irom uncle and his family has been our immediate neighbour for a very long time," said Gopal.

Gopal's words felt like music in Arun's ears. So, finally he will have the chance to be in close proximity with Esha. Esha smiled, as she could read his mind very clearly. Arun winked at her. By now Rashid had stretched himself well in the front seat. He seemed to be feeling a shade better now that he was enjoying the view of the city. To keep himself amused, he fiddled with the CD player of the car. Suddenly, a female singer's voice in local language was amplified by the car stereo. The music had soft nodes and the singer's voice sounded quite melodious. All other audio CDs in the dash board were also of local songs, therefore, Rashid let the song play. Even Esha requested to increase the volume for more clarity. It was a fast number and the music was on the western beats.

"What language is it?" Rashid enquired from the driver who was driving quietly.

"It is Manipuri language," said the driver. Rashid was taken aback as the driver had just answered him in English. Surprisingly, his diction was not at all bad. To further test the guy, Rashid continued, "Do you listen the English music also?"

"Yes. A little. But, mostly I prefer the Manipuri songs."

"Do they have so many songs in Manipuri?"

"Yes, a lot of them. Look, you see those large hoardings along the sides. They are of the latest Manipuri movies. Most of the songs are from these movies," said the driver.

Even Arun and Esha listened to the driver with interest. The poster girls on the hoardings were attractive and looking at them for a while made Rashid feel better. If only Ammi knew what was on his mind, she would have disowned her dear son.

Max got down after the main circle crossing of the city. He said that he will first go home and then later come over to Dhayan Singh's house.

"But then, when will you come to Hashnam's house?" asked Rajiv.

Max burst out laughing. "Rajiv! Dhayan Singh is his first name and the surname is Hashnam," said Max pointing towards Hashnam.

"Really, I missed upon that. Actually, you are more known by your surname," said Rajiv.

"So is his dad. Therefore, I recommend that all of you must call him Dhayan Singh during this trip or else the senior Hashnam may feel offended," said Max who had already collected his bag from the rear of the van and waved back to his friends.

Max's house was about twenty minutes from Dhayan Singh's house. He lived in the Kuki locality which was further away from the main market. During this time of the day getting public transport is not much of a problem in Imphal. Luckily, he soon found an auto to take him home. Memory of home filled him with overpowering warmth for his family and the childhood that he had spent here. As the auto stopped near the gate of his house, he saw his father sitting in the veranda reading the local newspaper. That was so typical of the old man. He had come over from Jaribam during the weekend. Father pulled down the newspaper and his eyes pierced towards his son. Max paid the auto driver and opened the gate. He could see that his father had grayed faster in the last one year. Mother had told him that off late, he was not keeping too well. His cuffing had increased and he also suffered from regular breathing problem. Seeing his son, Mr Lotzem seemed to be lightened up. Both father and son hugged each other.

"Marry, look Max has come." Mr Lotzem called his wife who was still busy in the household work. Before mother could step out into the veranda, Max had quietly moved inside the house. The moment he saw his mother he almost lifted her from the ground. Max laughter filled the house and it seemed that a lifeless thing had come alive. Only Max could do that. At least for his parents. The couple sat together to be updated by their son about his fast pace life. His sister Kim was still not back from the school and would only be returning a bit late. Mother had cooked special lunch for Max. Normally, as a routine the family lunch was laid a little early. In fact, his father as a matter of habit over the years preferred lunch by 8.30 in the morning. But today as an exception, he along with Mrs Lotzem waited for their son to come. Max was touched. He quickly freshened up and joined his father for the meal on the dining table. The dining hall was small and the table occupied substantial amount of space. Mr Lotzem was not in much favour of it, when it was purchased two years ago. However, he relented to the wishes of his children. The table was special for Max, as it was designed and made by one of the local boys who had gone to primary school along with him. Although, his friend unlike him did not pursue his education but now was a well established furniture businessman. He was almost like a family and gave due regards to the senior Lotzem.

"So how long are you on leave?" asked father extending the bowl of curd to his son.

"Well, I will be here for about ten odd days. We got to be back at the institute by first week of the next month."

"How about your friends you mentioned?" asked Mrs Lotzem joining in the conversation.

"They have also come along with us. Presently, they are at Dhayan Singh's house. I plan to take them to our village. Actually, they are all very keen on it."

"Oh! But the house has been locked for quite some time and your uncle may not have really found time for its maintenance. To my mind, it may not be a very good idea to take them to the village after all. As such, I am not very comfortable regarding your visit to the village," Mrs Lotzem said with a concerned look.

Before Max could respond, Mr Lotzem said, "Don't worry, I will pass it to your uncle to get the house prepared for your friends. Just confirm the dates when you want to be there."

"Thanks Dad."

Although Mrs Lotzem did not persist over her argument, still, her displeasure was quite evitable on her face. By the time the lunch was over, Noody came inside the room. She had been remarkably well trained and refrained from entering the room when the members of the family were having their meal. Noody was nearly three years old and had seen added in the list of the family members by Kim. She was a pomeranian. Noody generally stayed quiet and was a great companion for Kim. Rather, the only time she barked during the day was when the food was being served in her plate. She was quite furry. In spite the fact that Kim brushed her coat regularly still her stands were seen everywhere in the house. Interestingly, the senior Lotzems has adjusted to her company. However, Max did not like her. Especially, after the creature had chewed his hush puppy shoes during his last visit. Much to Max's annoyance, Kim had stood in support of her and rather blamed her brother for keeping the shoe near Noody's favourite sleeping place. The memory of the past also seemed to be fresh in Noody's mind, who immediately barked aggressively the moment she laid the eyes on the intruder. However, Mrs Lotzem intervened timely and took Noody out of the room before a duel could start between the two. She feared that once again, Noody must not become the cause of tiff between the brother and the sister.

Kim generally was back from the government school by four in the evening. Some six months ago, she had been granted a permanent appointment as a science faculty for senior secondary classes. Although, her parents were happy regarding their daughter's job but then were equally worried regarding her marriage. Off late, Kim insisted that marriage was not on her mind and she needed more time to professionally settle herself. As such, the family had not received much of marriage proposals in the recent past. The Lotzems feared that Kim was almost following the footsteps of their eldest daughter who had already declared her stand to stay single. As a matter of further concern for the Lotzems, in the last few years, Kim had also become quite short tempered. In fact, Max actually found it difficult to communicate with her. They often had arguments ranging from Max's pranks, to Kim's marriage and Noody's future in the Lotzems house. The only thing that was a common platform between the two was the love for music. Therefore, in spite of all the differences, Max had brought some latest English number CDs for Kim. He knew how much his sister loved to add to her collection of songs. With regards to Kim's marriage, Max truly hoped for a right match for her who would keep her happy. But, like his father he too did not want to force things upon anyone.

As usual, Max also brought some presents for both his parents. Quite naturally, they thanked him and told him not to really bother with such gifts. However, deep within they were touched by such gestures of their son and felt real proud to be his parents. One more person, who was always proud of him, was Father Alison and Max knew that he would be eagerly waiting for him. He was very close to estimable Father Alison, with whom he confided almost all his close secrets. Max gave the entire credit of his achievements to Father Alison. Even though, they had great difference in age, still they were almost like friends.

Sunday mornings, due to increased attendance at the church were busy for Father Alison. He truly loved his job and a deep look into the eyes of this altruist gave a clear sense of spiritual contentment that he enjoyed. Supportive of his appearance was the fact that the Father was a very well read man and had travelled to many places around the world. He was very fond of singing and the gospel songs had mainly been promoted and popularized within the area due to his personal initiative. Max had on number of occasions recommended the Father to record the songs and put them for sales. However, the Father was never in favour of any commercial activity. He always joked regarding the powerful impact of his live performance and that these songs were only a medium to connect to god, the experience of which was priceless. When Max was a young boy, it was Father who had encouraged him to sing and play the guitar. Father's own guitar was the most precious gift that Max had received over the years.

By the time Max entered the Church, Father had already retired to his personal library. Max knew that Father Alison never slept during the afternoons and would not mind his intrusion. A single knock at the door and the alert voice of Father Alison welcomed the intruder.

"Come on in," he said.

Max slowly moved inside the room and saw a radiant smile on father's face. Father Alison got up from the chair and warmly hugged Max.

"I knew you will be here. Marry had told me in the morning that you will be reaching today."

"Mom has never been good with secrets," said Max. Father warmly held Max's hand as he guided him to the chair. Max handed him the book he had purchased as a gift for the Father.

"You never forget to add on to this library. God bless you," said Father.

This time, Max had brought a book on the Chinese customs and traditions. They both had unanimously concluded during their previous discussion regarding the need to educate oneself about various facets of this rising global power. Interestingly, in Manipur in the past ten years the Chinese products had taken over a sizable portion of consumer market. The reduced competition of Indian products in the same segment had been a cause of worry. Many more within the region certainly shared this common viewpoint.

In the next one hour, Max updated Father Alison regarding the life at the management institute. They also spoke about the latest trends of business at the international level. Max was always surprised by Father's updated knowledge.

"Father, you sure can join a management institute as one of the professors. You indeed have great erudition of the market and financial issues," said Max.

"Well, I guess I am rather happier to be with my people and serve them to attain a more fulfilling life. However, it is you my son who needs to make the correct choice."

Max understood as to where the discussion was heading. Father, from quite sometime had been cajoling Max to finally get settled in Manipur after completing his education. That way, he will be able to actively contribute for the upliftment of the state and its people. But Max had his own share of reservations. Firstly, there was limited scope of business opportunities in Manipur. Even suitable employment as per his qualification seemed to be a difficult proposition. In case, even if he started his own venture, as was propagated by the Father, he didn't have that much money. Then, there was fear of the outfits demanding the extortion money or some other related trouble. Although, the general interference of the outfit had reduced over the years, but still, they were active and prevalent both within the urban as well as the rural areas. Finally, all his friends who were doing well had opted to settle outside the region. So, why should he restrict his growth opportunities?

"Hey Father, my friends from the institute have also come along with me," said Max trying to divert from their present discussion. Father Alison smiled. He knew Max far too well.

"That's great. Max, you must get them to our church sometime."

"I will Father. Well, I must leave now. My friends are expecting me in the evening. Good day Father and I hope you like the book."

"Oh yes! In fact, the next time we meet I will tell you some details of the culture and traditions of China. Thanks for coming," said Father as he waved at the boy who was leaving the courtyard.

During winters, the sunset in Manipur is generally by 4.30 or 5. In fact, the traffic movement in Imphal city also gets restricted after the last light. Thus, Max had decided to leave for Dhayan Singh's house early and spend the night along with his friends. It may sound so normal for people from other parts of the country. However, twenty years ago such a thing was unheard in Manipur. A Kuki boy staying in a Meitei's house was next to impossible. Mostly, the communities in the state restricted such close interaction amongst themselves. But with time, all these things were slowly changing. Today, marriages amongst various communities had become quite acceptable. These were signs of a progressive society which Father Alison often spoke about. However, there were still people, especially of the older generation, who latched on to the orthodox view. Luckily, Dhayan Singh's family was broad-minded, well-educated and had always welcomed Max in their house.

Max informed his parents about his plans and packed up his stuff for the next day. Mr Lotzem was in Imphal for a week to finish some work in the education department. This would give the father and son more time to spend together during the next few days. Before Max left, Kim also returned from school. She seemed to be in good mood and was genuinely happy to see her brother. Max promised her to be at home tomorrow and before leaving handed over the CDs.

Dhayan Singh's house was in a posh locality in the heart of the city. His father, Mr Indra Singh Hashnam, had retired last year as the Chief Conservator of the state forest department. They had a joint setup. Both his paternal uncles had adjoining houses next to their own house and the families seemed to be closely netted. Uncle Irom owned a transport company and two patrol pumps in the city. The other, uncle Tomba was a senior professor of mathematics in the Manipur University. Dhayan Singh's father was the eldest amongst his brothers. His grandmother stayed along with his father. Amongst the younger generation, uncle Tomba's eldest son was a doctor in the army. He had recently been commissioned in the forces. The remaining kids of the household were generally of school going age. It would rather not be an understatement to say that the Hashnams were actually from the affluent class of Manipur.

Dhayan Singh's van led them to the house. There were a number of family members who were present in the house. One by one, each of Dhayan Singh's friends were introduced to the members of the house. It seemed as if too many people were simultaneously speaking to each other within a constrained place. Shilpa who was till now inside the house also came out in the corridor. She saw Esha and both the girls hugged.

"Thank God, you were able to make it for my marriage," said Shilpa.

"You look so pretty."

"Thanks."

Rashid by now seemed to be in a much cheered up mood. He quietly admired the double storey house and especially liked the well-maintained lawn. There were a number of trees within the compound which gave quite a green look to the entire house. The adjoining houses of Dhayan Singh's uncles were commonly linked with a pathway. The strings of garlands were covering the entrance and the porch area depicting the festive mood of the house. The tea was served in the lawn itself while the domestic help of the house took the belongings of the guests to their respective rooms. Interestingly, the elderly male members of the house were dressed in the traditional white kurta and dhoti. The women folks were dressed in more colourful attire. This was more so as in the morning there had been the engagement ceremony in the house. The groom and his relatives had just left a short while ago. As per the Meitei tradition, the groom's side during the engagement visits the bride's house to offer new dresses to the bride. The fusion of modern culture has further added the ring ceremony during this event. The family pundit and the photographer who had captured the precious moments were still present. Mr Indra Singh Hashnam, Dhayan Singh's father, was busy coordinating the next day's events with the family pundit. Two days later was Shilpa's marriage. The photographer was still busy clicking the photos and the newly arrived guests were also covered under the lens.

Soon Dhayan Singh's mother announced that the lunch was ready and the guests could quickly freshen up before the meal was served. Shilpa had already taken Esha to her room and the girls were admiring the dresses that were brought by the groom's side. The rest of the group was to stay in uncle Irom's house. Gopal took Arun, Rashid and Rajiv to their respective rooms. Uncle Irom's house was done up very tastefully and reflected the affluence of its owner. There were at least five or more bedrooms in the house. The boys had been allotted two rooms on the first floor. Before Rashid could limp through the stairs, Rajiv had shifted his own luggage in one of the rooms along with Arun. This left Rashid with the option to share the room with his host, Dhayan Singh. Rashid had pathetic snoring habit which was well known and scary for all his friends. He almost whistled through his inlet and outlet valves in a manner resembling a MiG-29 during a crash landing. Therefore, the blunt of sleepless nights had to be faced by the host.

"So what's scheduled for the day, Gopal?" asked Arun.

"Irom uncle has organized cocktail for close friends and family in the evening. Day after is the D-day for Shilpa didi. The marriage ceremony will commence in the evening when the groom arrives," said Gopal.

"What is being served in the cocktails?" asked Rajiv who was always game for a drink.

"You are going to get a diet coke. And yes, don't get funny ideas. As such for your knowledge, Manipur is a dry state where sale of alcohol is not permitted," said Dhayan Singh, who just entered the room. He looked at his younger brother who took the hint that it was time for him to leave.

"Mom said that the lunch was ready, so don't be late," said Gopal as his passing comment.

"Uncle is going to do so much... the cocktails. And, the dear brother will continue to restore the sanctity of the dry state," teased Rajiv.

"Don't worry, Uncle Irom has already invited all of us for the cocktails barring Dhayan Singh," said Rashid who finally managed to reach the room.

"You guys will never improve! It's perfect if Uncle Irom has already extended the invitation to the boozers," said Dhayan Singh.

The food was perfect. There was a dish made of bamboo shoots which was quite spicy and well cooked. For the non-vegetarians, the fish curry and rice was the delicacy. Rashid especially gorged on to the fish curry, as if, he was the final terminator for the species. There were several other guests in the house for the meal. As per Gopal, the celebrations were in due process for the last three days. There were aunties, uncles, grandparents and large number of kids. They conversed in the Manipuri language. In fact, the background music from the speakers was also in Manipuri. However, to communicate with Arun, Rajiv, Rashid and Esha; English and Hindi were also spoken by many.

To Arun it seemed to be a totally different world. He observed that the people in general were very polite. Even if, someone was not formally introduced, still he greeted them with a warm smile and obvious nods. His eyes were searching for Esha. Although,

Dhayan Singh had told him that Esha was along with Shilpa and her friends. The girls will take some more time to come for the meal. He had the urge to walk up to Esha but then decided to just call her.

"Where are you?"

"Well, in the same house as you."

"Please, come out."

"Arun, I am with the bride and she needs some more time before she gets ready," she teased him as the urgency in the voice on the other side seemed to be so prominent.

"Bye."

"Now you are being unreasonable. Love, remember its Shilpa's marriage and not ours. And by the way, I have not come here to fly kite but just to be with you. So don't you say that Bye."

After a pause Arun could only muster, "OK."

Esha smiled and said, "What OK?"

"I love you."

"Love you too and please don't get so restless. I'll be with you shortly."

Rajiv was with his camera and clicked the photographs of the little kids who were dressed in their traditional attire. The kids were running in all possible directions and had befriended their new found admirer. They were screaming on top of their voice in Manipuri, which ironically was beyond Rajiv's understanding. Still, he seemed to be doing a good job of keeping the children busy and also drew the attention of some of the mothers present. Rashid who had finally kept down his plate after the hearty meal also mingled with the children's gang. They found his limping to be quite amusing. In fact, a small boy started imitating Rashid's walking style which drew a lot of laughter amongst the gathering. By now, the bride and her friends joined in for the meal. Esha was also part of this group. She filled her plate and finally came to sit next to Arun.

"You had your lunch?" asked Esha.

"Yes."

"How mean! Why didn't you wait for me?" said Esha who had changed in a salwar suite. She was looking so radiant and beautiful.

"Why is it that you get to pull my leg so often?" said Arun.

"So what's the programme for the evening?" Esha asked knowing that she had antagonized Arun far too much.

"Well, they have planned a cocktail. Rashid and Rajiv are fairly excited about the same. They have the personal invitation from uncle Irom for the party."

Apart from Rashid and Rajiv, even Max also keenly looked forward for the booze sessions. However, Dhayan Singh did not touch a drop. He was a typical sportsman and had maintained a teetotaller status in spite of all the allurements in the institute and otherwise. Arun sometimes took a drink or two when forced. However, he was famous to fall sleep after two strong drinks.

"You know what; Shilpa has selected such a beautiful dress for her wedding. She will look very pretty."

Knowing how much Esha liked to dress well for all formal occasions, Arun asked, "So what are you wearing for the marriage?"

At times such small tricks do wonders. For the next few minutes, Esha spoke about her plans in terms of dresses, ornaments, footwear and makeup. Arun just kept nodding, hardly assimilating the content of her detailed descriptions. He loved listening to Esha when she was excited about something. And on such occasions, the dress for the function was the most important thing on the mother earth. He was thinking of discussing about Esha with his parents to get their consent during his next leave. He knew they will surely approve his choice.

One person who will feel hurt regarding his marriage proposition with Esha will be his mausi who had actually started the witch-hunt almost a year back. Each time he went home, mausi would work out all possibilities for Arun to meet the daughter's of her kitty party friends. Mausi loved to maintain uniformity in her work, especially, her fixated ideas regarding the perspective girl and her family background. Arun's father although not vocal, deplored her but his mother encouraged her sister's enthusiasm. Arun's adamancy to indulge in the mausi's game plan was considered by his mother a serious threat to the emotional cord between the two families. Both of mausi's sons managed the garment shops in one of the premium markets of Delhi. She had successfully married them within her kitty party circle. Thus certainly, mausi had experience in match fixing that could not be challenged. The girls that mausi match fixed for Arun in the recent past were from the so-called affluent Punjabi families settled in Delhi. Generally, their father owned large shops in the posh localities in Delhi. The girls were mostly very fair and dressed in expensive outfits. They were amazingly aware of the price tags attached with the materialistic items in the vicinity. Be it cars, jewellery, clothing, etc...., they knew all prices. They were open-hearted and generous to upgrade Arun with the knowledge which had come to them so painstakingly. Still in the end, Arun extended his regrets to forgo such promising opportunities. After Arun and Esha got involved, he had tried hard to avoid close quarter debacle with mausi. However, her dedication to find a bride for Arun was very overpowering. In fact, during his last visit to Delhi, he did go to meet a girl on mausi's insistence. Yet again, he said a firm no. He didn't mention about the episode to Esha. The guilt of the same had bothered him for quite some time. From then, he had made up his mind to finally call it a quit as far as mausi's game plan was concerned. Today again, in this house where marriage ceremony was to take place, he was reminded of his resolve.

Esha was almost through with her meal when Dhayan Singh came to confirm Max's arrival. It was still bright outside; however, Dhayan Singh insisted that by 5 o'clock it would be sunset. By now, most of the guests had also left and the next event was to start sometime later. Esha opted to rest until then. The rest of the group also closed into their rooms. Through the terrace along their rooms they saw the complete view of the city. Imphal city was quite well spread. Hashnam's house was located in the heart of the city. The famous Kangla fort was clearly visible from there. As per Dhayan Singh, the Raj Bhawan on the Governor Road was also very close by. In fact, tomorrow they were scheduled for the local site seeing.

"In case you want any assistance, please do let us know," offered Arun.

"Thanks. You all made it to Shilpa's marriage, well that's good enough."

"So, where is Max?" asked Rashid whose back seemed to be much better than before.

"Well, should be here anytime," said Dhayan Singh.

The rest of the evening they spent formalizing the plans regarding their trip in areas in and around Imphal. Max, who arrived shortly, extended his contribution. Tomorrow in the morning, they would go around the city and see some important places. Dhayan Singh confirmed that a dedicated vehicle and driver will be made available to them.

Rajiv dropped Jeffrey Archer's latest novel and had started reading a book on Manipur. This book on Manipur was given to him by uncle Tomba. He had actually gone to uncle Tomba's house to get the book. Uncle Tomba was a very well read man. He had maintained a library in his own house which had all varieties of books. The library room had large wooden shelves all along the wall with various books neatly placed. Most of the books had leather covering which uncle Tomba particularly ensured. In the centre of the room, there was an elegant black leather sofa-set which was comfortable for long reading hours. In one of the corners, uncle Tomba had placed his computer to access the internet. On the wall facing the entrance door, there was a large painting. The painting depicted the 'Pung Cholom' dance form in which the male dancers had 'pung,' a form of instrument, which they played while all four of them synergized their bodies in the mid-air. Their expressive eyes seemed to be interlocked and reflected each moment of joy during performance. They wore the lemon colour kurta, dhoti and turban. It was a very beautiful painting which depicted the freedom, life, spirit and grace of the people of Manipur. One more thing that caught Rajiv's attention was the idols of Radha and Krishna which were auspiciously kept at one of the corners. The room also had the aromatic fragrance.

"Uncle, you have a very well-maintained library. I would love to sit here for hours together if time so permitted," said Rajiv.

"Well, thanks. I'll take it as a compliment. Good to see that people in your generation are fond of reading books. Ironically, from the time internet usage had increased, people have generally stopped reading printed books," said uncle Tomba.

"In fact, when I entered I thought that your collection of books will be purely related to your academic field. But here, I see books on culture, history, politics, autobiographies and many other digressed subjects."

"Yes. Yes. You will also find books on sports. Dhayan Singh especially in our house is fond of those types of books. The medical books are largely contributed by my elder son who is a doctor."

"The painting is also very good. The expression of the eyes seems to reflect so much life. Where did you purchase it from?" said Rajiv who was still admiring it.

"Oh! That was made by my wife. She is a very talented painter."

"Indeed. The work seems to be of a professional. Does aunty puts the paintings on sale?" asked Rajiv.

"No not really. She hasn't painted for quite a while. Although during her younger days she did contribute her paintings to some of the art galleries."

Rajiv nodded as he was fairly impressed. Before coming to Manipur, Rajiv never bothered to see much difference between his two friends, Hashnam and Max. But now he realized that both represented two different sets of communities. The Hashnams being the Hindus had more traditional form of living. The Kukis largely seemed to be followers of Christianity. There could not be a better person to explain all these things in detail than uncle Tomba.

Uncle Tomba firstly explained about the Meitei community. The Meitei inherited the Mongolian features. As per him, in the past the Meitei religion was based on animism. With time the 'Vaishnavite Hinduism' was adopted in which various gods and goddesses were worshipped with special importance to Radha and Krishna. The plains in Manipur were inhabited mainly by the Meitei who ruled the state and had a formalized kingdom from 33 A D onwards. The main livelihood of the people was agriculture. Amongst other communities, the Kuki is also called the Khongjois. They are widely settled all across Manipur but especially occupy the south-western, south and the south-eastern hills. They are originally believed to have migrated from China. Then, there is the Naga community. The Nagas are believed to share common ancestors with the Meiteis. There are many clans of Nagas who have come under common umbrella over the years. They mostly occupy the north-eastern, north and north-western hills of the state of Manipur. In addition to these three predominant communities in Manipur, the others include the Lois who claims to be the original inhabitants of Manipur. Then there are Muslims, Sikhs and Nepalese who have a fair representation in the social fibre of the state.

Rajiv was also curious regarding the spread of Christianity in the region of North-East. So he asked uncle Tomba, "Tell me uncle, how Christianity had such a wide reach in the region?"

"Well, primarily the Naga and the Kuki converted to Christianity over the last two hundred years," said uncle Tomba.

"What brought about this change?"

"Well, in 1870 the British government extended its influence in the region. They primarily wanted to guard their economic interests in Assam. However, they felt that no substantial progress could be made towards the east, if the hostility with the people in the hill region was not brought to an end. Thus, the British spread English education amongst the hill people. They perceived that in this way the hill people will be incorporated with the economic activities of the British in the region. Slowly, under the British patronage a number of missionaries of the Christian community also expanded their activities in this area. This led to large scale conversion of the Kuki and the Naga tribes to Christianity. Today, both these communities mainly follow this faith."

"That's great! I always wondered as to how there were so many Christians in this region. Thanks for updating me."

"I'll recommend you to read this book. It will surely broaden your horizon regarding various facets pertaining to the region of North-East," said Uncle Tomba as he handed over a book to Rajiv.

"By the way, now that you have raised the issue of the spread of Christianity in the region, let me tell you an interesting belief of its followers. The Mizo tribe believes that they are descendants of the tenth tribe of Israel in the house of Ephrain. Even as per the Old Testament of the Bible, the Israelites are the chosen people for whom god entered the covenant. However, during those times the people were unfaithful to god and so god dispensed them in far off places. These people worshipped woods and stones until they reconnected to god in the British times. Popularity of this theory further helped to spread Christianity in the region of Northeast."

"Oh! Really? This was not known to me. And yes! Thanks for the book," said Rajiv.

By the time Rajiv got back to the room, Rashid and Max were almost ready for the evening cocktail. Arun had been out for some time and his destination was not much of a guess. Outside it was a little nippy and Rashid had covered himself with a few layers of winter clothing. The much amusing part in his winter-wear was the woollen earplugs.

"Where did you manage those rabbit ears?" asked Rajiv.

"Well, I purchased them sometime back." Rashid's tone was already on the defensive mode.

"And you actually think that you should wear your entire winter costume today itself in the cocktails. Rashid stop embarrassing us. What will Dhayan Singh and his family think?" said Rajiv with both his hands up in the air.

After much pleading and argument by Rajiv, Rashid finally agreed to forego wearing the ear plugs. Gopal soon came to escort them for the cocktails. Dhayan Singh had told his friends that traditionally the girl's side did not organize such functions but with changing times the trends were also changing. The get-together at Irom uncle's house was in the hall on the first floor. Indra uncle and Tomba uncle were teetotallers and preferred to skip the cocktails. Even Dhayan Singh was not there. He was busy in some household work. As for Arun, he was still missing in action. Anyhow, the trio were themselves company and Irom uncle proved to be a good host. Uncle had invited few of his friends and relatives. The best of scotch was on house and the grand drawing room was quite cosy and comfortable.

Arun and Esha had finally found time for themselves. Gopal had brought Arun to their house. There was dominating presence of the women folks in the house but then the terrace area on the second floor was peaceful. The terrace roof was covered by a thick fibre sheet and a number of green plants further enhanced the ambience of the place. There was a rot iron swing which was large enough to comfortably accommodate three people. Dim multi-coloured bulbs in the terracotta hanging lamps added to the sanctity of the place. There were a cluster of city light in the background and the sky stood clear with sparkling stars. The soothing folk music played somewhere in the background. It was neither too loud nor too slow. Perfect. But, in a language that was not known to both of them. Still it had its own magical charm. The wind had a little chill but was quite bearable. Arun sat next to Esha on the swing. The swing swayed in slow momentum without force expedited by its occupants. She was wearing a red and black salwar suit and cream cardigan. There was a reflection of the light on her hair, making her look all the more desirable. The little index finger of her left hand was touching Arun's hand. Both were so very conscious of this touch which gave a feeling of so much warmth.

"I find the place to be very beautiful. In fact, Shilpa told me a number of places that we must visit in Imphal. So are we going out tomorrow?" asked Esha.

"Yeah! Dhayan Singh has organized for our local sight seeing. Max will be accompanying us. He has also tied up with his friend, Daniel, to take us for the Sangai festival in the evening."

"I hope you guys will give me some time to shop around in the city. Shilpa has told me a number of items that are must pick type."

Esha for the next hour talked about her experience in the house of Hashnams. She had befriended some of Shilpa's friends who were also staying put for the marriage. Girls as such are universally gifted to communicate amongst themselves on various topics which are beyond understanding to a common male. However, they are generous to readily impart the knowledge to the patient listeners. Arun was indeed a very patient listener who could maintain very receptive expressions in spite the fact that the comprehension of the extended data was to the minimum. This was his biggest asset which had put him in advantage over many others. Esha adored him for his this particular god gift.

As per Esha, today was the first marriage function in the house of the Hashnams. It is what we in the other parts of India consider as the engagement ceremony. Here it is called 'Heyingpot'. Before their arrival, the rituals had been performed. As per tradition, the members of the groom's family had come with gifts locally known as 'Kwa'. The items are handed over between the fathers of both the bride and the groom. In the evening, amongst the close relatives of the bride the sweetmeat is distributed.

"That's very interesting. It pleases me to see that you have developed great interest in the marriage ceremonies. Ours should be facilitated with such close quarter experience. So, when should I officially propose you," teased Arun.

"Don't be naive."

"OK. Coming back to your talks, tell me, do the girl's side only receive gifts or do they also give something," said Arun still teasing Esha. He was now sitting closer to Esha and was almost holding her hand.

"You are teasing me".

"No. No. I am dead serious and listening to you."

"OK. Stop laying your hands on me and listen. Even the girl's side sends gifts to the groom. Tomorrow, Gopal along with Tomba uncle will carry Kwa and flowers for the groom. This is considered as a formal invitation to the groom for the marriage."

"Oh! Great! But tell me, when will your own brother formally invite me for our marriage?" said Arun who burst out laughing and held Esha much closer.

Suddenly, the door from the room to the terrace opened and Gopal came in. Seeing him, Arun let go off Esha. To cover up Arun said, "Well, we were just talking about you."

"Yeah! Even Dhayan Singh bhaiya says that I land up where actually I should not be. Mom told me to tell you to come over for dinner."

Arun and Esha quickly followed Gopal. Esha had already given the glaring look to Arun which had sobered him. Normally, the dinner in the Hashnam family was over by 7.30 in the evening but today due to the large gathering in the house, the timings had extended. Rashid, Max and Rajiv also joined in for dinner. They had just come from Irom uncle's house. Dhayan Singh was part of the catering department and was busy in ensuring that the guests were served warm food.

"Any help required Hashnam," said Rashid in almost the top of his voice.

There were suddenly a number of heads that turned. Max was first to realize that Rashid had lost the control over his tongue.

"Actually, we all in the institute address Dhayan Singh with the surname," said Max, almost extending a quick explanation.

Irom uncle was the one to laugh loudly and added, "All of us are known more so by our surnames. Come on, pick up your plates."

However, there was no denying that Rashid was tipsy and seemed to be extremely happy. He had a mountain of rice on his plate and had topped it up with the fish curry. With his spoon he was attempting to dig into the fish cuisine. However, the accuracy was poor and the rice was spilling from the plate. As a quick remedy, Rashid left the spoon on the side table and used his hand to stuff his mouth with the fish. Rajiv could not stand and witness the so called 'tamasha'.

"You fool. You will die right here if any of the fish thorns get hooked on in your throat or wind pipe. Leave the dam fish alone," hissed Rajiv into Rashid's ears.

It took a lot of cajoling from Arun's side to make Rashid finally leave the fish on his plate to its own destiny. Although the entire group, including Esha, was feeling a little awkward on Rashid's tipsy state, but then, others in the gathering did not seem to note much. This was reasonably so because there were many more like Rashid in the gathering. Dhayan Singh also confirmed that this was part of good hospitality extended by Irom uncle. He was as such famous in his circle to offer drinks to people to their hearts content. The entire Hashnam family was aware of this quality of Irom uncle. Rajiv and Max only survived due to their capacity which had been built up with practice over a prolonged period.

Not with standing their present state, they had become close friends of Irom uncle. In fact, Rajiv had taken Irom uncle on board to manage country liquor for himself during their next session. Someone in the gathering today had told Rajiv that the rice liquor of Manipur was very famous, largely consumed by the locals and was good in taste. Ironically, inspite the state being a dry state the country liquor is much in use.

By the time the majority of the guests left the Hashnam house, it was around 9 o'clock. As per the normal timings adhered by the people here in general, it was very late. The group also called it a day as they had a busy schedule in the morning. Max shared the room with Arun and Rajiv. As for Rashid, he was far beyond the state to be bothered as to who slept where. Once he entered the room, he just threw himself on the bed and was off to sleep.

Arun was holding Esha's hand. She was giggling and stood under the tree which had those beautiful red flowers. She pointed towards the flowers. And before she could say anything further, Arun left her and moved towards the tree. He selected the bunch of those red flowers that he intended to pluck for Esha. Before his hands could reach the bunch, his eyes closed due to the sudden brightness of the sun. Then he heard Rashid's voice. He was calling for Dhayan Singh. With forceful effort Arun opened his eyes. He could not correlate. He saw Rashid standing almost over him and in the background there was glare of a bright tube light. As he turned his head he saw Rajiv and Max who were fast asleep. It slowly started coming back. He was in Hashnam's house and had gone to sleep sometime back. By now, Dhayan Singh also came in from the adjoining room.

Rashid had got up in the night and wanted to use the toilet. Both the rooms had a common bathroom and were adjoining the room in which Arun and others were sleeping. Dhayan Singh had helped to get Rashid to the toilet and now he was hovering over other's head to reach back to his bed.

"Rashid just get lost," said Arun who was fairly irritated by Rashid.

"Where is my bed?"

"Hashnam take him out of here."

"Rashid come."

"I want to have water."

"Later."

"No now. Please, I am thirsty."

Rajiv and Max lay well wrapped up in their blankets and so lifeless that they looked more like the Egyptian mummies. Dhayan Singh almost physically lifted Rashid and took him to the other room. It was nearly 2 o'clock at night and getting water for Rashid would have woken up the entire household on the ground floor. Dhayan Singh walked up to the lobby near the drawing room and opened the refrigerator. It was stocked with the soda bottles. He picked up one and brought it for Rashid. Rashid drank half of it and wring the bottle before going off to sleep. Arun had a disturbed sleep and was not too happy with the conduct of his friends.

In the morning by the time Rashid got up, the other seemed to be ready. He felt a little pain in the back but vaguely remembering the episodes of the previous evening.

"So what's the plan for the day dude?" Rashid looked up at Arun to begin a conversation. However, Arun preferred to walk out off the room then to answer him.

"What's wrong with him man? I hope, all's well between him and Esha."

"Rashid don't drink if you cannot hold. I heard that you made a fool of yourself last night," said Rajiv.

"Look, who is advising."

"OK. OK. Just chill. You guys better get ready and have your breakfast. The driver will be coming in shortly to pick you up," said Dhayan Singh.

Dhayan Singh's mother was personally involved to get the

breakfast prepared for the guests. Most of the family members had already had their first meal. Esha was with one of Shilpa's friend. The girl was doing her internship from the regional medical college in Imphal. Her parents were close friends of the Hashnams. Rajiv found the girl to be real cute but saw 'Tell me something new' look on Esha's face. Still, he walked to where the girls were seated for the breakfast.

"Hi Esha! You look great. May I click few of your photos?"

"Go ahead," she said with her best smile. She knew that Rajiv wanted to click the photo of the girl next to her and if possible break a conversation with her.

And there he went, just as predicted. "Excuse me miss, can I also take you in the frame?"

"OK."

The girls smiled while Rajiv clicked the photos. When he came to show the photos on the digital screen of the camera, Esha quietly said, "Rajiv lay off, OK! She is already engaged and her father is an important politician of this place."

"I guess I need to be miles away from you if I ever want my love life to begin. Anyways where is Arun?"

"He is waiting for us near the vehicle."

Max had planned to first take them to the Kangla fort. The subsequent destinations included the famous polo ground, the museum and then the nearby market. Max would in the evening take them to his house and to Father Alison. He had also managed the tickets for the Sangai festival. As far as Shilpa's marriage function was concerned, the big day was tomorrow. Thus, they could be out for the entire day. At about 10 o'clock, the group reached for the Kangla fort. The place was ruins of the old palace of Kangla. There was a waterbody along the periphery of the fort. The landscaping was covered with rich green grass. During this time of the year, the flowers were blossoming and the entire place had a beautiful ambience. There were huge gates at both the entrances of the Kangla fort. Max confirmed that some of the important government employees had their residence within the premises which added on to the factor of additional security. The driver stopped the vehicle next to the temple which was part of the assets within the fort. At the entrance of the temple, there was a huge sized pair of white cows made of concrete cement. The stairs led to the temple which was quite well maintained. They offered their prayers and Rajiv clicked the photographs once they came out of the temple.

Next to the temple, there were two huge grounds which seemed to be used for organizing functions. One of the grounds even has the sitting facility in its arena. Then, there was the museum of the Kangla fort. Rajiv promptly purchased the tickets and paid additional charge to carry his camera inside the museum. The museum had a wide collection of the art and craft of the state which was well displayed. The walls were covered with photographs depicting the history of Manipur. A section of the museum housed the costumes traditionally worn by the locals. Then, there was a section in which the dresses of the warriors along with their weapons and arms were kept. Some of the ancient documents which seemed to be well preserved were also displayed. Overall, the museum was aesthetically maintained and the group spent almost an hour going around the entire place.

"It looks as if an entirely different world existed here. So rich in their culture and traditions," said Esha.

"Correct. Until, I guess the British came over to get them integrated with rest of their empire," contributed Rajiv.

"When exactly did the British come over to this region?" asked Rashid who had already opened the bag given by Dhayan Singh's mother and was digging his teeth on a fairly oversize apple.

"Well, the British rule was established in Manipur in 1891 and later it was merged into Indian Union on 15 Oct 1949. At that time, it was administratively placed under the territorial council.

Later in 1963, a legislative assembly under the Union territory act was formed. Manipur attained its complete statehood on 21 Jan 1972. With this, a legislative assembly of sixty elected members was established," said Max.

"Wow. How do you know so much? It seems that you have done a good homework to be our guide, no?" said Rashid.

Even Arun and Rajiv were impressed with the information that Max has just shared.

"Esha, please take the bag off from this monkey before he even eats the bag," said Rajiv. Rashid had again fiddled into the bag and successfully found some bananas in it.

Esha, Arun and Max burst out in laughter seeing Rashid limp away towards the vehicle as Rajiv practically chased him.

"Lay off. I didn't have proper breakfast."

Immediately after the fort visit, the group headed for the famous polo ground. The polo ground per says was located in the middle of Imphal city. Max told them that it was the oldest existing polo ground in the world today. However, the infrastructure to accommodate large strength of spectators around the ground seemed to have been slowly upgraded over a period of time. In its present form, it looked like any other modern stadium with best state of the art facilities. Initially, when polo was introduced in Manipur, the ruling class improvised the local dress to suit the requirements of the polo players. Even now, a majority of players wore the same traditional attire. Each year in succession the polo tournaments are organized by the Horsing and Polo Association of Manipur in which more than fifteen local teams participate. The state police team and army team are also active participants. The polo tournaments are very popular amongst the locals.

By the time they all reached the central ground within the stadium, they found two teams actually practising for the mega sports event. Incidentally, there were few spectators of the game. In place of horses, the players were riding the ponies.

"Why are they not using horses in the game?" asked Arun.

"Well, even I am not aware of the logic of using the ponies," said Max.

Esha said, "Look there are some people sitting in the stadium. Why don't we ask them? They surely will know about it."

"Yeah, that's a good idea," said Rajiv.

Both Arun and Rajiv climbed the stairs to reach the podium where they found some spectators who could actually tell them about the game and its rules. In the meanwhile, Esha, Max and Rashid stood admiring the ponies that were running from one extremes of the ground to the other. Each pony rider had a polo club in his hand and they were attempting to control the rolling ball. Their aim was to gallop towards the goal post. It seemed to be quite similar to the game of hockey or football. The only difference was that the players were riding the pony and each team comprised of just seven players. To control the game there was also a referee who too was riding a pony. In addition, just outside the ground there was a pony rider who in place of the polo club had spear in his hand. He was galloping the pony with full speed from one end to the other on a track along the ground and in the mid route attempted to pick up a target object from the ground. When he reached closer to his objective during the practice, Esha and others realized that the rider was a very young boy. By all calculations, he would not have been more than twelve or thirteen. He had a good coordination of speed and stealth while he rode his pony.

Arun called for Esha. The trio turned towards the podium and realized that Arun and Rajiv were waving and indicating them to join. An elderly man was standing along with them.

"So, finally they have found someone who can extend some information regarding the game," said Max.

Max and Esha moved towards the stairs which led to the podium. Rashid preferred to stay where he was.

"Rashid, you don't want to come," said Esha.

"No. You guys continue. I will give some rest to my back," said Rashid. As such, the handbag with the eatables was still with him.

Arun introduced the fresh arrivals to the old gentleman. Max spoke to him in Manipuri. The man was fluent in both English as well as Manipuri. However, for the convenience of his target audience he mainly spoke to them in English. As a prelude to his previous discussion with Arun and Rajiv, he gave the background of the game and the ponies.

The ponies were of a unique variety and are only found in the region of Manipur. They are active and naturally quite energetic. Over the last few decades, the species has drastically reduced in strength. Under the wild life regulations, if the count of any species falls below the mark of ten thousand, it is added in the list of endangered species. As per the data collected in the recent past within Manipur, the number of these ponies was assessed to be about fifteen hundred only. Therefore, the state government felt that deliberate attempts must be made to enhance the strength of these ponies. Keeping this aspect in mind the game, polo, was reintroduced with fresh enthusiasm in the state. The responsibility of breeding the ponies and promoting the game was taken over by the Horsing and Polo Association of Manipur. Today, once again the game has become popular within the state. In fact, a few foreign participants have also started coming in Manipur to witness and play this game. Encouraged by these developments, a number of tournaments are being organized for polo game around the state. In November end, yet again, one more tournament was scheduled. The teams present at the ground were practising for the same event.

They all thanked the old gentleman. He was actually part of the organizers who were involved with the conduct of the forthcoming tournament. Before leaving, they got a few photos clicked with the practising teams and the ponies. Arun, Rajiv and

Esha even managed to get their photo clicked sitting on the pony. Esha was in the centre while the boys positioned themselves on the sides wearing the colourful headgears. This time Rashid was the photographer.

Closer to the polo ground were the famous shops which are locally called as 'Ima Keithel' in the Khwairamband Bazar. Interestingly, it is the only market in the world where all the stalls are run by the women folks. There were numerous shops which were selling garments of the latest design. However, the displayed stuff was not branded and seemed to be of a slightly lower quality. As per Max, a large amount of products on sale were of Chinese origin. The local retailers purchased such stuff through Moreh which was the border town between India and Myanmar. Apart from the Chinese clothes, there were also traditional dresses of the Meiteis which were displayed for sale.

"Esha do not spend too much time here, else we will not be able to cover up all places as planned," said Arun.

"OK. But you please stay with me."

Arun told the others that they will meet them at the vehicle parking after forty minutes. Knowing Esha, it was certain that the young couple will be spending more time in the garment section. The others moved ahead. There was a section within the market where eatables were being sold. In addition to the commonly available items as in other parts of the country, here, there were some unique items for purchase. They included flowers of different varieties, roots, rice based snacks, frogs, insects, variety of fishes etc. Then, there were the famous Naga spears and knives of all shape and sizes. Max told his friends in much detail about the local people and their lives in Manipur. Rajiv and his camera seemed to be busy. In a market full of mostly ladies, he found more reason to click photos. Rashid had already requested Esha to purchase some gift items for his sisters within his specified budget. Apart from that the only place which interested Rashid was the section where eatables were being sold. He had already gone around a number of stalls tasting the local items without purchasing any. He felt he deserved a pat on his back for his intelligence but somehow his jealous friends ignored him.

Within the market area, there was also a section for electronic goods. Yet again majority of China made products were on display. Interestingly, most products seemed to be the replica of the original ones and looked real good. There were mobile phones, computers, televisions, music systems, mixers, etc. Even, things like generator and bicycles were on sale.

"How come there is so much accessibility of the Chinese products in the market?" Rashid asked Max who had almost become like an encyclopedia on Manipur.

"I guess the region is much closer to China?"

"That is definitely a satire. After all, this area is an integral part of India."

"Yes. Indeed. However, if the Delhi-Agra highway is closed for a single day, it will be covered in detail by all news channels. But here, even a road block of more than hundred days does not draw much attention. People's indignation has crossed the stage of self pity and they have adjusted to their circumstances, I guess."

"I wonder how people here managed with the road communication getting disrupted so often. It must be really bad?" Rashid asked.

"Yes. During such blockades petrol is sold in plastic bottles at triple the cost in black market. So is the state of the gas connections and such essential products. It is these Chinese products that come from Myanmar, which rescue the people through such terrible times. This is also one of the reasons that these goods are preferred in the region. Although, development changes are noticeable in Manipur but still much more is desired to develop the state," said Max.

"I guess you are right. Until, the aspirations of people within a particular area is understood, even, the government cannot bring about much substantial changes in their lives," replied Rajiv who was almost in the thinking mode.

"If the strategic analysts are through with their debate, can we have something to drink?" said Rashid.

"Well, it's almost lunch time. I propose lunch at one of the famous hotels in the city. In fact, Arun and Esha must also be waiting for us at the parking. Rashid if you could hold your thirst for some time."

"OK. No issues."

By the time Arun and Esha came to the parking area, the others hanged around in the nearby bamboo shop. A number of decoration as well as utility items made of bamboo were on display. Max told them that bamboo products had a unique place in the lives of people of Manipur, irrespective of their cultural diversity. Even, Max had prophecy in making bamboo items. Once they visit his village, he will display his skills to make various items out of the bamboos.

It took Esha and Arun some more time to reach the parking. Arun was carrying the shopping bags. Yet, Esha wanted to revisit certain shop. This time she requested Max to come along with her. She had already selected a silk sari but the cost quoted was a little high. She wanted Max to confirm if the price was justified.

"I hope we did not pay her too much?" said Esha, who finally came back along with Max.

"No. No. The price was reasonable. Actually, all these items are hand carved and require lot of efforts."

"Show me what all you purchased," said Rashid.

"Well, I will but once we reach back home."

"Did you pick up something for my sisters also?"

"Yes I did."

"Thanks Esha," said Rashid.

The traffic in the city had congested and it took them about twenty odd minutes to reach Hotel Classic. Enroute they crossed a large number of security personnels at various points. This was the only possible sign which indicated that the state was still very volatile for untoward activities. The security personnels were undertaking random vehicle checks to add caution against the anti-social elements.

"How is the security situation within the city?" enquired Arun.

"Well, it's quite in control. In fact, the city has been largely incident free for quite some time," said Max.

"What kind of incidents takes place?" asked Rashid.

"Well, sometimes some blast or firing may take place. In fact, last year a fire fight had taken place right in this area."

"Max, stop scaring us," said Esha.

Max started laughing on seeing the serious faces of Rashid and Esha. He did not want to scare his friends but then the facts were facts and could not be denied.

"Hey listen; let's go back home if the area is that unsafe. As such, we are not that hungry," said Rashid.

"But I am. And as far as you are concerned, the whole bag of eatables that aunty gave has been solely eaten by you. In fact, I saw you munching around in the market also," said Rajiv.

Finally, the group entered the restaurant. As such, it had been quite a walk in the market and all were a bit hungry. The hotel menu had a large variety for selection. In fact, they even served several North and South Indian cuisines. In consultation with Esha, Rajiv and Rashid ordered a hearty meal. Before entering the hotel, Rajiv had quietly paid the driver for his quick grub. The restaurant had a counter for bakery items also and before leaving Esha insisted to carry a cake for the Lotzems. Max's house was a short distance away from there. However, he decided to take his friends to the church first to meet the Father. As such, it was in the afternoon that the Father will have no other commitments. He had already confirmed Father's availability. Many a times, father went out to the neighbouring villages and would not be at the Church. By the time they got down from the vehicle, the Father came out of the church to greet them. He was wearing his white rope and had a very pleasing smile. Father must be in his fifties but looked much fitter and younger. He welcomed Max's friends to the church. The mountains seemed to be much closer from this part of the valley. In fact, this locality was at the extreme western edge of Imphal Township. Beyond this, it was all hilly area. Overall, the place had a very scenic location.

The church was painted white with a golden cross on the top. A large wooden door with intricate carving led to the large hall where the mass prayers were performed. Close to the central wall of the hall there was a large statue of Jesus Christ. Right below the statue there was a podium from which father usually conducted the prayers. The hall had wooden flooring and spacious benches made of old Burma teak which could easily accommodate at least hundred people at one time. The group gathered near the place of worship and the father conducted a small prayer for them. For most of them, it was their very first visit inside the church premises. Only Esha and Max had previously entered a church. The place had the fragrance of incenses that were still burning. There were few murals of Jesus Christ which were also placed along the walls of the hall. Overall, there was a religious sanctity of the entire place. As per Father Alison, the maximum attendance in the church was on the Sundays. Even the children were present to form part of the coir. Max told his friends that father had a great voice and could play a number of musical instruments. Guitar was his favourite. In fact, the guitar that he had was also gifted to him by father when he was just fifteen years old.

"Yes I remember that. In fact, that was Max's prize for being in the coir without missing a single Sunday throughout the year. He used to be our lead singer and guitarist," said Father Alison with pride.

"Father, he still is the lead singer and guitarist. But now, of our institute only," said Rashid.

Father Alison laughed. "I am happy to hear that Max," he said.

Father now took the group to his study cum library. He instructed his attendant to get coffee for all of them. Father's collection of books was fairly impressive and Rajiv went around checking the books which were neatly displayed on the heavy wooden racks. Max narrated the events of the day to the Father. Father Alison had an extremely important asset. He listened to people with utmost sincerity and interest. This encouraged the others to freely share their experiences with the father.

"Well, it was a great chance for you to see the polo teams. The last time I saw the polo game was some five years earlier. But let me tell you, the sport over the last few years is again becoming popular amongst the local people. This, I know rather well because on Sunday's a number of youngsters sneak away from the church service to witness this game." Father laughed at his own joke.

"So tell me, how are you finding this place? Max says that you guys have come to the Northeast for the first time, right?"

"Yes father we all are experiencing the beauty of your state for the very first time. Max has promised this to be just the start and there is much more to see in the state," said Arun.

"Yes, he is right. I have lived almost my entire life in this area and I find the place to be so beautiful."

"But Father, isn't the state badly affected by the militants and is also much neglected?" said Rashid.

"Yes and no. Yes, there is militancy that still exists. Yes, there is slow pace of development in the state. But then, the positive aspect is that with time the militancy is on a decline and the development is on a rise."

It seemed that Max wanted to avoid any further discussions on the issue of state introspection by Father. Father too got the hint and invited them to have a look at the facilities within the church premises. A fully functional kitchen garden had been created in the church's backyard. Father was fond of growing vegetables and benevolently sent them for consumption to some of the poor families in the neighbourhood. By the time they came to the music room, Father's attendant brought them the coffee. In the music room there were a number of instruments. Father was extremely passionate about music and had been teaching musical instruments to volunteer children in the neighbourhood.

"Father, how much time does it take to learn the basics of an instrument?" asked Esha who was checking on to each piece of instruments kept in the room.

"Well, frankly it depends upon the individual. Some are fast learners and some of them are extremely slow. However, an average person will need about three to four months to understand the basics of any instrument," said Father.

"You know Father, I always wanted to play guitar. But then, never really got much opportunity," said Esha.

"I didn't know that Esha." Arun also joined in.

"In fact, whenever, Max used to play the guitar at the institute, the loss of not learning the instrument was much stronger."

"Well, had you told me so, I would have taught you the basics by now," said Max.

"OK. If that be so, Max it's an order from my side that you will teach Esha the basics of guitar the way you learnt from me years earlier. OK?"

"OK. OK. I will."

"That's very nice of you, Father. Thanks Max and don't you forget your promise. Can I request Father and you to sing a song for us?"

All others also joined in this demand and Father along with Max agreed to sing a gospel song. The song was in praise of the god and how he looks after his disciples. It was a beautifully worded song which actually touched the heart of the listeners. The meeting with Father Alison was short but Father had tied a cord with almost all of them. Before the group left, Father gifted a small Bible book each to Rajiv and others. He blessed Esha and Arun for a wonderful future together. They all promised to meet the Father again before leaving Manipur, if the time so permitted.

The next destination was Max's house. Both his parents were waiting to meet Max's friends. The family background seemed to be very modest but there was lot of warmth in the manner they were welcomed in the house. Max's father raised a number of queries regarding their institute and the future that each one hoped. He could not hold himself from praising his son. Max had to face difficult times during his growing years but still he had worked really hard to reach the place where he was today. Max was yet again uncomfortable to find himself the centre of the conversation. He hinted his father to change the topic of discussion. By now, his mother had arranged tea and snacks and insisted that Max's friends stay put in their house for the night. There was no doubt in his friend's mind that Max had inherited his mother's style of laughter. Esha gave the cake to Lotzem aunty on behalf of the group. She seemed to be a very nice person who really cared for her son. Max's sister Kim had still not come back from the school, although Mr Lotzem anticipated her to return anytime. Kim had especially made the cookies and the cake for Max's friends, the taste of which was appreciated by all. As for Rashid, he had some capacity of stuffing and did true justice to the cake and cookies served by Mrs Lotzem.

"Max told me that you all want to go to our village," said Mr Lotzem.

"Yes uncle. Max says it's located in the hills and has a very scenic view. I really wish to click some rare photos of the interiors of Manipur," said Rajiv.

"That's great. In fact, Max also has not gone to our village for many years. However, my brother still stays in the village and has his own house. We had moved out of that place some years ago. Actually, very few people will be able even to recognize Max, unless he gives his family details. My father had made a house which I inherited but that is mostly locked. By the time you all get there, I will get it prepared. I have already told my brother to look into all necessary arrangements," said uncle Lotzem.

"How far is your village from Imphal, uncle?" asked Rashid.

"Well, by bus it will take about five to six hours but in your own vehicle it would work out to be about four hours drive. Actually, the last stretch of twenty kilometres is not in good condition. But, I am sure you guys will manage it."

"Dad we got to go now. Actually, I have planned to take them for the cultural programme at the Sangai festival. I will be staying in Dhayan Singh's house tonight. Tomorrow is his sister's marriage. After that I will come back to stay with you."

Max's mother told them to wait for a little while longer as she went inside one of the rooms. Mr Lotzem also excused himself and after about ten odd minutes the couple returned with some packed gifts. They handed each one of them a gift pack.

"Aunty that truly is a very warm gesture but we possibly can't take gifts. You have already done so much to take care of us," said Esha who was looking towards Arun.

"Yes aunty, please. This really is not required. We wanted to meet you so we came but please do not tax yourself," added Arun.

"Nothing doing. All of you are like Max to us. So do not say no. As such, all these things have been made by your aunty with her own hands," said uncle Lotzem whose wife stood next to him and nodded in approval.

Quickly, understanding the emotional aspects attached with the gift, Esha thanked Lotzem aunty who hugged her. Esha asked aunty if she could open the gift. Aunty smiled and nodded in consent. It was a Kuki shawl made of woollen material. It had a combination of bright red and black colour. Not only was the shawl beautiful, traditional but was made with lot of efforts and love.

Interestingly, Rashid wanted to gain the inside knowledge as to how aunty had weaved the shawls. His questions seemed to be endless. Finally, only when Rajiv asked him as to when Rashid intended to open up his own small scale shawl making industry did the guy backed off. Before leaving, each one thanked aunty for her thoughtful gesture. Finally, the group bid their farewell to the elderly couple and headed for Dhayan Singh's house. The plan was to freshen up and then leave for the Sangai festival.

By the time they reached Dhayan Singh's house it was almost last light. Although, today there was no ceremony in the house, still, it was crowded with a number of friends and relatives. Uncle Irom was sitting in the veranda entertaining some guest when the group entered the house. Uncle Irom enquired about the events of the day. Rajiv showed uncle the digital photos on his camera of the various places that they had visited. Rashid seemed a bit tired. Maybe, his back was after all troubling him a little. But then, he refused to acknowledge his fatigue fearing that he may be excluded from attending the Sangai festival. Esha went to change and displayed the items which she had purchased to Shilpa and her mother. They approved her choice and unanimously claimed that she will look pretty in the traditional sari. Soon Dhayan Singh's mother made tea with refreshments for all.

"Are you coming along with us for the festival?" Arun asked Dhayan Singh.

"No yaar. I still got to take care of certain arrangements. You guys continue. But don't get too late. Tomorrow is the main day of Shilpa's marriage. And yes, Max is arranging for your dinner outside tonight."

Max had tied up the evening programme with Daniel and his friends. The Sangai festival is organized on the central ground of Imphal city. Today, there was the cultural programme in which artists from various districts of Manipur state were to participate. Each group had a performance of fifteen to twenty minutes in which the culture and tradition of the different communities within various districts would be depicted. By the time the group reached the venue, it was almost dark. However, the entire location was brightly lighted up. It seemed so much festive with all this rush of people. In fact, the quantum of crowd was clearly evident from the number of vehicles at the parking. By the time the group reached the entrance, Daniel was already there to receive them. Today, he was looking quite different in his appearance. He was wearing bright blue cotton trousers with a contrast yellow colour jacket. His hair style seemed to have also undergone a change. Overall, he looked very western in his dressing style. He was accompanied by someone whose name was Pakmi. Pakmi was an artist from the Manipuri film industry and seemed to be popular amongst the locals. There were a number of enthusiastic young girls and boys who came to get his autograph or to just click a snap along with him. Pakmi seemed to be happily obliging his fans who were flogging around him. He also met Max's friends with equal warmth. Incidentally, Max and Pakmi had studied in the same school. Although, Max had been two years senior to him, still, they were good friends.

"The guy seems to be a big star. Just look at the way the girls are flogging on to him. Lucky chap," whispered Rashid into Rajiv's ear.

"Yes. You are right. He seems to be quite popular amongst the people. In fact, Max told me that this guy is the lead star in a Manipuri movie released recently. Look at his physique; he seems to be a body builder. You better watch out what you speak to him. All people may not be as accommodating as your friends. OK."

"Are you taking a dig at me?"

"Come on Rashid. I am sure you have more grey matter than him. Why get complexes?"

Daniel confirmed to Max that the cultural programme would begin shortly. Today, Daniel's band concert was not scheduled and he would be with the group once the cultural programme gets started. Max guided his friends to the venue which was an open auditorium with concrete benches in the arena. Arun had purchased a few packets of popcorns. He handed the popcorns packets to others and settled next to Esha. Rashid under the dim light read out to Esha the scheduled programme from the information brochure that he had picked up at the entrance. The event would last for the next two hours.

"You seemed to be really enjoying yourself," said Arun to Esha with a broad smile.

"Well, I didn't expect so much of activities in this place. In fact, I perceived the place here will be in isolation and all wildernesses. But it seemed to be very pleasant. You saw the way the guys and girls dress up here. I am impressed."

"Oh come on. Not with that yellow jacket that Daniel is wearing."

"Well, I was rather thinking of gifting you one like that. You will look so cool," laughed Esha and held Arun's hand. She knew that Arun will never dare to wear such loud colours.

The centre stage was occupied by two beautiful announcers who were welcoming the people for the programme. Rashid cleaned his spectacles as if this will increase his zooming capability. His excitement was also reflected with the speed with which he was munching the popcorns. He kept nodding his head simultaneously to confirm to Max his keenness for the additional information that was being shared with him. Rajiv had quietly moved ahead in the row of spectators. He was busy clicking the photographs. Esha's head was leaning on to Arun's shoulder by the time the first group of artists came on the stage.

The group dance was performed by the girls for whom the boys held and moved the large bamboo sticks in rhythm just above the ground level. The music was accompanied by frequent whistle sound in the background. It was quite impressive to see the synergy with which the act was performed. The announcers thanked the concerned district organizers for the act, on completion. The next act was a solo performance. In this, a boy used three large animal bones which he flicked in mid-air on rotational basis. Each time one bone was in the air, it seemed that the performer will lose control. But then, the entire act was performed flawlessly. Next, a group song was presented in Manipuri language. It was very melodious and there was wide cheering in public in support of the singers. Max explained his friends that the song depicted the feelings of two lovers who had met each other after a long time and wanted to spend their remaining life together without any further separation. Esha and Arun seemed to be under the spell of the music as they sat even closer almost hugging each other. Their romance was finally in the full bloom. There were some more announcements that were made. A few of the dignitaries amongst the audience were extended acknowledgement for their presence during the programme. Next, was the display of the traditional dresses that are worn by people of various districts within Manipur. In this, one couple each with a small child participated. They also carried few items made of the bamboo to depict their traditions. Each male participant carried some spear or weapon to symbolize the need to be armed within the various tribes.

Subsequently, there was a small skit which was also performed. In this, a hunter along with his wife and child encounters a tiger in the middle of the jungle. He bravely protects his family as he engages the tiger. In the dual that follows, the tiger is killed. In previous times, killing of the tiger was considered an act of great bravery amongst the tribes of Manipur. Soon, when a word is spread about his act of valour amongst the peasants working in the nearby paddy field, they honoured the man and his family. This script depicted the sense of honour and bravery that is deeply rooted amongst the various tribes.

Rashid was impressed with the artist who acted as the tiger on stage. The tiger had leaped from one end of the stage to the other and in the entire act his movements on his four legs seemed so effortless. By the time the acts got over, the popcorns were also over and Rashid clapped with full enthusiasm. Next the Meitei dance was performed, in which the participants moved rhythmically reflecting Radha-Krishna who are considered very auspicious by the Hindus of this state. Then followed a dance presented by young boys with the Mrithang. It reminded Rajiv of the painting made by Tomba aunty which was placed in the library. It seemed as if the time passed at a rather fast pace. The announcers finally invited all the participants on the stage to sing a collective song for the peace and harmony within the state. There was a huge strength of artists. Their presence made the stage look so lively and colourful. And adding to the mood of the crowd, all performers carried candles for their last parting song. Although the song was in Manipuri, still the spirit of unity behind it was so strong that its message touched the hearts of the entire audience. Max's friends felt equally moved and felt blessed to witness such strong spirit of oneness in a place that the world perceives as disturbed and full of conflicts.

"You two can leave each other for some time now. I have something important to discuss with Esha, if you may excuse us," said Rajiv looking up at Arun.

"OK. But don't you get the poor girl in any trouble."

Arun along with Max moved towards the exit. Rashid could not control his curiosity and asked Rajiv if he could be of any help. Only after his call went unnoticed, he followed the exit.

"Esha, you saw the girl in the group song standing on the extreme right? The tallest girl? She is so photogenic. I really wish to click some of her photos from close quarters. If only you could come along with me to the back stage to meet her," pleaded Rajiv.

"Rajiv one day you are going to land in trouble and take me along with you. Why me, Rajiv?"

"You see, if you come along none will feel awkward. And you know I just want to click her photos only. She is so very traditional in her looks."

"OK." Relented Esha and followed Rajiv to the back stage where the entire artists had gathered after the end of the programme. They were soon able to spot the girl. She was standing in a group. The music was still being played and Esha had to almost shout on top of her voice to speak to the girl. Her name was Naomi. She was indeed a very beautiful girl. Esha told her that her friend was a photographer and wanted to click some of her photos. After a little hitch, the girl agreed to meet them once she changed her costume. It was mutually decided to meet at the eating stall outside. Esha and Rajiv thanked her and moved out. In addition to the cultural programme, stalls displaying various products for sale were also organized and had heavy rush. A large crowd had moved over towards the stalls where different items were being sold. While the others proceeded towards the stalls, Rajiv stayed near the eating joints waiting for Naomi.

Sometime later Naomi came out wearing jeans and a bright coloured jacket. She had long hair and a fair complexion. In fact, she was a little shorter than Esha, who herself was reasonably tall.

"Hi, my name is Rajiv. Thanks for meeting. Actually, I saw you on stage and felt that I need to click some of your photos, if you so permit. You have such a photogenic face," said Rajiv who seemed to be very conscious of the girl's presence. He further told her that he was passionate about photography and had come to visit his friend in Imphal. He spoke about himself and asked about her, as much as was possible in a short period of five to ten minutes.

Naomi was from Taminglong, a place in the southern district of Manipur. She had come along with her friends to participate in the Sangai festival. Otherwise, she was a student in her final year of graduation. Soon, two of Naomi's friends also came over to join them. They were amused to see a boy from outside getting so interested in their friend. Rajiv was introduced to the girls by Naomi. He offered them coffee as they settled in the nearest eating joint. The girls had planned to leave for Taminglong tomorrow. Their cultural programme was over and they were expected to be back home by their respective guardians. Rajiv clicked some photos of Naomi who felt a little hesitant in front of her friends. He wished if Naomi could sit there for some more time. But then, the girls had to leave. There were no more reasons, Rajiv could bring out that would hold Naomi any further. He had to let her go. There was nothing common in between them. Still, he felt something that drew him towards this girl. He will remember her for a long time. She will be part of his sweet memories of Manipur. Rajiv could have asked for her phone number and other details but something inside told him to let it go. Any further move would destroy this very moment. He thanked the girls. Shook hands, especially a bit longer with Naomi, and eventually bid goodbye to them.

Now Rajiv sat alone in the stall. He ordered for one more cup of coffee. The place was pretty crowded; still, he was all by himself. His friends were nowhere in sight. Probably they were shopping around in those stalls. He did not have the urge to go there. He was happy as well as a bit sad. Happiness was for meeting Naomi and sadness came with the realization that she had left. At times, it is difficult to comprehend the reason for people to meet and then suddenly drift completely apart. No amount of logic can explain such events and the rational of such brisk contacts wherein people touch each other's emotional cords. Rajiv felt sure that even Naomi had liked him. This generated a mixed feeling. Should something more have happened between the two of them? Was such a thing possible? Would it have made him happy? Was there any future between the two of them? He sipped his steaming coffee and blankly looked in the far distance undisturbed by the crowd around him.

Rajiv was tapped on the shoulder which brought him back to the world of the mortals. It was Daniel. Pakmi was also along with him.

"So how was the programme?" asked Daniel.

"Well, it was just great. In fact, I have been thinking about it only."

"Good. Where are Max and others?"

"Well, I guess they are still hanging around near those stalls," said Rajiv.

"Hey Rajiv, you really have got a very good camera. Can I have a look, please?" said Pakmi whose eyes caught the glimpse of the bright maroon coloured frame of the gadget.

"Sure. As such, you are the man who stays in front of the lens." Rajiv extended the digital camera to Pakmi and told him about its general features. On seeing the photo of Naomi on the digital screen he was once again reminded of the goodbyes that they had exchanged. Pakmi clicked some photos to get the general hang of the camera and then handed it back to Rajiv.

"Are you interested to drink something other than your coffee?" asked Daniel.

The offer seemed to be good and the trio moved from the coffee shop. The others were still strolling from one shop to the other. A large number of stalls had clothes or the electronic items displayed for sale. In the central alley near the roundel, there was display and sale of various exotic plants. It included the orchids, which were in beautiful colours and sizes. In addition to the orchids, there was also a large variety of plants of rare species that were put up on display. Arun and Esha spent a lot of time admiring the plants.

"Whenever I will have my own house, I shall purchase all such plants," stated Esha.

"I hope, even I shall also find some space in some corner of your house," said Arun who was just standing next to Esha.

"Maybe," she smiled and moved ahead.

For last one year Esha and Arun had been emotionally involved with each other. Their relationship was an open secret not only amongst their friends but also within the institute. Although, Esha was not very verbal but she did have her own ways to express her inner feelings for Arun. She took care of every little aspect that mattered to Arun. She would be the one who reminded Arun about the birthdays and anniversary of his dear ones. She would be very concerned if he was not well. Her voice would distantly change if Arun forgot to call her or meet her beyond a day without sufficient reason. She had to take his advice before she made any major decision. They had openly acknowledged their love for each other. Some close and intimate moments had also passed between them. But none had ever discussed their future together. Maybe, both of them were presently involved in their academic pursuit and the actual professional life was yet to unfold. Thus, the topic of future together was left without discussion between them. However, this had to be finally considered at some point of time. Both were aware of the fact, but, were postponing the issue till appropriate moment came their way. From the time, they had come to Manipur the thought about their future together was constantly playing in Arun's mind. The only thing he had been contemplating was whether to discuss the matter first with his parents or to directly confront Esha. If he did not confront her here then back in the institute, life will be busy again. As such, in next six months they will be finally taking on their respective job assignments. Only the exact destination of their job commitment stayed unknown.

"There are lots of beautiful decorative items up for sale. Some of them are quite unique. See that tusk shaped wooden piece which has the carving of the tribal man and the woman. Do you think it is good?" asked Esha to Arun.

"Yes it is. You must purchase it for your house."

There was a deliberate emphasis on the word 'your' by Arun. Esha could see the evident remark.

"Mr Banker, are you there? Why do I have a feeling that you are somewhere else?" said Esha who was now smiling at Arun and almost held his hand.

"I am OK," said Arun immediately realizing that he was not being fair with her.

"You want to go back. Maybe Arun, you are a little tired," said Esha with concern.

"No. No. I am just fine. Promise. Let's go to the other side of the stalls once you purchase those tusks. They indeed are looking quite good and unique."

They purchased a few more items together and Arun was again back to his cheerful self. Max and Rashid had also gone around the entire stalls and finally joined Esha and Arun. Rashid had purchased a local ointment. He was assured by the seller that its use would quickly cure his back pain. The ointment had a stale smell; however, Rashid was almost convinced of its effectiveness. He also advised Arun to purchase a bottle of this unknown concoction, but Arun did not relent.

The group finally decided to move towards the stalls where eatables were being served. As such, the crowd in the festival had also thinned down indicating that it was time to have a quick grub and depart. Rajiv was still not traceable, therefore, Arun called him on his mobile. Rajiv confirmed that he was with Daniel and his friend. They will reach the eating joint shortly. The others took their seats and fiddled through the menu card.

"Hey, I am really hungry. Let's order something," said Rashid.

"Rashid our main accountant, Rajiv, is still missing. So let's wait," said Esha.

"The accountant must be on liquid diet with least respect for our hungry stomachs."

"Do I hear someone speaking evil about me? Who is this bad spirit in our group?" Rajiv said in a loud dramatic tone. He was followed by Daniel and Pakmi.

Now, Rashid was the one who seemed to be a bit agitated. He walked and came in close proximity of Rajiv. This whole act drew Esha's attention. She looked at Arun and almost pleaded him to intervene before a dual triggered between the two. However, Max and Arun decided to stay out of it.

"Bad spirit? Ha. Bad spirit is in your breath. You alcoholic! Should I tell Esha? She will develop new sense of respect for you," hissed Rashid and started sniffing Rajiv as if he was a trained tracker dog.

Rajiv immediately realized the damage Rashid could cause to his image in the present circumstances. He immediately put his arm around Rashid and took him to a corner. Rajiv now almost pleaded Rashid to keep quite while his other two companions took seats next to Max.

"Yaar, Rashid please don't create a scene," said Rajiv who was keeping his voice as low as possible.

"OK. But you better not try to bully me."

Rajiv could finally get Rashid off his back by luring to purchase some chocolates and further promised to avoid drinking during the balance of the trip. By the time they both returned back to the table, they posed as if they were the thick of pals and therefore nobody wanted to ask anything further. The dinner was ordered. It seemed that Rajiv, Daniel and Pakmi had already had their grub as none of them ate much. The others ordered for the Chinese cuisine. Max told them that there was variety of non-vegetarian items which were being sold at the neighbouring counter. Rashid did not believe that it actually included frogs and dog's meat till he himself went and saw the displayed items.

"So are you guys going to attend the rock show? It's from tomorrow onward," said Daniel.

"No. Actually tomorrow we are busy, but then, we will surely come over someday to attend your concert," said Max.

Pakmi told them that his latest movie was due to be released in another two months. He had been working in the Manipuri films from the last three years. In fact, he even had an offer to participate in some singing programme which was being recorded in Mumbai. He had yet to confirm his availability for the same. Pakmi had a tattoo which was quite evident on his neck. Esha found the colourful tattoo quite impressive. Pakmi flaunted another one which was there on his left forearm. Pakmi told her that she could also get one made for herself in case if she was interested. Arun jaw dropped the chowmein when he heard the possibility of such a thing being put under consideration by Esha. His imagination drew a wild figure of Esha with tattoos all over her body. If Esha ever got tattooed, he will curse Pakmi for the same. However, he joined the others to wish Pakmi good luck and hoped to see him as a bigger star some day. After dinner the group decided to return back to Dhayan Singh's house. Dhayan Singh had being calling them throughout the day to check if they were fine and enjoying themselves.

It was almost 10 o'clock by the time group returned back. Most of the people in the house had slept, except Dhayan Singh who was still waiting for his friends. Tomorrow was a busy and important day for the Hashnam family. The group too was excited to attend the traditional Meitei marriage.

By seven in the morning it was bright outside. The sun rays seeping in through the curtain folds were almost falling on Rajiv's face. He unwillingly opened his eyes. There was nobody else in the room. He had seen her. She was laughing and talking to him in her native dialect. He really could not understand anything. Still, he knew that she loved him. Her large expressive eyes said it all and required no further proof for any assurance. She looked sparkling in that yellow outfit. Or was it cream? Then suddenly she was gone leaving no mark of her physical presence. There was a sense of deep loss. Or was it only an attraction? If it was, then the person, the timing and the feelings were all so wrong.

"Stop scratching your head and get ready," said Arun in a loud voice who knew that his friend was still in his dream world.

"Where are others?" asked Rajiv still yawning and seemed a bit reluctant to get up.

"Well, others are ready much in time and are having their breakfast. You too better come down fast. And yes, just to remind you, today is Shilpa's marriage."

"Oh yes! I will be there shortly."

As soon as Rajiv got ready he searched the entire room to locate his missing camera. He clearly remembered that yesterday in the evening it was hanging around his neck. He couldn't have actually misplaced it. The last photos were clicked by Pakmi and then the camera was again hanging around his neck. Where could it go? He must have kept it somewhere here. Did he leave it in the vehicle yesterday? He was not very sure now. He must look for it. It was not only expensive but had a lot of photos which were clicked with painstaking efforts.

By the time Rajiv came down into the main courtyard, there was a large gathering of people present all over the place. He quickly moved towards the dining hall in Dhayan Singh's house. While heading towards the dining hall he greeted the acquainted ones and nodded to those he had not met before. To his great relief there it was! However, who it was with, brought a sudden gush of anger. There were few of Shilpa's friends who were sitting along with Esha and Arun. Rashid was busy clicking their photographs. He was proudly handling Rajiv's camera. Rajiv felt like strangling him to death but somehow controlled himself.

"Good morning Rajiv. I thought that in spite your being late, your camera must not miss the chance of capturing the important moments of the marriage, therefore, I brought it along," said Rashid who still could not trace any anger the way Rajiv looked at him.

"Thanks Rashid. You are always so thoughtful. From here on, I will take over the obligatory duty of clicking the photos." He almost snatched the camera from Rashid's hand and indicated him to step aside for some serious talks.

Rashid was smart and smoothly said, "Oh! Not to worry. I am in no hurry. You can get me the chocolates that you promised, whenever you happen to go out." He knew that he had cornered Rajiv more than he would accept and decided it was better to back off and stay away from his firing line for a while. Sometime later, Rajiv sat down for breakfast next to Esha and she got him introduced to some of the girls around. This helped to brighten up his mood a little, although none were as attractive as Naomi.

The house which was the venue for the marriage had been beautifully decorated. Dhayan Singh was still engrossed into the last minute details. The entire courtyard had been covered with garlands on the sides. Varieties of flowers were used for making those garlands. A red carpet was laid with sitting arrangement done on the left side of the courtyard. As per Irom uncle that corner was primarily prepared for the groom and his close family members. The groom along with his friends and relatives was expected to arrive by 10 o'clock. Arun and Max had accompanied Gopal to the local market to purchase some bakery items required during the day. Right from the early morning both of them had been assisting the family to organize for the event. They were also involved in serving breakfast to the guests. In fact, Dhayan Singh's mother was deeply touched by the gesture of both these young boys.

A majority of the guests present in the house were dressed in the traditional attire. The men were wearing white coloured kurta and dhoti. They also carried a white shawl and had a white turban over their head. The ladies were wearing a shawl called 'Innaphi', a Phanek and a wrap around shirt called the 'Sarong'. Even Rajiv and Esha had also changed into their formals. Rajiv wore a dark coloured formal suit with a bright tie and Esha wore a sari. She indeed was looking beautiful and a show stopper of the whole event. As far as Rashid was concerned, he was hell bent to wear the traditional dress of the Meiteis. Finally, Dhayan Singh had relented and managed a pair of the dress for him. The second issue of concern for Rashid was tying of the Dhoti. Dhayan Singh again came for his rescue. However, Rashid was not very comfortable with the way it was tied around his waist. Still, in the end of it all he was looking different, if not actually smart. He planned to get his photos clicked in this traditional attire and send them to his sisters. Maybe, the photos will be a hint to his mother that she should start looking for a girl for him also.

Arun, Max and Gopal were the last to get ready for the function. Arun wore the woollen blazer with the trouser that Esha had purchased for him. About half an hour before the arrival of the groom the others got together in the courtyard. Soft Manipuri music was being played in the background. The bride was still in her room. Even Esha was with her to extend any assistance, if required.

"You are looking smart," said Rashid to Rajiv to break the ice between them due to his last act.

"Even you are not looking so bad," said Rajiv after a little pause.

"Well, then you will surely not mind to click a few of my photographs in this dress. Actually, I have no objection."

"You really think that I will even click a single photo of yours. Rather, I will delete any photo of yours in case it exists in my camera. You blackmail me, carry my camera without even asking and then you want favours with this snobbishness," said Rajiv who was staring at Rashid to dare take the challenge.

"Cool down, 'Angry bird'," smiled Rashid knowing well that Rajiv was actually pissed off with him.

Arun who was overhearing asked both of them to end the childish play. There was congregation of the hosts at the entrance of the house. Some women folk also gathered there. Gopal told Rajiv and others that the groom and his relatives had finally arrived. Rashid, Max, Arun and Rajiv also moved nearer to the entrance to get a closer look of the welcome ceremony. Rajiv's camera was yet again in action. Dhayan Singh, his parents and close relatives were all there to receive the guests. Just outside the house, the groom and his relatives got out of the vehicles.

They were guided towards the house by an elderly person. Gopal who was standing close to Arun and others gave his running commentary to update them. As such, Gopal had promised them to explain the entire procedure of the marriage. He explained that this person along with the groom is traditionally called 'Bor Shennaba'. He is supposed to guide the groom during the course of the entire ceremony.

"Bor Shennaba. Bor Shennaba. Bor Shennaba." Rashid said almost in a chorus.

The groom was a fair looking smart young man. He was rightly paired for Shilpa. The groom was dressed in the 'Mangshok', attire worn during such ceremonies. The guests were led by six women from the groom's side. Each one of them was carrying the ceremonial items. One of them brought a dress for the bride which she duly handed over to Dhayan Singh's mother. Mrs Indra Singh took the gift with utmost humbleness and respect. Behind these six leading women there was a short and plump woman who was Shilpa's to be mother-in-law. The groom followed his mother. Gopal confirmed to his captive audience that this order of march of the guest was strictly adhered in the Meitei marriage.

Behind this gathering, on the side near the boundary wall, the priest from the bride's side along with Dhayan Singh lit a bonfire. Seeing Dhayan Singh near the fire, Rashid commented, "I hope he is not overdriven by his emotions."

"No. No. This is part of the marriage ritual. It is called 'Mei okpa'. Actually, the fire is lit to dispel evil spirit, if any, from the groom," said Gopal.

"Mei okpaaaaaaaaaa," repeated Rashid a little loudly.

"Quiet. Lower your voice," said Arun who was conscious of some guests who were closely observing them.

"Well, I am only trying to learn a few words, 'Mei okpa'," said Rashid defensively.

"Tonight I will perform 'Mei okpa' by burning you in your bed if you continue speaking any further. This will actually call off the real evil spirit from the house," said Rajiv. Rashid spontaneously moved rather closer to where Arun stood.

"Bhaiya, as a matter of fact for this bonfire one requires pine leaves and herbs. Plywood of the bed would not be the right choice," said Gopal maintaining a poker face.

The priest sprinkled some rice on the fire which was also part of the ritual. After this the groom and his close ones moved further inside the courtyard. They were formally welcomed by three women including the bride's mother. Mrs Indra guided her to be son-in-law to pay tribute to the Tulsi plant which was planted within the courtyard. By now young girls of the house came giggling and surrounded the groom. Interestingly, with this new found attention, the groom seemed a little self-conscious. The groom was further led to the place which was embellished beautifully with colourful garlands especially for him to sit. Before the groom sat, the priest sprinkled some flour on the floor near the place.

Suddenly, the cheering of the young girls present in the courtyard drew everybody's attention towards Shilpa who was being brought by her friends for the ceremony. She was looking stunningly beautiful. Shilpa was wearing a very heavily embroided green colour traditional outfit. Beside her there was another girl who was looking equally gorgeous. Arun was staring at her. It was Esha no doubt. But then she had never looked so beautiful. She was in red and golden colour saree and her hair were tied in the neat French knot. Her skin was radiating and her eyes looked beautiful with neatly defined makeup. To Arun she looked almost like some Diva from the silver screen who he actually stared stunningly with his mouth open.

Esha immediately caught Arun's expressions and could not resist a smile. She gesticulate him to close his mouth. Even Rashid observantly noticed Esha's transformed look.

"Oh god! What has she done to herself? She looked like a ...," said Rashid.

"One more word Rashid and I promise you that I will rip apart your dhoti and use it to hang you by your neck on the nearest available tree," said Arun looking pretty annoyed.

"Come on. No offence. She looks.... She ... I mean ... even I want ..."

"Just shut up."

"OK," said Rashid and now stood closer to Gopal.

Shilpa was made to sit next to the groom by the priest. Rajiv went a little closer and took photos of the bride and the groom. There were some hired photographers who also directed their cameras at the young couple. There was a videographer and his assistant who were also trying to capture the special moments. The priest finally started the rites. Gopal told them that these rites were called 'Nahei Nashenba'. However, this time Rashid did not repeat the word. He only did the lip-sync covering his face so that Rajiv could not catch him.

Next, the priest called Dhayan Singh's parents for the next part of the ceremony. The bride's mother tied the hand of both the bride and the groom together. As per Gopal, the thread-binding of the young couple is called 'Langja Taret'. It is made of seven smaller threads. Mr Indra Singh stood next to his wife praying in consonance with the priest for the long life of the bride and the groom. He also offered some money as a sign of good luck. Soon one by one other relatives came and bestowed their blessings upon the young couple. To make adequate space for them, Esha stepped towards Arun who stood along with other friends at some distance.

"You are looking very attractive and beautiful. Never saw you like this. Your eyes also look so different," said Arun.

"You actually made my day. I let the beautician have a free run to apply her craft so that the concomitant effects are liked by you. Otherwise, you know I do not put on so much makeup."

"When did you manage to go to a beautician?"

"Well, she had come to assist Shilpa. By the way, you too are looking no less dashing. The trousers are a perfect fit with that combination."

"Thanks for the compliment. But I feel slightly uncomfortable as I couldn't find my belt for the trouser. It is a bit loose on my waist."

Gopal told them that the next ceremony was called 'Mitan Nga'. This means releasing of the fish in water. For this, three women moved together through the centre of the courtyard towards the pond where the young couple was sitting. The leading lady was holding a lantern and the other two held a live fish each in their hands.

"Are they supposed to eat it raw to form a bond?" asked Rashid.

Ignoring the comment, Gopal told them that the fishes will be released in the pond by the young couple. It is believed that any impending sorrow and suffering that may happen to the young couple will be carried away by the two fishes. As per a second version, it is also interpreted that the two fishes depict the bride and the groom tied in nuptial bond. The fishes released in the pond reflect the life that the couple will possibly lead in the future.

Once released in the pond the fishes swam together, on seeing that, the entire gathering applauded witnessing the good omen. Next, the priest untied the thread from the bride and groom's wrists and handed it over to the bride's mother.

"Now is the time for the main ceremony," said Gopal.

The priest chanted the mantras while the bride moved around the groom for seven times. During this event, the flower petals were showered on the groom intermittently. Even Esha and the others too joined in the ritual. It was an emotional moment for the entire Hashnam family. Dhayan Singh and his father's eyes were moist. It was a rare sight to see Dhayan Singh with tears in his eyes. Even Esha had some tears in her eyes, which Arun couldn't miss to notice and was pretty sure of their time, to come soon.

"Don't you want to know what is this ceremony called?" said Rajiv looking up at Rashid.

"Can't be called 'Mei okpa', I guess," added Rashid.

"No. No. It is called 'Leichiba'. And bhaiya, I must compliment you for such a sharp memory," said Gopal.

"Thanks."

"Hey Rashid, even I am impressed. Let me click the photo of the genius between us," said Rajiv.

This cheered Rashid. He readily posed for the photograph. For a better pose he also picked up one of the children in his arms who had imitated his limping walk on the first day of his arrival in the house. During last two days, Rashid had actually befriended a number of small children and was quite popular amongst them. Even, the mother's of most of the children found Rashid to be quite funny. Actually, this image was almost opposite of the one Rashid thought his personality generated. He still liked to believe that people got attracted to the persona of his personality. After putting down the child, Rashid felt that his dhoti got little loose from the waist. He turned to adjust. There it was. Arun instantly recognized it.

"You crazy guy! The last place I expected to find my trouser's belt was over your waist. Rashid how can you? Give it back," shouted Arun who could hear Esha burst into laughter.

"Later, my friend. This is not the right time to ask for your belongings. You will still manage but not me. Please be a little understanding. Please." Rashid said with conviction of true rational and understanding. Arun knew that in front of Esha the argument could not be extended any further.

As such, the garland-exchange between the bride and the groom was about to take place. Shilpa placed two garlands at a time around the groom's neck. There was cheering by the gathering for the couple. After this, Shilpa sat next to the groom and he removed one of the garlands and placed it around her neck. Again, there was cheering from all around. Gopal told Arun and his friends that the marriage ceremony had now officially concluded.

The bride and the groom were finally taken inside the house where as per traditions they were welcomed by both their respective mothers. Here Shilpa offered sweets to the groom. This part of the ceremony was called 'Kangshubi Lannaba', as per Gopal. The entry of the groom and the bride was symbolic of the belief that the almighty resides in the body of the mankind and thus spreads the off springs.

"Wish you heartiest congratulation for Shilpa's marriage," said Arun to Dhayan Singh. Others in the group also joined in to wish Dhayan Singh, his parents and uncles their good wishes.

"I guess now we can officially meet the groom," said Max.

"Yes. Yes. Why not? Come, I will get you all introduced to my brother-in-law," said Dhayan Singh.

"Hey Max, where have you been hiding? We did not see you at all during the entire marriage ceremony," said Rashid.

"Well, I was with Dhayan Singh's grandmother. She can barely walk and was watching the ceremony sitting there on the terrace," said Max indicating towards the direction of the grandmother.

They all went to meet the groom. By then, Esha brought the collective gift that they had purchased for the newly weds. They handed over the present and were introduced one by one to the groom. He must have been of their age. His name was Vimol Singh Koijam. He had done his engineering from Delhi and was assisting his father in his business in Imphal. Their house was just five kilometres from Dhayan Singh's house. It was an arrange marriage however they had known each other for quite some time. The young couple was radiating true happiness.

There were other guests too who wanted to wish the young couple, so the group moved back to the courtyard. By now, tea and snacks were being served. Gopal told them that soon Shilpa and her husband will be leaving for their house. As per customs, there will be a small get-together in the groom's house in the evening. Dhayan Singh and his parents will be attending the same.

"Max, will you come along to get the vehicles prepared for their departure?" said Dhayan Singh.

"Sure."

"Do you want me to come along?" asked Arun.

"No thanks. Max knows where the vehicles are. So, you guys just enjoy yourselves," said Dhayan Singh who left along with Max.

Soon the newlyweds and relatives of groom's side were all set to leave. To understand the emotions of the girl's family there was no interpreter required. Shilpa hugged her parents and cried. Even Gopal was crying. Dhayan Singh wanted to avoid eye contact with his sister but when she came running into his arms he too lost control over himself. With tears the bride bid farewell to her family members. Uncle Irom and Gopal also went along with Shilpa to leave her to her new home.

A major event in the Hashnams house was finally over. It was indeed a great opportunity for Dhayan Singh's friends to come and be the part of a Meitei marriage. Rajiv had captured the entire moments of the ceremony in his camera. Somewhere, the marriage had also touched the fine cord of the inevitable between Esha and Arun. Their relation had reached the point of no return. In an unspoken manner both realized this fact. Only the way ahead for them had to be mutually explored. And in this trip the possibility of a new commitment seemed to be on both minds. Rashid in the meantime had changed into his jeans and was in the company of the young kids. At times, it was difficult to predict Rashid. Max was already inside the house to assist the family in coordinating the subsequent events.

It had been a very long day for all of them as they witnessed the creeping darkness of the night sitting in the courtyard. Esha went to change and agreed to meet the boys after sometime. In the next hour, most of the guests had left the house. Even the Hashnam's were getting ready to attend the function that was to take place at Shilpa's new home. Dhayan Singh's mother had catered for their dinner. Thus, the group was left to themselves for the evening.

"So Max what's your plan for tomorrow?" asked Rajiv.

"Well, I intent to spend the day with my parents. Even Kim has got a day off from the school. You guys will go to Moreh. And yes, Dhayan Singh also plans to accompany."

"So what's great about Moreh?" asked Rashid.

"Not much. It is a small town on the Indo-Myanmar border. It has been converted into a free trade zone between the two countries. One does not require a passport to travel inside a limited area within Myanmar. That means that you all can visit Tamu which is the first township of Myanmar from the Indian side. However, permission by the authorities manning the joint border has to be taken before crossing, which Dhayan Singh will get organised."

"Wow! So tomorrow we are going abroad. To a foreign land! You know what; this will be my first official trip to any foreign country. How far is it from here?" asked Rashid who seemed to be fairly excited.

"Don't worry; you will not suffer jet lag. And yes, we will have to come back from there by evening," commented Rajiv.

"Why. Can't we stay there for a day or two?"

"You are free to match pace with the last Mugal Emperor Bahadur Shah Zafar who lived the remaining years of his life in Rangoon," laughed Rajiv while Rashid threw a pillow at him.

"Hey stop behaving like kids," intervened Esha.

"OK. OK. Sorry Rashid," said Rajiv. Even Rashid sobered down to listen as to what Max had to say.

"Moreh is about four hours drive from here. You will have to leave a bit early so that you are able to come back on time. You will find a lot of Chinese products which will be on sale from that side. In fact, the Myanmar market hasbeen heavily inflexed with the Chinese items. There was a time when Myanmaris preferred to buy maximum number of Indian goods. But today, the precedence has changed. More and more items are being pumped into Manipur through Myanmar by the Chinese. I personally feel that this will adversely affect our long run national interests. The policymakers cannot turn a blind eye to such things."

"But from what I know, Moreh is part of the international corridor which will connect South-east Asia with the European markets," said Arun.

"Yeah. On paper the project sounds so very impressive. But then, the reality is quite different. Due to frequent bandhs and political instability a number of policy makers are recommending to change the alignment of this corridor so as the region of Manipur gets left out."

"But then it's not fair. If the region has problems, then they must be suitably addressed. And the solutions have to have time bound implementation or else they hold no value and relevance," said Esha.

"I agree with you," added Arun.

"You all may be right but then the mainstream planners for the country do not feel so sensitively about the region. In a way, those people there are not linked with events here. Look at us. We also had no idea about this place till we came here. We too considered it to be only a backward place which was disturbed and not worth living. Let me tell you, this is the perception that needs to be changed. And this modulation can only come when the awareness regarding the region is extended on a larger platform. Maybe, once I return back I will use the photographs of this place to create awareness of this region amongst people belonging to other parts of the country," said Rajiv.

"I am impressed. I thought we were on holidays. But see this guy; he is slowly working to develop his long-term prospects of a professional photographer. You have already covered the Meitei marriage, now go and cover the Naga and the Kuki rituals also," said Rashid.

"Well, I guess for the first time you are talking sense. Max why don't you tell us something about the Kuki marriages? I am sure the customs will be different from the Meitei culture," said Rajiv.

"Yes Max, tell us something about your culture. It surely will be enriching," added Esha.

"Are you guys sure? Then don't complain that you got bored," laughed Max.

Seeing the genuine interest of his friends, Max began. "Majority of the Kuki and the Naga communities converted to Christianity over the years but then some of the old rituals are still in practice. In the Mizo tribes, that means the Kuki clan, the marriages per se are performed under following formats. 'Nularim', under this system the girl formally courtships the young boys of her age. Marriages resulting from such alliance are considered legitimate and are socially recognized."

"Wow! Will the girls also consider an outsider?" asked Rashid.

"Definitely not, especially with a desperado like you," added Rajiv.

"In another form of arrangement for marriage, the family of the girl that doesn't have a son may admit a prospective son-in-law to the family. He then becomes like a son to the parents of the girl," Max said ignoring the interruption.

"I think this form of marriage will be fine for you Rashid?" said Arun again taking a dig at his friend.

"No way! I have no intention of working in somebody's field for the rest of my life," said Rashid. He vigorously nodded to further add his confirmation over his statement. However, he still asked, "By the way, what do you call such type of marriage?"

"Well, it is called 'Makpa Chung'. But, the one in which the boy has to actually work for the girl's family is called 'Kongla'. This type of marriage is seldom practised in the area."

"Next," said Rajiv.

"'Iawn Puan Phak'. If due to some untoward circumstances, the couples are not able to marry, then under this arrangement they are free to live together in the girl's house. If the boy at some later stage decides to walk out of the relation, he is supposed to pay a heavy price," said Max

"It seems, all these arrangements are made to ensure adequate security and safety for the girls within the society," said Esha.

"Yes Esha, you have actually hit the nail on the head," Max said with excitement of explaining the logics.

"However, there are some marriage arrangements, wherein a pre-condition is put which may be of disadvantage to the girl. Like under 'Sazumeidawh' the payment to bride is not made, if the man decides to leave her. But, such types of marriages are not very common in the society."

"I am happy to hear that," added Esha.

"In case the involvement of the young couple before marriage leads to pregnancy of the girl, then the boy is socially committed to honour the marriage. This culminated marriage is called 'Luk Khung'."

"That sounds interesting," said Arun.

"Well. Under the marriages there is also a provision of elopement. This is primarily to ensure that true love between people is not suppressed. In this, the love couples who elope are later given recognition within the society."

"Any more forms of marriage Max? It is very exhaustive," said Rashid.

"Yes. Lastly, is the 'Levirate'. In this form, the man marries the widow of his deceased brother," said Max.

"This type of tradition is also practiced in other parts of the country. They primarily aim to provide security to the girl and her children, if any," added Arun.

"As a concluding point I wish to inform you that in Mizos, no marriage can take place unless the bride money is paid to the parents of the girl. This is contrary to what the Meitei follow or is followed in other parts of the country," said Max.

Dhayan Singh's aunt, Mrs Tomba was at home and had taken the responsibility to serve dinner to the group. Esha went to the kitchen to assist.

"Hope you are not bored of eating the fish. In fact, I was telling Dhayan Singh to get Chicken for you all from tomorrow," said aunty.

"No. No. Aunty, we are enjoying everything that you are cooking. Dhayan Singh and Shilpa were telling me that you are their best cook in the family."

"These kids! They are fond of exaggerating things. Whenever they want to eat something different they always come to me. Actually, amongst the ladies I am the only one in the house who cooks and eats non-vegetarian."

"But aunty, I saw even others eating fish for the lunch," said Esha a bit surprised.

"Oh! You may not have noticed. In Meitei families the fish is considered to be a vegetarian item. Look, like you eat eggs in other parts of the country but still stay vegetarian, likewise we eat fish and are vegetarians," said aunty understanding the difference of culture that they shared.

"So aunty what are the speciality of food items here?"

"Well, we eat more of fish, bamboo shoots and vegetables. My elder son who has recently joined the army is fond of chicken, pizza, continental and North Indian food. So I even cook those items."

"How about sweets? They are my weakness."

"Amongst the sweets you must taste Kabok. It is made up of molasses and rice. You must try it before you leave. I will prepare it for you."

Mrs Tomba had been married for over twenty-eight years. She must have been almost the age of Esha's mother. Before marriage she was a student of modern art. She had done her post-graduation from Guwahati University and had decided to pursue painting as full time career. Initially, she had worked with few of the renowned names in this field and then subsequently even managed to get her own paintings displayed in the art gallery of Guwahati and Shillong. But then, destiny had something more stored for her. In one of the college cultural exchange programmes, Professor Tomba came to Guwahati with a group of students. They fell in love and later got married.

"For a very long time, people in our circle used to tease us that we married after drawing inspiration from a Hindi movie in which Dharmendra and Sharmila Tagore were the lead actors," said Aunty.

"Had you actually seen that movie before marriage?" asked Esha who found Aunty to be very lively.

"Yes, I had seen it as a teenager. But, never really thought that I will marry a professor," giggled Aunty.

"Do you regret leaving a career?"

"No. Life has been very blissful. Tomba is the only man I ever fell in love with in my entire life. And yes, I am lucky to be his wife," smiled Aunty.

The dinner was laid in the dining hall. Although, today the food had been prepared by the cooks hired for the marriage. Aunty closely observed the way Esha helped in laying it out.

"Esha, I feel that you are correct with your choice. Arun is a good boy. You too will not regret. Wish you luck beta!"

Esha did not expect aunty to be aware of her involvement. She would have been a bit embarrassed had it been someone else bailing out the cat. But aunty definitely meant her good. She smiled at her.

"Go and call your friends, the dinner is ready."

Once all the guys came down for dinner they settled in the dining hall. Esha looked at Arun. For the first time, she wondered as to how many in the Hashnam family were aware about her relationship with Arun. She loved him. There was no doubt that his feelings matched the same passion as hers. Still, the commitment for the future was unknown. She had actually not seen so far in the future.

Apart from Rashid others ate less. He seemed to be happily getting used to of eating the fish curry. Some of the young ones in the family also joined for the dinner. Their parents had left aunty as their guardian. They all sat next to Rashid as he told them as to how he once ate an elephant in the jungle. After dinner the children were sent to bed by aunty. Her younger daughter was the main ring leader. Sometime later, Max took his friends to meet Dhayan Singh's grandmother. She lived in Indra uncle's house. Due to her age and also customs she stayed in the house. Grandma was ninety-two years old. She had a hearing aid which she best liked to keep on the table and spoke as loud as possible. Fortunately, her mind was sound and she did not suffer from any aliment other than being hard of hearing. Grandma wanted to know as to which all places each one of them hailed. Her Hindi was fairly poor but Max explained her things in the Manipuri language. Grandma told them that she had not gone out of Manipur for the last forty years. She asked them as to whether they were enjoying themselves in Manipur? She also wanted to know if they had witnessed Shilpa's marriage. There was so much that the old woman wanted to speak and ask. Arun was reminded of his own grandma. In old age, there is hardly anyone to talk to these elders. When they find someone paying slightest of attention to them, they like to keep continue their monologue. It seems as if they are really hungry for companionship. At times, one feels sorry for their condition. Arun decided that tomorrow the first thing he will do was to call at home and speak especially to his grandma.

Sometime later, the Hashnam family also returned from the get-together organized by Shilpa's in-laws. After latest updates from the family members regarding Shilpa, the group decided to break off. As such, tomorrow they had a long day ahead.

"Esha, good morning beta. All set to leave?" asked Indra uncle.

"Yes uncle. Dhayan Singh had told us to be up and ready by 6 o'clock."

"Your aunty, I guess is also preparing breakfast for you all in the kitchen."

"Well, she shouldn't bother. We will eat something en route."

"No. No. It's always better to have the home made food. As such, there is nothing much to eat en route."

"In the middle of marriage we all have really bothered you."

"Not at all. In fact, we all are happy to have you all here with us."

Uncle Indra was an early riser and in spite of the busy schedule of the last few days, managed to stick to his timings. Soon the others in the group also came to Indra uncle's house and after breakfast were ready to leave for Moreh. Uncle told Dhayan Singh that in case they got delayed, they must call back. He would make some arrangements for their stay, if required. Uncle had served in the forest department and to get such things organized was not much of an issue for him. Aunty had over-ensured things and had also made a big hamper of eatables for them. Rashid started fiddling around with it the moment their vehicle left the house. Max got down from the vehicle after sometime at a road junction leading to his home and promised to meet them shortly.

"Is there some ATM en route?" asked Arun.

"We can check. But mostly during such early hours they may not be functional. Do you urgently require cash?" asked Dhayan Singh.

"Yes. He wants to gift something to Esha," said Rashid.

"I never said that," said Arun looking at Rashid.

"But I logically assumed so."

Esha smiled and thanked Rashid for being so concerned. This prompted Rashid to get after Arun as to what he would gift Esha if he actually did planned to gift her something.

"Hey wise guy. Why don't you let us know?" Arun asked Rashid.

"But you are her boyfriend not me."

"That's why you have pain in you're … you're …," said Rajiv.

"Mind your tongue."

"Not there yaar, but your eyes, Rashid," completed Rajiv. The boys laughed and Esha looked outside.

"No pain OK! I wish them all the very best." He almost sounded as if he was giving his farewell speech.

"Let's actually take Rashid's query a little bit seriously. Dhayan Singh, what can one purchase from Myanmar per se?" asked Rajiv.

"Actually, that's not very easy to answer. Myanmar does not really have factory products oriented exports. But yes, there is one thing that gives them an edge. Myanmar is an excellent market for the ruby stones. In fact, they cost much less than their value in the international market. However, you got to be smart to identify the genuine stones," said Dhayan Singh.

"See. Now what Arun must purchase for Esha has been so amply cleared. Esha you can thank me to generate this topic if you so desire," said Rashid feeling so smart with his words.

"Come on Rashid and you guys. Stop cornering poor Arun. This is not fair," said Esha.

"Yeah. Esha is right. No more talks of provocative nature. OK," added Dhayan Singh.

By now they had crossed the outskirts of Imphal city. The valley seemed to have rather opened up as they drove towards Moreh. There was large area of paddy cultivation on both sides along the road. However, during this time of the year the crops had either been harvested or were duly under the process of being cut. Thus, the empty fields further enhanced the visibility of the entire place. The scenic view of the hills was seen on both sides of the road which had rich greenery. Dhayan Singh told his friends that the general elevation of the adjoining hills was from two thousand to two thousand five hundred metres. Almost seventy-seven percent of the geographical area of Manipur state was covered by the rich forest.

"Is there no cultivation in the hill region?" inquired Arun.

"There is, but is limited. Actually, the hill tribes of Kukis and Nagas traditionally produce the crops for their own consumption and have not commercialized the production for sale. For meeting their food requirements they widely practice 'Jhum' cultivation. This basically means the shifting cultivation. Crops like maize, sesamum, potato, ginger, tapioca and vegetables are grown under this method of farming. Otherwise, the soil in the hill area is acidic in content and proves to be good for cultivation of other horticultural crops such as pineapple, pears, plums, lemon, oranges, banana etc," added Dhayan Singh.

"Which are the main crops that are grown in the plains of Manipur?"

"Well, the soil in the plains is flooded most of the time. Therefore, it is best suited for the rice cultivation. In addition, a number of vegetables can also be grown," said Dhayan Singh.

"So, this means that there is river basin water present which leads to flooding," said Rajiv joining in the discussion.

"You guys always land up with discussion on heavy topics. OK. So be it. Well, Manipur has got mainly three river basins. They are the Barak river basin, Manipur river basin and the Chindwin river basin. In case you guys want to know more, then I will advise you to discuss the state dynamics with uncle Tomba."

"You are right. In fact, I have already taken a book on Manipur from him. It did cover some of the issues that you just mentioned," said Rajiv.

The driver played in the car stereo the CD's of English and Hindi songs that Dhayan Singh had given him as per the general liking of his friends. En route, they halted at two or three places on Rajiv's insistence. He wanted to click the photographs of some of the local people and their houses. The road to Moreh was not very wide. Still, there was frequent traffic of load carrying vehicles en route. As they travelled further, they found a number of security forces that were deployed along the road. In fact, there were also a few check posts where vehicles were being checked from security aspects. Mostly, the focus was on vehicles which were carrying goods. Even their vehicle was stopped at one post but was allowed to move ahead after the authorities verified the concerned papers with the driver.

"There is lot of security in the area. Anything of concern?" asked Rashid.

"Nothing. This security is routine. They primarily stay on vigil to ensure that untoward incidents can be avoided," said Dhayan Singh.

"Hashnam, do you feel at times that the deployment of central forces in your region is not justified? You know the kind of human rights issues which come up. And yes, then there is always concern of the special powers that have been delegated to these forces," asked Esha.

"Let me put up this way that all is not too well here. At times, the force executed by the security forces is not proportionate. But then, the blame cannot be squarely put on them. There are elements within the society who are dangerous and require to be curtailed. However, the positive aspect of life in Manipur is that things are stabilizing and improving. Therefore, it is time for looking at developing advantages than to cry always and every time for what we do not have," said Hashnam.

"But what about the issues of people like Manorma Devi and other such issues?" asked Rashid.

"Yes these issues do exist. I am not denying it. And they are important and very sensitive issues. But then, there are also good things that are taking place in Manipur. We must give due importance to those issues also. It is imperative to encourage people who put in efforts to make such changes happen. Too much of criticism will only slow our steps towards change and development. And then, how will we get tourists like you to visit our state. I hope you all are enjoying your stay in Manipur ," smiled Hashnam.

"I guess you are right. In fact, barring the extra security in various places, the area by and large looks quite peaceful," said Esha.

"See, the rail link to Manipur from Assam is under progress. The road networks are expanding. Mobile range is available in the most remote places of the state. There has been a drastic improvement in the air connectivity of this place. The central government had directed the entire cabinet ministers to digress ten percent of their allotted funds to the region of north-east. Are these not positive signs of improvement?" asked Hashnam.

"OK. OK. I guess, we all are fairly convinced with your logical plea," Rashid intervened. He opened the hamper and extended the snacks to all.

By about 10.30 AM they reached Moreh. The village was frankly not very impressive. The driver along with them had prior visited this place and was quite clear as to what they should see first. He took them to a by lane and stopped the vehicle.

"Bhaiya ji, first you take them to the temple and then we can go to the market," said the driver to Hashnam.

"OK."

All of them got down from the vehicle. Rashid stretched himself as if he had been released from a squeezed canister. Rajiv noticed that Rashid's limp was gone. Maybe, the local oil he purchased from the festival had done this wonder.

"You know, this place where majority of people are Christians has a temple. And, the uniqueness of it is that it's a South Indian temple," said Hashnam.

"Stop kidding," said Arun.

"No. Let me explain. Actually, this area is inhabited by sizeable population having origin links with Tamil Nadu. During the British times, they had got their employees from Tamil Nadu along with them to Burma (now Myanmar). These Indians facilitated in establishing the British economic interest in Burma. Over the years, a substantial population of Tamil people settled within Burma. Once the British left, some of the Tamils decided to move back to their native places. However, others decided to continue staying in Burma. There were a few who also settled in this side of Manipur. This temple is looked after by them."

"That's indeed very interesting," said Esha.

As they moved towards the temple they observed that residents in the vicinity were mainly Tamils. Their dresses also reflected their ethnic affinity. A majority of women were wearing saris and had gajra on their oiled hair. The men were wearing shirt with the traditional lungi. There were coconut trees which were planted around the place. Soon they were at the entrance of the temple. Here too there were large numbers of coconut trees in the close vicinity. The main gate of the temple had an arch which had cemented carving of the gods and goddesses in bright multi-colours. There was a huge courtyard within the temple premises. The temple structure had a main temple and then on the sides there were two more structures where the devotees offered prayers. The group moved on towards the main temple area. At the entrance itself they had taken out their footwear and the marble floor seemed to be a bit cold.

A priest was present near the centre idol of the god and goddess. This dark skinned person must have been in his fifties. In spite of a little chill in the air, he was wearing only a lungi and was bare from the top. Chandan was sported on his forehead and he was wearing large earrings. The priest had fresh flowers and items used during prayers on a large tray. He chanted mantras once the group came closer and bowed at the idols. After the prayers were over he gave them the *prashad.* There was intricate carving and paintings on the walls and sides of the temple. The place had sanctity and looked so peaceful. From there, a good view of the valley in the front and the inhabited area on to its side was seen.

"Panditji, for how long have you been the priest of this temple?" asked Arun.

"Well, my entire life has been devoted in prayer to the god and goddess of this temple," smiled the priest showing his snow white teeth.

"So, were you born here?" asked Esha while Rashid was munching the *parshad* and eagerly listening to the conversation.

"Yes. My family has been staying here for many years. This is our home. Do you find it strange?" this time the priest questioned them.

"Yes. I mean, I had never heard or read about the Tamil settlers in Manipur. But tell me, do you have no links with Tamil Nadu?" asked Esha.

"No. No. We do have links with our ancestral place. In fact, my wife was born and brought up in a village near Chennai. My elder son is presently working in a factory in Chennai," said the priest.

"Do you not feel like leaving this place? I mean go back to the place where your forefather's came from. This place is not even developed and is so far off from the rest of the country," commented Rashid.

The priest took a minute before he answered. Then he said, "My father was the priest of this temple before me. Both my parents lived and died here. Many of my dear ones live here. This is where I belong. Why should I leave this place? Nobody must leave his land. This land is my mother. I will die in her arms."

"Sorry, if I offended you Panditji. I just found your community inhabiting an area so far away from your place within your own country a little unheard. I meant no offence," said Rashid.

"Son! I understand what you meant. You all seemed to be educated and well meaning people," added the priest.

The priest asked them the purpose of their trip. He was delighted to know that tourists find this place good for visit. He told them that this small town had also suffered due to insurgency but today it was a more stable place. The various communities in Moreh had over the years learnt to live with each other. But yes, they all paid a considerable price over the years to reach this state. He was hopeful that once the trade route between India and Myanmar was further improved the pace of development will also increase within this region.

"So is there any South Indian restaurant in this place?" asked Rashid. Back in the management institute he had developed a taste for the South Indian food items.

The priest laughed. He said, "Yes, there is one but may not be to your satisfaction. This is a small place and not many outsiders come here. Actually, the restaurant is run by one of my relatives. I will tell someone to take you there if you so desire." Arun and Rajiv were not much keen to visit the so-called restaurant. But then, Rashid insisted and the others relented.

The priest called for a small boy who was playing with marbles in the courtyard and instructed him something in Tamil language. Assumingly, he told the boy to guide them to the restaurant. The boy nodded. They all thanked the priest and left. The little boy wore a red track pant and a blue shirt. The track was almost above the ankles and had holes which suggested that the change was required. The boy smiled and indicated them to follow. His blank expressions to their questions confirmed that he did not understand their language. Even Dhayan Singh became helpless to generate response in the local Manipuri dialect. As they walked behind the boy, his curious playmates also joined them. Even the locals watched them with amusement and curiosity. It almost looked like a procession by the time they reached the place. The restaurant was a big disappointment. Its owner seemed puzzled to see such an unexpectedly large gathering of customers. The boy was their volunteered interpreter. Dhayan Singh too came for the rescue. The shop owner understood Manipuri and confirmed to Dhayan Singh that he did serve the south Indian food. But presently, nothing much was available. It will take him some time to prepare items as listed on the austere board outside.

Now, seeing the state of the restaurant even Rashid backtracked to eat anything. Suddenly, he had a loss of appetite. Rajiv insisted that Rashid must order for something. Especially, after such a big procession of children being their fan followers. Rashid decided to stay invisible. Finally, Rajiv paid for hundred idalis and asked the shopkeeper to give them to the children. Before leaving, he clicked a group photo of all the young boys and girls who had congregated there.

"That was very considerate of you Rajiv," said Esha who was appreciative of Rajiv's small gesture.

"I agree," added Rashid.

They moved back towards the general direction where the driver was supposedly waiting for them. However, this time they walked through a different lane. It seemed that sometime back the local authorities had made the half-hearted efforts to construct a concrete road. The rubbles on route were the supporting evidence. There were few shops in route. A tailor shops which was being run by a few girls, caught Esha's attention. The girls were local Manipuris. There were few bright coloured female tops which were displayed for sale.

Noticing Esha's interest in the shop, Arun said, "Esha, in case you want to go inside the shop we will wait."

As any normal girl, she did not waste the opportunity. It was good about fifteen minutes by the time Esha finally came out of the shop.

"Did you like something?" asked Arun.

"Well, they have chiffon tops with good embroidery. But looking at the place the price was too high."

"How much was the price range?" asked Hashnam.

"It was close to fifteen hundred rupees."

"Not much. The people in our state, especially the girls spend a reasonable amount on tops and vestiary," said Hashnam.

"Yes, I guess you are right. In fact, even in the interiors of Manipur it seems that the girls do dress up quite well. Above all, most of them have a pleasant smile on their faces reflecting true happiness.

It didn't take much time to locate the driver who had parked the vehicle under the big shady tree on the roadside. Their next destination was the main market which extended between the common land jurisdiction of both India and Myanmar. There was free movement of market vendors and buyers from both the sides through a common entrance gate. During this hour of the day, there was huge rush in the market. As they were about to enter the market, the driver told Hashnam that he will have to get a pass made to enter Tamu. Tamu a small town of Myanmar was about fifteen kilometres from the border and a permit to travel in own vehicle was required from the authorities of both the countries. Hashnam decided to accompany the driver to get the formalities completed while the others went around from shop to shop. Rashid was very excited with the idea of stepping into the land territory of Myanmar. He ensured that Rajiv clicked few of his pictures with the Indo-Myanmar sign boards in the background. Even here, the majority of the shops were being run by the womenfolk. Most of them were young girls who themselves were dressed quite fashionably.

"Some of the girls here have very sharp features unlike the locals from the region," remarked Arun who was walking along with Esha.

"I hope you have not selected someone for yourself," teased Esha.

"You bet I have. She is a great girl but at times passes nasty comments."

"Can I meet her sometime?"

"Yes. She is around but you got to see a little harder."

"Your choices are never simple. Always complex," laughed Esha and held Arun's hand.

The market was yet again full of Chinese products. There were large variety of items which were on display. For instance to cater for the forthcoming winters, a number of woollen clothes and jackets were on display. Then there were the footwear, blankets, electronic products, decorative items, food products, furniture, paintings, cycles, jewellery, etc. Most of the shopkeepers had prophecy to communicate both in Hindi as well as English. Although, none within the group had any wish list for purchases, still they spent a lot of time moving around the shops which were aligned almost in rows and were spread over a number of lanes.

Esha purchased two bright coloured stoles and a decoration piece for the Wadleys, her local guardians. It was a brass statue of Buddha. Arun on Esha's approval purchased a tapestry for his mother. The tapestry had a black background with a large dragon embroidered in cream colour beads. The border was intricately done and looked elegant. The payment was readily accepted in Indian rupees which had better market evaluation then the currency of Myanmar.

"You are alcoholic, aren't you?" said Rashid. Nothing could miss his eyes, he knew.

"Just shut up and lay off you sniffer dog," said Rajiv who thought he had left no trail behind.

"I will tell everyone. Let them all know as to how much you are dependent on alcohol."

"Even you drink. Don't you? That day in uncle Irom's house you got badly sozzled."

"That was because I don't have your type of appetite for drinks. You keep looking for opportunities for drinking. And you don't dare to incorporate me in your games, you manipulator," added Rashid.

"Come on Rashid, chill! I am just purchasing few cans of beer, OK. And they are not for me .Today, in the evening Max has planned to take us out for the rock concert. I thought that we must take something for Daniel and Pakmi," said Rajiv trying to sound rational.

"Oh! You could have told me before. Why sneak away from friends if you can share the secrets?"

"Should I take few extra cans for you also? As such in the concert you don't want to survive on lime water or milk. Come on damn it, we are here on holidays," said Rajiv.

"OK. OK. Got ahead but see to it that Esha does not come to know," said Rashid who was proud of his ability to be accommodating for others.

They saw a girl at the counter of a shop who was wearing a bright red coloured ring. On inquiring the girl confirmed that the gold ring had a ruby stone and cost about sixty thousand rupees.

"It indeed is a beautiful stone. Is it OK if I gift one to you?" said Arun.

"Are you OK? Ah! You actually took Rashid's comments very seriously in the morning. Come on, why do you take all such things so seriously?" said Esha.

"Well, I guess you are right. My first ring to you can't be this." He said without thinking much.

However, Esha was taken aback with what Arun just said. "First Ring". Oh god. Was he planning to propose her for a lifelong commitment? What will she say if Arun actually brought up this issue? She had been so wrapped up with life within the campus of the institute that there was actually no time to plan for all such things. Yes, she loved him. There was no one she had met till day who had stolen her heart the way Arun had. But marriage was something she had not seriously considered. As of now, they both were in the crucial junction of their professional life. Nothing could be predicted of the future ahead for the next six months till they pass out of the institute and take up some job. On the other side, her heart told her that one really can't be full of calculations regarding love. At times, you just got to listen to it. Before the two of them could say anything further, Hashnam joined them.

"Look, here you guys are. I kept looking for you in all those shops. Where are others?" asked Hashnam.

"I guess still shop-lifting. They agreed to meet at the border gate in thirty minutes," said Arun.

The trio moved back from the market place and waited for Rashid and Rajiv to return. The two of them came after sometime. Rashid was wearing a bright green coloured shoe with high ankles which he had purchased from the local shop. They were quite loud in looks. His trouser seemed to be wet around the ankles. Arun could not resist himself and asked, "Rashid who forced you to purchase these shoes and why is your trouser wet?"

Rashid pointed towards Rajiv who had mischief in his eyes. "Actually my foot went in that drain…," he said.

"Not drain. It was the sewage line and it badly stinks," added Rajiv.

"You bloody loud mouth. Anyway, my shoes after the wash were wet so he told me to purchase these local shoes," said Rashid who was carrying a packet which had his wet shoes.

"The choice could have been a bit sober," commented Arun as he put his hand on his nose, almost imitating Esha and indicated Rashid to remove his bag from his visual vicinity.

"He told me that for tonight's rock show these shoes will look real cool and then they aren't very expensive."

"Are we going for the rock show tonight? Nobody told me," said Esha feeling offended for being kept out of such decision making.

"Actually, Max also told me in the morning that he will try to coordinate for the show today. In case it is taxing for you then I will get it cancelled," said Hashnam.

"On my dead body," said Rashid.

"And that too with shoes on," added Rajiv.

"OK. OK. If you all had your share of tongue lashing then we can proceed for Tamu," said Hashnam.

"You are always riding on the high waves. Bloody positive chap you are. Let's hit for Tamu," said Rajiv with enthusiasm while the others smiled and followed.

Arun had to convince Rashid that his shoes in the bag were really stinking and must be kept in the boot space of the vehicle. The route towards the check post was under construction and the vehicle had to be driven with caution. However, there was luckily limited traffic on the road. At the border crossing check point they had to wait for about five odd minutes while the driver went to validate his papers. The route ahead went through the forest belt and the road also became two-lane. Hashnam told them that the road was constructed by the Indian authorities and was called the Indo-Myanmar friendship road. The traffic regulation in Myanmar subscribes to right hand driving which Rashid found to be quite interesting. A number of Chinese made two wheelers and cars were plying on the road. Along either side of the road there were a number of sign boards in English as well as in the Myanmar language. Otherwise, the general ambience of the place seemed to be no different from any other township within India.

After about ten odd kilometres, the outskirts of the Tamu city became distinctively visible. There were bamboo huts to start with and the more they moved towards the city, a number of cemented houses could also be located. Most of the houses were coated with bright colours. The driver finally stopped the vehicle in one of the main market areas. There were shops all around the place and there was reasonable traffic on the road. Hashnam lay the term wherein they will stay for an hour at Tamu and then move back. Yet again most of the shops displayed the Chinese products. This fairly gave an idea that the economy of Myanmar was quite dependent on the Chinese support. Rajiv purchased some chips and bottles of cold drink from one of the shops. In another shop, a variety of cheese was on sale. Arun and Esha tasted the cheese. However, they had to pull back as Rashid too joined in and the chunk of samples being tasted increased in size. Arun before leaving had to purchase some grams of cheese finally, to avoid undue embarrassment.

"Let me click a group photograph of yours. This will always remind you of Myanmar and your trip towards the Northeast," said Hashnam.

By the time others got together, Hashnam managed to get a volunteer from amongst the public who agreed to click their group photo and joined in. This was probably their first and last trip together to a foreign country. The lunch for the day was what Hashnam's mother had packed for them. After strolling in the market for some more time the group finally decided to move back. The return journey seemed to be much longer. Even Rajiv and his camera took rest. At half way distance to Imphal, they took a tea break and expected to timely reach back before the last light. While they were still thirty kilometres short of the Imphal city, the vehicle had a flat tyre. The driver tried to replace the tyre but the supporting rod used along with the jack broke. The nearest mechanic shop was about two kilometres away. Therefore, the driver took lift from a two wheeler owner and went to get the rod wielded. The others had no option than to wait. The sun was down and the darkness started setting in. A few lights could be seen in the vicinity. There was a general store shop which was at some distance. Rajiv decided to get some chocolates for Esha and others. There were few people who stood for purchases at the shop. Rajiv suddenly saw Naomi near the counter of the shop when he still was a few yards away. He felt he had goose flesh. She was wearing a blue coloured jeans and a green cardigan. Her long hair were straight and falling on to her side making a portion of her face visible. She had told him that she would be leaving for Tamiglong. Maybe, she had changed her mind or did she lie to him? Anyway, this could be his chance to meet her again. Was god playing up his role? Has destiny decided to hold something for him here? His mind was running wild and he finally decided to walk up to the shop and confront her. Now, has back was towards her and he thought he would tap her on the back. But then, maybe she would unnecessarily get alarmed and may even not like it. Suddenly, she turned and stood in front of him. She looked at him and her face reflected her annoyance of being countered at close vicinity by a stranger. Rajiv's face had a look of disappointment. The girl left in a hurry.

"You freak, why were you ogling at the girl? Pervert." Rashid hissed at Rajiv who thought he was doing the right moral policing.

"No yaar. I mistook her for someone else," said Rajiv.

"Nice way of covering it up. Had I not been here, god knows what you would have done," added Rashid.

"Shut up. One more stupid word from your mouth and I swear I will hang your tongue with the fluorescent laces of your shoes."

"Such threat won't work. I will tell everyone," said Rashid who withdrew towards the vehicle.

By the time Rajiv returned back to the vehicle, Rashid had already narrated his side of the story in which he was the prime witness. Rajiv had a drooping face. He looked towards Esha and said, "I thought that it was Naomi."

No one spoke anything. Arun who knew about Naomi through Esha indicated Rashid to keep shut. Rashid also realized, sensing the general mood that for his own good he must stay quiet for a while.

"Happens Rajiv. But maybe, you will have someone better in life," said Esha after sometime.

The driver came along with the mechanic and they got the tyre changed. They were at the outskirts of the city when Dhayan Singh received a call from his father. He confirmed that they were about to reach back home shortly. It had been a long day, still, all of them agreed to head for the rock show provided Max had made the arrangements.

"I think before we plan the evening, let's first speak to Max," said Arun as he dialied Max's number.

Max confirmed that the concert was as per schedule and that he would wait for his friends at the venue at sharp 8 o'clock. After the programme was over he would come over to Dhayan Singh's house for the night. While Arun was still talking to Max, Dhayan Singh took the phone and told Max that he should be ready to move along with others to Loktak tomorrow.

The moment they reached home Dhayan Singh informed his parents regarding their plan to leave shortly for the Sangai festival.

"Aren't you all tired after such a long journey?" asked Dhayan Singh's mother.

"Not at all aunty. Rather we are very excited to go for the concert," said Rajiv.

"Yes. Yes. At your age there is no question of feeling tired. When we were young, well, even I could manage a busy life. Go ahead, have a good time," said uncle Indra.

Aunty smiled as she realized that all of them seemed to be undeterred for any change in their plan. She went in to prepare for their quick dinner. She insisted that unless they had proper meal, she will not let them go for the concert.

"If we eat so much then how will we drink?" whispered Rajiv to Dhayan Singh.

"But my mother's condition is non-negotiable," smiled Dhayan Singh.

They reached the parking area of the concert venue at sharp 8 o'clock. Max and Pakmi were waiting for them. Today, Max was actually dressed in the funkiest attire. He was wearing a jean with a silver chain hanging on both sides of his hips. Even the black shirt that he wore had a silver lining. The matching shoes were black with high heel and side chain. His hands were full with ornamental strings. The hair were gelled and made in a different style. Overall, one look and Mr R R Vankatash and Ramchander would have issued his suspension order from the institute. Still, there was no doubt that he looked smart and ready for tonight's performance. His companion was also dressed in similar matching attire.

"Hey! Look at these two. I think they look real cool," said Rashid as he approached Max and Pakmi.

"Thanks dude," said Pakmi while Max smiled.

"What do you think about my shoes?" asked Rashid who was wearing a sweat shirt with a hood over his jeans.

"That you have enough guts to wear it in public," commented Rajiv into Arun's ear while simultaneously Max said loudly, "They look just great."

Max told them that the concert was to start in another half an hour. Daniel and his group will be performing today.

"Even Max will be part of the performance," added Pakmi.

"Wow! We all will look forward for your show," said Esha.

There was a stage on a raised platform where the artists were to perform. It was covered with a variety of musical instruments. There were flashlights on the stage and speakers were placed all around the area for amplifying the impact of the music. There was gathering of more than five hundred people. Although, some seating arrangements were catered, however, a large majority of people preferred to stand. The crowd mainly comprised of the youngsters between the age group of eighteen to twenty-five. Such a show in one of the most remote parts of the country which is perceived to be culturally backward was quite unimaginable. The group was fairly impressed. In this region, music seemed to be quite an integral part of people's life. By the time the crowd settled, the first musical band started performing their opening song. They mainly played the songs from the collection of Metallica. There was huge uproar amongst the audience. Arun, Esha and Dhayan Singh stood together. The ones missing in action were Rashid and Rajiv. Both of them had gone along with Pakmi on the pretext to say hello to Daniel and his team.

"This tastes good. Where did you purchase it from?" asked Pakmi taking the first sip from the beer can.

"Well, I got it for you guys from Moreh," said Rajiv.

"Thanks dude."

Max had refused to even touch the beer till his programme was not over. This left Rajiv, Pakmi and Rashid to do justice to the dozen cans of beer that Rajiv had purchased. The place where they were sitting was isolated from view of the general public but from here they could see the stage. Daniel passed the final instructions to his group of six performers who now took on the stage. It also included Max. The crowd roared to welcome this new entry for their live performance. They started with a Manipuri song. This was the first song of the evening in the local language. The response of the audience was appalling. People clapped in the air and joined the group to sing the song. Max was the lead guitarist and was at times jumping on the stage to draw in the crowd to repeat the lyrics.

"Check out to the way he is performing. I hope he has not gulped down a few cans quietly," laughed Rashid who seemed to be thoroughly enjoying himself.

Daniel and his group performed for good about forty odd minutes in which they gave six songs. Next, the stage was taken over by another band. Back stage Rajiv and Rashid congratulated Max and Daniel for their group's fantastic performance. Now Daniel and Max were also offered the beer cans to celebrate their wonderful performance. Pakmi had quietly mixed some rum in their drinks. They drank for some more time and enjoyed the concert. Finally, Rajiv urged them to move to the place where Arun and the others were waiting.

"Yaar, I found the beer to be good. It was so sweet. But tell me, why my head doesn't spin?" asked Rashid.

"Maybe, you have become a hardcore boozer," said Pakmi who was swinging from one side to the other and seemed to be really very happy.

"Or maybe because you only drank the fruit beer," added Max.

"Fruit beer? Does it not have alcohol?" This time Rashid seemed to be surprised.

"Yes and No. Yes it was fruit beer and no it did not have alcohol," said Rajiv shrugging his shoulders.

"The rest of you had proper beer, right? In fact, you mixed it up. And you gave me fruit beer. Rajiv you owe me an explanation," said Rashid feeling very offended.

"Rashid calm down. There were three reasons for you to be given fruit beer. Firstly, you hardly know the difference. Secondly, it is cheaper and you are never in for contribution. Thirdly, I wanted you to stay sober and avoid feeling screwed up with a hangover tomorrow," said Rajiv with all sincerity.

"This stays unsettled between us," said Rashid almost fuming.

The rock show continued further for about an hour and finally the group decided to call it quit. It was a memorable evening and all had their own share of fun. It was almost ten thirty by the time they reached home.

The next day they all consensually agreed to move out a little late. It was almost 10 o'clock by the time they finally left the house. Today, their destination was the Loktak Lake. The lake is located about forty odd kilometres from Imphal city in the southern side of the Manipur state. It is the largest freshwater lake in the Northeast region of the country. The flight route of all planes to Imphal airport crosses over the Loktak Lake. The lake from the aerial view looks oval in shape and extends to about twenty-six kilometres in length.

"So tell us something about the lake?" said Rajiv.

"Today, the description can be in bit more detail. As such, today both our local guides are accompanying us," added Rashid looking at Max and Hashnam.

"Well, recognizing the bio-diversity and socio-economic importance of Loktak Lake in 1990, it was designated as the wetland of international importance under the Ramsar Park convention."

"Wow! Does this help to draw tourism?" asked Arun.

"Not really. In fact, few years back the area around the lake was occupied by militant outfits. Due to their fear nobody really came to visit the lake," said Hashnam.

"Let's turn back. I have no intention of having fun at the cost of my life. You guys have no responsibilities. But I have to look after my two younger sisters and a mother," said Rashid feeling a bit agitated.

"Relax Rashid. Why do you have to jump guns? Listen to what Hashnam has to say," said Rajiv.

"Rashid, some seven years prior the security forces had launched a massive search operation in and around the lake and the militants were either eliminated or had to leave the place. From then on, a special force for the protection of the lake has been created. It is called the Loktak Protection Force."

"See, now the place is safe for the visit," added Max.

"But how safe is it actually?" asked Rashid still doubting the security of the place.

"OK. Let me tell you that four years prior water sports of international level were organized in the Loktak Lake. There had been heavy influx of people to witness the games," said Hashnam.

"Now it sounds better," said Rashid.

"And yes, the southern portion of the lake has Keibul Lamjao National Park which is a unique floating park," continued Hashnam.

"Floating park you said?" asked Esha who was also listening to the conversation with keen interest.

"Oh yes! Floating park. Actually, even the lake is full of the floating marshy land masses. They keep changing position during the day. However, you can walk on them."

"Well, I am really excited to see the lake."

"We should be there in another thirty minutes," said Max.

"And yes, the National Park is house for the local deer who are called Sangai," added Hashnam.

"OK. That's why the festival we saw is known by the same name," added Arun.

The route to the destination did not seem to be as long as it was yesterday. They came to a market place from where a road digressed towards the lake. Max told them that from the market another road went to the Subhas Chandra Bose's Indian National Army Museum. They will be visiting the same as they return from the Loktak Lake.

From the turning beyond the market area, the road was not in a very good condition. Hashnam told them that the move of heavy vehicles on the route had led to the poor state of this patch of the road.

"Heavy vehicles. Why is this lake area taking the load of so many heavy vehicles?" asked Rashid.

"Well, there is a large culmination of weeds in the lake which require periodic cleaning. These vehicles are used to support this maintenance. Once we reach the lake, you will see for yourself the kind of efforts that are required for upkeep of the Lake," said Hashnam.

The mere sight of the lake was really beautiful. It had clear blue water. Indra uncle had arranged for their move within a security camp which was located at a hillock along the lake. They identified themselves and were permitted within the camp. Once, they reached the view point at the high ground the entire Loktak Lake was clearly seen. It was a very large lake and the reflection of sun rays added to its beauty. They were offered tea and refreshments and then proceeded for boating. There was a motorboat available to take them along the lake.

"During the rainy season the locals put round fishing frames in the lake for catching fishes. Once, the weed comes around the frame they look like green concentric rings over the lake," said Max.

"Oh yes. I did see the photograph of the lake with those green rings displayed in the lounge," said Rajiv who was busy clicking the photos of the lake.

The floating biomass looked like small islands. Some of them were big in size. On one of them someone had even made a bamboo hut. The breeze was blowing and added freshness to the place.

"Come let me click a good photo of you two. If you don't mind Rashid, please move out of the frame," said Rajiv to Esha and Arun and smiled at Rashid to do the needful.

"If we are single that doesn't mean you will keep us out of the photo frame," commented Rashid who shifted to one side in the boat and looked offended.

"Don't be pissed off. I will click a photo of all of you after that," added Arun.

The boat slowly went from one corner of the lake to the other while the group continued its photo session. Esha tried to put her hand in the water. When she was checked by Arun, she splashed some water over him. Rajiv folded his camera in his arms as if his little child will suffer pneumonia.

"If you fall in this lake I bet you will drown," said Arun.

"If you have noticed, my life jacket is just a hand away, Mr Banker."

"Yeah. But the water will be deep and cold."

"Don't worry Esha. He is trying to scare you. The water in the lake is not more than five metres deep. You get him wet, rest we will look into," added Hashnam.

"The driver of the boat says that he can stop next to the biomass if you want to walk on the same," said Max.

"Will it not be dangerous?" said Rashid.

"No. No. It is perfectly OK," said Max.

Rashid did not leave the boat. He also ensured that Esha stayed on the boat. The others got off on the biomass to get the feel.

Finally, the driver of the motorboat got them back to the mainland. Esha insisted to spend some more time around the lake and Arun had to relent to her request. While the other sat at the viewpoint, Esha and Arun went for the stroll. They took the pathway which went along the side of the lake. From a distance, now Esha's yellow top was an easy landmark for others.

"They look good together," said Rajiv looking in the direction of this love couple.

"Yeah. I hope their relation works out well," added Hashnam.

"She has quietly become a part of our group. In fact, rather we all are so use to her being around that our friendship will look void without her," said Rajiv.

"Even I agree. If she was not around, you're stupid pranks would have known no limits," added Rashid.

Arun was aware that they must be quite visible from the place where his friends were sitting. This refrain him from holding Esha's hand. However, she was walking so close to him that her presence was unavoidably overpowering. She looked so beautiful and so carefree. In the institute, the precedence was accorded to more functional aspects and very little time was spent together. There were quantification standards which always played in the mind. However, here Esha was rather carefree. She didn't think twice before splashing water over Arun on the boat. The temperament was quite unlike Esha, who always preferred to maintain a cautious reaction.

"I will associate this trip with all the beautiful moments that we two have spent together," said Esha with a smile.

Arun kept walking along quietly thinking over Esha's words. She had put her thoughts across so simply.

"You know, your presence in my life still looks like a dream. Sometimes, I feel that one day I will lose you. Well, can't really think of a life beyond you," said Arun who too seemed to be carried by his emotions.

"Why do you say so?"

"Then tell me, do we have a future together?"

"Why do you ask such a thing?"

"This is because; off late such thoughts are always on my mind. I love you Esha and want to…"

"What?"

"Well, will you consider marrying me?"

This was the first time marriage was spoken about between the two of them. In past, they had only expressed love for each other but then the commitment of future was never brought out.

"Arun, let's not rush into this now."

"Are you offended," said Arun.

"No. Obviously not. But let us give some more time to this. I mean, the future is so unpredictable. After six months none of us actually knows where we are going to be."

"Precisely, and in this I don't want to lose you. Undoubtedly, there will be a professional future for both of us but what about our future."

"Let's go back."

"Well, the way I look at things between us, there is hardly any scope of going back," said Arun.

"Even I won't disappoint you. But as of now, the others are waiting for us. So can we please go back?" Esha almost pulled Arun and had a smile on her face.

"I love you." She added very gently as she walked besides him.

Neither of them spoke on their way back. But today, a new beginning was made between them. They had agreed to see a common future with each other. By the time they reached the lounge area others were waiting for them.

"Sorry, I hope we didn't keep you all waiting for very long," said Esha.

"Oh! Not at all. In fact, they are just about to lay the lunch for us," said Hashnam.

Mr Indra had also spoken to get the meal organized for them at this place. It was a lavish lunch. It was organized in the lawn from where lake was clearly visible. Post lunch, the plan was to visit the museum.

"So by what time are we going to be home?" asked Esha.

"Well, it should take us less than an hour in the museum and then we will be free," said Hashnam.

"This implies that we will have the evening free from any commitment?" asked Rajiv.

"Yes."

"In that case, why don't you come over to my place? Even Father Alison will be very happy to meet you all. Also, I can pick up some clothing for the next two days," said Max.

"What have you planned for the coming days?" asked Rashid.

"Well, you guys will leave for Kohima tomorrow and then come back a day later. Max will accompany you. I will have to make arrangements for Shilpa's first visit to home after the marriage. There will be some ceremonies at home. I hope you guys will understand," said Hashnam.

"That won't be an issue. In fact, both you and Max have really looked after all of us in a great way. Without the two of you, our trip would not have been so great," said Esha as the others nodded their approval.

"It's our pleasure to have you here," said both Max and Hashnam almost in a chorus.

The museum as a routine stayed open till five in the evening. However, by the time they reached the place there was hardly any visitor. Rajiv purchased the entry ticket at the counter and also paid for his camera. Hashnam had been to this place before and became their guide. He took them first to the memorial that was made within the premises of the museum. It was written that the first flag of Indian National Army (INA) was hosted here by Netaji Subhas Chandra Bose. The INA forces had advanced from Burma and fought against the British forces. Due to the lack of fire support, the INA force had to slow down its advance and was subsequently countered by the British forces.

The museum had various photographs of Netaji. Old guns, ammunition and dresses worn during the war were also displayed. Rajiv told others that a similar museum is maintained in Port Blair. He had seen the museum some two years prior on his visit to Andamans.

"Never knew that a museum of Netaji would be maintained in Manipur. My maternal grandfather had his association with the Indian National Army. When we were kids, my mother and aunty used to tell us about him," said Rajiv.

From the museum where they had rather spent quite some time, the group decided to directly head for the church, as Father Alison was waiting for them. Father had already confirmed to Max his availability in the church during the evening. It took them little over two hours to reach the church. Father had arranged for evening refreshments for all of them. Today, he was dressed in the normal trouser and a cardigan. He was indeed delighted to receive Max and his friends.

"So how has been your experience in Manipur?" asked Father.

"Well, Father every day has been a rollercoaster ride. It is indeed very exciting. There is so much that one has learnt about Manipur in such a short duration," said Rajiv.

For the next hour, Father listened to each one of them. Everyone had something to say and then pose their questions to Father. Max went home to get his belongings and soon joined others. Max informed his friends that Father in addition to his music classes and gardening was also involved with an orphanage.

"That's great Father. So how do you manage to get time for all such noble things?" asked Esha.

"Oh! I don't deserve this appreciation. There is a lady of our village who through the help of some NGOs runs this small orphanage. Still, their financial resources are very modest. Therefore, I sometime help them out. If nothing, I just go and spend some time with those kids. A few of them also show interest in music," said the Father.

It was almost dark outside and Dhayan Singh reminded them that they must timely revert back. As such, the next day would be quite hectic. Father Alison thanked all of them for their visit. By the time they reached home it was almost dark. Uncle Irom was sitting along with his elder brother in the veranda. Both the elders seemed to be discussing something important with complete seriousness.

"So how was your trip?" asked Indra uncle.

"Uncle, it was extremely good. In fact, we must thank you for getting our lunch organized today," said Arun.

After some pleasantries, the group members went to their respective rooms. They decided to get together again for dinner after sometime.

"I hope we did not intrude into the privacy of your father and uncle," said Rajiv.

"Oh! Not at all. They generally sit together during this hour of the day and talk. Even uncle Tomba joins them," said Dhayan Singh.

"The brothers must be real close. I and my brother care for each other but then we really do not sit together like this. It was good to see such closeness between the brothers," added Rajiv.

"Actually, my grandfather expired at quite an early age. Being the eldest amongst his siblings, my father had to step into his father's shoes. He gave his brothers unconditional support and in return they always gave him respect which an elder of the house deserves. Even now, both his brothers take his opinion over all matters of concern. Their evening gathering is a part of this ritual," said Dhayan Singh.

Esha had the entire room for herself. After Shilpa left, it was a little uneasy for her to be using her room but then Dhayan Singh's mother insisted. She said that as Esha was there they didn't feel all that lonely and bad. After changing, Esha went to assist aunty in the kitchen. However, aunty told her not to bother after such a busy schedule.

"You girls of today have some stamina. I would have actually got tired. Even Shilpa is also like you. She can jump around more than her brothers," said aunty.

"Do you miss her?" asked Esha. Aunty could just nod. The mere mention of her daughter made her emotional. She quietly wiped a tear off her eye and continued with her kitchen work.

Esha was reminded of her own mother. She had spoken to her and dad in the morning itself. However, it was almost five months that she had last met them in person. Sometimes, she really missed them. Seeing Dhayan Singh's family she was missing them even more. Uncle Indra brought his mother to the dining hall. Esha wished the old lady who had a smile on her face. Grandmother was the first in the house to have her meal. She usually was accustomed of sleeping early.

"My mother is asking, how you are finding this place?" said uncle Indra.

"Tell her that more than the place, I have loved the goodness of the people of this place," said Esha.

When uncle translated what Esha had said, the mother and son had a good laugh. Then uncle said, "Ma says you are a very nice girl. God bless you."

Gopal returned from Tomba uncle's house. He had been playing with his cousins. He was happy to see Esha.

"Didi, when did you all return?" asked Gopal.

"Well, a little while ago. And by the way, where have you been? We haven't seen you from almost the day of the marriage."

"Busy didi, busy," said Gopal as if he was an adult.

"Busier than your elder brother," teased Esha.

By now grandma had her dinner and uncle took her to her room. Aunty told Gopal to get the boys for the dinner. Gopal dutifully went to Irom uncle's house to get his brother and others for dinner. Aunty had insisted that Dhayan Singh's friends must have the meals at her place, in spite, Irom uncle and aunty's offer to be the host. Keeping Rashid's choice in view, aunty had made the Tuna fish for them. Irom uncle had once casually mentioned to Rashid that Manipur had hundred and thirty species of fish of which twenty-seven had commercial value. He had requested aunty to cook at least the top five in the countdown chart.

By the time dinner was through, Mrs Tomba also came in. Although each brother had his separate house with individual entity in the Hashnam family but they still lived quite cohesively. Tomba aunty told them that she had not been to Loktak Lake in the last ten years. Esha narrated her experiences of the day to aunty.

"Aunty, yesterday evening I had observed that the maid was sweeping the dirt inside the room. I tried asking her but then her Hindi was difficult to understand," said Esha who was chatting with Tomba aunty while the others listened.

"Oh!" laughed aunty and said, "Actually, that's the way the houses are cleaned here. In the morning, the dirt is cleaned outwards and during the evening the reverse order is followed."

"But why so?" asked Rajiv.

"Well, in case one drops any valuable on the floor during the day, the same can be checked next day in the morning before the dirt is thrown out of the house."

"Is this a ritual in every house?" asked Arun.

"Yes."

"That's interesting. Tell us some more rituals or beliefs that are peculiar to this place," added Esha.

"Let me think…."

"Tell them about the importance of bamboo in our households," prompted Dhayan Singh's mother who also sat along with them.

"OK. As didi just said, a Meitei house is considered unlucky without a bamboo tree. Each house will have a bamboo groove and the bamboos are cut only on the auspicious day under the supervision of the elders of the house."

"Do you believe in such superstitious sayings?" asked Rashid.

"Yes, same like any other place in the country. Even we have some superstitions," said Tomba aunty.

"Aunty, tell us a few," said Esha.

"Like seeing someone brushing his teeth when one is leaving the house is considered to be a bad omen. Also, if a person steps out of the house he must not re-enter if he has forgotten anything that was to be carried. The item is delivered to him by other family members outside the house," said Tomba aunty.

Adding on to what aunty had just said, Dhayan Singh continued, "Meiteis traditionally are extremely superstitious with regard to days and dates for setting out on journey in different directions."

"Now, I got it as to why you hardly moved out of the institute," said Rashid.

"Well, that was by choice and not due to superstition. However, I can tell you that if tomorrow you travel towards the west it will bring good luck to you."

"Really."

"Yes. And for that you and others need to catch upon some sleep so that you have a pleasurable journey," added Dhayan Singh with a smile.

The evening came to an end with the commitment to start for Kohima by seven in the morning. As the days progressed, the group members became all the more punctual. The main reason to be on time was that the entire Hashnam family, especially Dhayan Singh's mother, would get up much earlier to ensure that meal was prepared for them. Indra uncle would be busy giving all instructions to the driver regarding the places that he must take them to. Under such circumstances, it would not be right to break the general time-line consensually agreed upon.

It would take them about five hours to reach Kohima, the state capital of Nagaland. The highway road connecting both the states was the main lifeline of Manipur. All resources coming into Manipur were supplied through this route. Although, there was one more route which connected Manipur with Assam but then the road was in poor state of maintenance. Due to various protests over the years, Nagaland-Manipur route has witnessed frequent blockades. But today, it looked like any other highway road of the country with smooth traffic. The Manipur River was flowing alongside the road and on the foothills some inhabitation was seen sprinkled with large areas under cultivation throughout the route. Some of the hill areas were also occupied and could be compared to any of the best hill stations of the country. It was a bright sunny day; still, the low level clouds could be seen at various places. With so much greenery around, the ambience of entire place was very mesmerizing.

"One thing that I have observed about this place is that the general traffic is not rowdy. People do not unnecessarily overtake, especially from the wrong side. A proper queue is maintained where-ever there is a traffic block," said Arun.

"Yes you are right. People do follow the traffic guidelines properly and life in general isn't too busy. That's the way people here like it."

They took their first break a little ahead of a place called Senapati. Throughout the route at various places people were selling pineapples. It is the most common and much relished fruit of this place. Rashid was keen to taste and got the same for the others also. The seller cut the pineapple into smaller pieces and sprinkled some salt on it. It was very sweet and tasted good with this combination.

"I love this fruit. They say, it has a lot of fibre," said Rashid.

"Yes. But if you eat too much, it will loosen up your stomach," cautioned Rajiv.

Max told them that the fruit was largely grown on the hill slopes as the soil there does not have water logging. He indicated to the massive pineapple cultivation which was seen on the hills at the near distance.

The next place where they halted was the Mao gate. Beyond Mao gate is the jurisdiction of Nagaland state. In another few hours, they reached on the fringes of Kohima town. Max told them that en route there was a model village that had been made on the outskirts of Kohima city, in which the hornbill festival was organized in the month of December. Tomorrow on their way back to Imphal they will halt there. As of today, their first destination would be the war cemetery of Kohima.

The view of Kohima was very beautiful. Much before entering the city, one could see the major built up of the place. It looked at par with any other hill stations of the country. The houses had slanting tin shed roofs which were painted in various bright colours. The wind outside had a little chill and with the bright sunlight it was a perfect weather.

"It must be an old cemetery?" asked Esha.

"Yes, it was made in memory of the British Army soldiers who sacrificed their lives fighting the Japanese aggression. It has mix graves of the British and the Indian native soldiers," said Max.

The cemetery was located almost at the start of the city on an elevated area which gave an entire view of Kohima. There was a large roundel adjoining which the vehicles parking had been made. In the centre of the cemetery, there was a huge vertical pillar which had the names of all the martyrs of war. The necropolis around the grave of soldiers had been converted into beautiful lawns. The multi-coloured flowers all across the lawn further enhanced the ambience of the place. The area was very well maintained. Each grave had been properly marked. The name of the soldier, his unit, his date of birth and the day he died was mentioned. Rajiv clicked photos of all his friends around the place which had eye catching view. In addition to the group, there were many other visitors who were there at the war memorial.

"Did you notice that almost all the soldiers who died in 1943 during the war were between the age group of seventeen to thirty-five years," said Esha.

"Yes, even I noticed the same. Not much of an age to die. But then wars always lead to heavy disaster. Dying thousands of miles away from the homeland in the name of their country must be some courage and cognitive content," said Arun who was walking along with Esha through the cemetery.

"Sometimes, ones beliefs overtake the fear of making various choices. But then, the belief in itself is tempered by the circumstances. Today, one may find logic of a particular decision but the same may not look like the best choice after sometime," said Esha.

Arun could feel that sometime more was being conveyed by Esha. He walked quietly thinking what to say. Now the time for dogging off from reality was over in their case. So indefatigably he decided to hold the bull by the horns.

"Esha are you ambivalent regarding our future together?" he asked her.

"I didn't say so." Esha sounded defensive as if her mind had been read.

"So what's playing in your mind? Look, even I will also not like you to rush into things. Do take your time to think about our relation. I will wait. But, I just want to tell you that love has never been the captive of logics. No amount of rationality can justify your love for someone. Listen to your heart and all rest will fall in place."

"Don't take me wrong," said Esha with her eyes almost beseeching.

Arun felt the urge to hold her in his arms and pledge his commitment. But then, this was not the time to give assurance of his love. As a matter of fact, Esha needed the assurance of her own belief. This she would have to find within her own self. Arun will have to wait.

"I will never take you to be wrong. Please don't burden yourself too much over this onerous decision. Let us cherish the present moments, OK. Rest all can wait. I love you." He held Esha's hand and kissed it.

"I love you too."

The others had reached the acme of the cemetery. Rashid was obliging a young couple who had handed him their camera to click their photograph. Once all of them converged at the central lawn, they decided to head for the hotel. Uncle Indra had gone out of his way to confirm their booking. The hotel was twenty minutes drive from the cemetery and was centrally located next to the main market area. The rooms were pretty decent. Only Esha got the room for herself, where as the others were on the sharing basis. The group decided to freshen up and post lunch proceeded for the museum and the church.

From the room through the glass window of one of the walls, Rashid saw the traffic on the nearby road and beyond that the beautiful view of the city. For the first time in his life, he was visiting a place which could be called a hill station. He did not have the family affluence to afford such trips. He had heard of hills stations like Mussoorie, Darjeeling, Nainital, Ooty, and many more. But visit to such places was unimaginable with his financial background. Now things will change. Once he gets a job he will see such places of scenic beauty.

Suddenly, his thoughts were covered with the emotions of guilt. After the death of Abba, his Ammi had just lived her life for her three children. She had done all menial jobs to ensure that her children had a future. Even now, in a small dingy room she would be stitching clothes to make ends meet. She did not have the courage to purchase anything for herself. All her love and worldly desires were for her children. Tears rolled down Rashid's cheek thinking that Ammi would die living this life that was not fair to her. He promised himself that he will make his Ammi happy someday. He resclved that he will not travel anywhere for fun after this trip. He will first take Ammi for Haj. This was a desire that she was so scared to even imagine. As if, god had denied her the rights to even meet her.

"Hey Rashid, why aren't you out of the room? Others are waiting for you," said Rajiv. The moment Rashid turned, looking at his face Rajiv asked, "Are you OK? You don't look too well."

"No. No. I am just fine."

"Sure?"

"Yes."

"So let's go then," said Rajiv who knew that at times it was best to leave things unquestioned.

The museum was on the other end of the city. However, the driver was quite crude up and knew the route. The entrance gate of the museum was made up of boulder size stones. Somehow, the passage of the main building was quite narrow. Finally, the driver stopped the vehicle at the open space which presumably was used for the parking. The group walked to the museum's entrance.

Rajiv, the official accountant of the group, once again purchased the tickets for everyone. The museum was better maintained then the previous one they had visited in Imphal. The gallery had two-sided display of items depicting the culture of the Naga people. There were items of jewellery, household use, weapons, animal skins, clothes, utensils, historic write-ups, etc, which were on display. In addition, there were numerous cut-out models depicting the various tribes of Nagaland. It took the group good about an hour to go through all the floors of the museum building. Rajiv did not waste the opportunity and clicked a number of photographs in the museum.

After the museum, the group went to the church which was located at one of the highest points of the city. As per the driver, it was the biggest church of this region. Indeed, the church was massive in size. Its roof had been designed in such a manner that the place had good natural light coming into the main hall. The entire flooring was of wood finish. On the sides of the main hall there were confession boxes. In the main hall the prayers were conducted. By the time they all reached there, no mass prayers were scheduled. In fact, a portion of the church was under repair and a few workers were busy with their work. It was a Catholic church which had a capacity for mass prayer of more than four hundred people at one time. The group went around the place for some time and then decided to move for their next destination.

Near the main market, there was the famous Kida market. Esha had some initial inhibition to enter the market but then later relented. From the main road a stairway led to the Kida market. The vendors in the market had all assortments of insects for sale. All the insects were live. Some of them en umbered with their own load were moving in a constrained space and looked pretty scary. In addition to the insects, frogs, fish, snakes, turtles and other such species were on sale. There was a pungent smell pervasive in the place. None of them wanted to hang around the place for long and just walked across till they came to the end of the market.

"This market is one of its own kinds. It has been in place for number of years," said Max.

"Why do the people here prefer to eat such horrible insects?" asked Arun.

"Well, such things were consumed by the tribes to cover up their requirements of protein. Hunting was in place but then assured regular supply of animal's meat was not possible every time. That is how the consumption of such insects came in place. Later, with changing times when all such items were purchased by the people, the low price of insects in comparison to meat promoted the less privileged to eat insects. Others too eat insects but more due to the taste preference," said Max.

Once out of the Kida market the group entered the main market of Kohima. It was typically a hill station kind of market. There were a lot of branded shops in addition to those shops which were selling the Chinese products. In comparison to Imphal, there was a larger representation of men and women of affluent background who could be seen moving around in the market area. In place of Makhela or traditional attire, the western dresses were more prominently in use. There was more sense of freedom that was quite evident in the place which inspired more liveliness. When Arun shared this observation with Max, he said, "Yeah. In a way you are right. Nagaland has speedily returned towards normalcy over the years. Due to this the people of the state find better opportunities available to them for economic growth. Soon, I am hopeful that our state will also have such congenial environment."

"Can I see some Naga traditional items on sale?" asked Esha.

"Yes, there is one shop of handloom nearby. In addition, the decoration items will be available in many shops."

Arun, Esha and Max went inside the shop while the other two decided to have a cup of coffee in a nearby stall.

"So how do you find this place?" asked Rajiv.

"Oh! It's good. In fact, I will always have fond memories of this trip provided you promise to hand me over the soft copy of all the photographs that we have clicked together," said Rashid.

"That's a deal."

"You must have visited a number of hill stations."

"Well. My schooling was from a boarding school in Mussoorie. In addition, to that I have also been to Shimla and Nainital but I have very vague memories of those places."

"Why, were you so drunk?"

"Shut up. I was maybe five or six years old during those trips."

"So your parents didn't take you brats out much," again Rashid tried to crack a wise one, sipping his coffee.

There was a long silence and then Rajiv finally said, "You know what! I don't like speaking much about my personal life. But then, we have been friends for some time. Both my parents died in an accident when my elder brother and I were seven and nine years old. We studied in boarding schools after that, which one of my uncles arranged for us. Varun bhaiya is now working in America. We are not very close. So that's my family history."

There was a look of apology on Rashid's face. "I ......didn't mean....," he said.

"You don't have to be sorry. But please, don't play the Chinese whisper within the group. I don't like it."

"Point taken. But, can I ask you something? Why did you share it with me?"

There was a smile on Rajiv's face as he said, "Becausc, I happen to see a look on your face in the hotel which reminded me of myself."

"So we have something in common after all."

"Now you are insulting," laughed Rajiv.

After sometime others also came out from the shop. Esha had purchased a cast of Naga couple which depicted the Naga traditional attire. The sun was almost down and the breeze had become colder. They decided to call it a day and returned back to the hotel room.

Rajiv and Arun were sharing the room. Rajiv had put on the music channel on the television and the volume was pretty high. When Arun came out of the bathroom he could barely hear what Rajiv was asking. He indicated him to lower down the volume.

"So what's the plan for the evening?" asked Rajiv.

"Well, Max just said that this place does not have much of a night life. So, I guess we have to have our dinner in the hotel itself."

"Tell me something. Were you always like this?"

"Like what?" asked Arun who was combing his hair.

"A typical mama's boy. I am no preacher and have no reason to sniff around and advise people. But then, we are friends? No. Therefore, I just wanted to say that you must have some special moments with Esha. Don't behave as if you two are a part of a documentary being made on the Northeast region. Have some space for yourself. Take her out for dinner."

"I guess you are right. But, will it be safe? You know, taking her out at night," asked Arun who seemed to be seriously considering the suggestion.

"Yes sir. It will be just fine. There is a good restaurant next to this hotel. In fact, it belongs to the brother of the owner of this hotel. I have already put a word for you. He will make all arrangements. So go ahead."

"Thanks. But what about you guys?"

"Don't you worry, the bottle which Irom uncle just gifted will take care of our evening."

Arun spoke to Esha who agreed to be ready for dinner by 8 o'clock. There was not much of a crowd in the restaurant and the first floor was with limited gentry which included few couples. They took a table from where the entire city was visible. The city looked beautiful with all the lights.

"So what would you like to order?" Arun said extending the menu card.

"Well, let's get some coffee to start with."

"OK." Arun called for the waiter and placed the order.

Before the waiter returned with the coffee, they mutually agreed to order for some vegetarian food. Arun requested the waiter to serve the dinner by 9.30 PM.

"How often do you eat non-vegetarian?" asked Esha.

"Well, in my home it is made quite regularly. Actually, my father and sister are really fond of Chicken. Even I enjoy non-vegetarian but then I can adapt to all types of food varieties."

"My folks don't eat non-vegetarian," said Esha.

"Well, that's not a reason to feel sad. Each to his own," teased Arun.

"Do I look sad to you?" said Esha looking deep into his eyes.

"Consider it as a poor joke, OK."

"OK. Tell me something about your sister."

"Well, Parul is three years younger to me. Last year, she completed her fashion designing course and is working with a fashion house in Delhi. Presently, she has no plans for marriage," said Arun.

"So, you want to wait for her to get married before you take a call for yourself?" asked Esha who had caught Arun at a wrong foot.

"Well, I am not waiting for her decision but the decision of someone who need more time," Arun said looking unflinchingly at Esha who looked the other side.

The waiter got them the coffee and left. There was silence which none wanted to disturb. Arun held her hand which she squeezed tightly.

"Look, one day or the other we got to talk about our future. Maybe, the whole thing can be delayed but not avoided. OK. Let me put this the other way. We both have fear of uncertainty. Will it not be better if we just talk about it?"

"Arun, when we met during the start of the management programme, I was drawn towards you. Then, you candidly expressed your love. I could not believe that we two will have a love life. But it happened. At times when I am with you, your presence still looks like a dream, too good to be true. I feel I am really a lucky girl. Now you have rightly proposed marriage. Well, what more can I ask for? But then Arun, there are some more aspects attached with my life. I can neither ignore them nor avoid their presence. My parents, especially my father, always dreamt that their daughter will make a name for herself. Like all parents, they too would want moments which will make them feel proud of their kids. How can I deny them this basic? We still are just students. The world will open for us shortly. Let me find my place in that. And then, we will live our dream of our future together. Any commitment from my side at this point of time will raise your expectation. If I fall short of it, it will disappoint you. Arun, I do not want the foundation of our relation to be made over disappointments. When I look at you, I draw the strength of my life to face each day with the happiness which you sprinkle all around me. In my own way, I too want to remain as strength of your life and not as a weakness for which you compromised," said Esha.

"Wow! I never thought from that angle. It was infatuation which became love and then desperately aimed for marriage. I guess you are right. There are other aspects which also deserve consideration. But tell me, someday, will you marry me?" Arun said looking deep into Esha's eyes.

"Arun let me promise to you today that if I ever have any space for a man in my life, it will be only you. I love you," said Esha.

"OK. But, will you like to meet my parents? I intent to share my little secret about you with them," said Arun.

"Sure. I will definitely look forward to meet them. And yes, the next time I visit my folks, they will surely know about you, Mr Banker, and also about their daughter's inclination".

They both had just here in Kohima graduated in terms of their involvement in the relationship. Esha had agreed for a future together but the timings of the same had to be worked out. The waiter started laying the table for their dinner. It was a well cooked meal and both enjoyed it with an enhanced appetite.

Max, Rajiv and Rashid watched the cricket match being telecasted on one of the sports channel. There was a small restaurant on the ground floor of the hotel. They had their quite dinner there and were again back in the room. Rajiv had befriended the room attendant and managed to get the Times of India newspapers of the last one week. From the time they had come over to the Northeast, they had hardly found time to watch news on television or read the newspaper. Rajiv read the paper while the other two continued surfing the television channels.

"Hey! There is no news of the love birds. I hope they will find their way back to their rooms," said Rashid.

"Why can't you stop being so intrusive?" said Rajiv.

"I agree," said Max.

"Hello. I just made a casual query. OK," said Rashid.

"Rashid, have you ever dated a girl, ever?" Max asked.

"Well not really. Though while in college, I had a crush on a girl," said Rashid.

"Really! Then what happened to the poor girl?" Rajiv said as he dropped the paper from his hand.

"Well, I was not brought up like you. In Muzaffarnagar, it was a big thing to even speak to a girl. She used to study in Girls College which was next to my college. I used to see her walking along with her friends to the college. At times, she used to look at me. I feel she knew that I used to track her. She had long hair and tied it in a single plait. I still remember that she used to wear bright salwar suits."

"So did you propose her?" Max asked.

"Propose? Well, I never could muster the courage to speak to her. Once, she dropped a book at the bus stand. I picked it up. Next day, through my younger sister, I sent it across to her."

"Did you know her house?" asked Rajiv.

"Yes. Her family lived in the same locality," said Rashid.

"So did she not ask your sister about you?"

"Yes she did. But still, I never had the guts to speak to her. I thought, the day I become something I will speak to her. But then God didn't want it that way."

"What happened?" asked Max.

"Well, two years ago she got married. Sometimes it hurts," said Rashid with emotions. Rajiv burst into laughter and teased, "Shit happens. Sometimes, my friend."

"One last question, OK! What was her name?" asked Max.

"Zoya. OK. Now that you all had your share of fun, tell me about your love life. Rajiv your turn," said Rashid.

"Well, I don't know what to tell. I never really stayed committed towards any girl for a very long time. Actually, I am not good to handle emotions. Most of them used to tell me that I was not good enough to ever take on any responsibility. But then, that's the way I have always been."

"How many did you date?" asked Rashid.

"Stopped counting after my twelfth."

"How many did you sleep with?" asked Max.

"Lost count."

"Pervert, you will burn in hell," said Rashid who almost meant it.

"Relax. Just joking. I am not Tiger Woods who could afford to play so much."

They all laughed knowing that of all what Rajiv had said only ten percent would be true otherwise. Rest, one could run his imagination on both the extremities. The next in line to talk about his love life was Max. Although, initially he tried to dodge off the question but finally came up with his story.

Max had stayed in Delhi for sometime before he joined the institute. In one of the coaching classes that he attended there was a girl. Her father had recently retired and settled in Chandigarh. She stayed in a girls' hostel. They were originally from Nepal. The girl cleared her management entrance exams for a university in America. And she left. He was in touch with her through mails for sometime but then somehow the contact broke. He wasn't sure whether he loved her or not but there was definitely some chemistry between them. She also liked to spend time with him. But then, it did not work out. They both had very different backgrounds so the drift wasn't much of a surprise. Through friends he later came to know that she was seriously involved with an American chap who was along with her in the university.

"So that means that all three of us had a fucked up love life. One couldn't speak, other couldn't express and the third didn't know whom to speak and express to," laughed Rashid.

"I guess you are right. But then, love happens when it has to happen. You don't have to chase people around," said Max.

"Are you taking pot shots at Rashid and me?"

"No. But look at our friend Arun. Esha and he had to fall in love and it just happened. They look like people who should be together. Seeing love between them makes you feel that somewhere true love does exist," said Max.

There was a knock on the door. Max opened the door. It was Arun and Esha.

"So, how was the dinner?" asked Rajiv.

"Well, great. The restaurant had good ambience and a nice view of the city," said Arun.

"How about you guys? Did you have your dinner?" asked Esha.

"Oh yes. A long time ago," said Rashid.

Max declared that tomorrow they would leave for Imphal. En route, they will halt at the model village. Esha was the first to say good night and left. The others also decided to call it a day. Arun had just entered his room and opened his shoes when he heard a shriek. He felt it was Esha. Who else could be? He rushed towards her room and banged the door. He called her name. There was a panic in his voice as he continued to bang the door. By now the others also came out and joined Arun. What could have happened? Was she in some danger? Was she hurt? There were a number of questions that were running in Arun's mind.

"Let's break the door," said Rajiv.

"No, I can open it," said Max and inserted the wire attached with his key chain. He opened the lock; however, Esha had bolted the door from the top also. Before they could contemplate the idea of forcible opening the door, Esha opened the door.

"What happened? Why did you shout?" demanded Arun.

Esha gave a sheepish look as she was little embarrassed to see all the boys outside her room.

"Actually, there was a big lizard in my bathroom. I am scared of lizards," she said.

"My God! After going around the Kida market you are still scared of lizards. You could have caught her and probably got a good price for it in the market," said Rashid.

Everyone laughed which eased out the tension. By now, the receptionist also came to the lobby to check if all was well. He returned when he was told about the fiasco, much to Esha's embarrassment. Apart from Arun, the others also returned to their rooms.

"Well, in case you feel scared to sleep alone then I can always give you company." Arun said with mischief in his eyes.

"And how many girls have got such offer before me?"

"Well, nobody was as scared as you."

"No. I was not."

"Yes you were." Arun put an arm around her waist and held her close.

"Don't get ideas," giggled Esha.

"My offer is still on."

"You pervert."

"We can just talk or play ludo if you like."

"Go away."

"Think about it."

"Good night."

"That's not fair," smiled Arun removing his fingers from her neck.

"Go." said Esha and placed a kiss on his cheeks.

"You're going to give me sleepless nights," said Arun as he released Esha from his arms.

He moved along the corridor and then turned. He saw Esha still standing close to the door. He said "Do call me if the lizard comes across."

"Not the best choice. Good night. I love you."

Arun waved at her and was back in his room. Rajiv had already changed and was surfing the channels. He smiled at Arun.

"I was impressed with the way Max opened the lock. I thought his hands were only good on the cords of the guitar," said Rajiv.

"Well, in my panic mode I really didn't notice much. But yes, the guy has a lot that we still don't know."

Rajiv was the first to get ready in the morning. He ordered lavish breakfast for everyone. Right from boiled eggs, to scrambled eggs, to omelette, everything was ordered. The toasts were fresh and options of milk, coffee, tea and juice was available. He had passed especial instructions at the counter that the food be served steaming hot.

"Who ordered for this crap? The whole thing looks like Ramchander's choice. I would have ordered for some Aloo Paratha." These were the first words Rashid uttered as he entered the restaurant.

Rajiv smiled and said, "Rashid it's not a very nice thing to say, especially, when the person who has placed the order is holding a flask full of boiling milk."

"Are you threatening me?" said Rashid but his voice was less challenging.

"Well, medically it is believed that liquid above the boiling temperature can lead to third degree burn? Come, what's your choice of eggs for the breakfast."

"That is not civilized." The rest of the comments Rashid preferred to speak within his own mouth which he had already stuffed with scrambled eggs.

The next to come for the breakfast was Max. He had applied hair gel and his wet hair was almost standing like that of a porcupine. After the pleasantries, his plate was filled without any comments.

"Did you observe Arun seemed to be in quite a romantic mood? For the first time I heard him sing a song."

"Oh no! I can't deal with two mad men in this trip," said Rashid.

Ignoring his comment Rajiv asked, "Where is he?"

"I guess getting Esha for breakfast. At least, that's what he told me."

Soon, Arun and Esha also joined them for breakfast. Rajiv cleared the hotel bills and by 9.30 AM they left Kohima city. About ten kilometres from the city, on the right hand side there was a big entrance gate to the model village. There was a guard at the gate but he did not bother to stop their vehicle. The drive was upslope and then there was a big roundel. In the background of the place, on the right side, there was a huge hillock on which a large white hoarding was displayed. It read 'Hornbill'. The driver parked the vehicle around the roundel. There was a model village that had been constructed. It had numerous huts. Each hut was unique in its construction. Max explained that each hut depicted a certain form of hut construction peculiar to one set of tribe. However, the common thing was that almost all of them were made of bamboo and wood. The huts were constructed in a series. Although, some huts were small and some were big. Between three to four huts there was a garden that was well maintained. The garden had slabs placed on the sides for people to sit. The slabs were made with the combination of stones and woods. From all the huts and especially from the garden location, a stage was visible.

As per Max, during the Hornbill festival, various cultural programmes are conducted on these stages. People watched the programme sitting in the enclosure next to these stages or even sat in those gardens from where the view of the stages was clear. There were number of such stages and overlooking them were the huts. Each stage was peculiar in its own way and so were each hut. Visitor's booked and stayed in these huts during the Hornbill festival. However, it is much difficult to manage living space in this campus during the festival in general. A larger strength of people coming from outside prefers to spend the day in Hornbill festival and then subsequently reverts back to their respective places.

Within the village, there was also a large shopping complex where there was provision of many shops. During the festival the entire space is fully occupied. The shops sold clothes, decoration items, food stuff and many more things. The general gentry of the festival were the youngsters who came from all across Nagaland and Manipur.

"I wish we could have come during the festival. It must be so lively. The place itself has got such beautiful setup," said Esha.

"For that you just need to adjust your return schedule by only a month," said Rashid.

"I guess that will be asking for too much. By the way Rashid, thanks for the scarf," said Esha while the others looked at Rashid. Esha wore a blue scarf.

"What? I purchased two for my sisters and one for her. She has been kind enough to shop on my behalf in Imphal," said Rashid.

"Don't be defensive, Rashid. It was just that you shocked us all. After all, a miser like you doesn't give gifts too often," said Rajiv.

They all laughed and got their group photographs clicked at various places in the model village. After some time, they decided to revert back for Imphal. Max planned that they will halt at Senapati for their lunch and then subsequently move back to Imphal. Dhayan Singh during their trip had called a number of times to check if they were all doing fine. Yet again, he called and Max gave him the latest updates. The drive back to Imphal seemed to be much longer this time.

"What are those red stars that I see hanging over so many houses?" asked Rashid.

"Well, people here are preparing for the Christmas," added the driver.

"Really! But Christmas is almost after a month."

"Yes. But it is a very important festival of the Naga and the Kuki tribes who are mainly Christians," said Max.

"So apart from Christmas what all is celebrated in Manipur?" asked Esha.

"Good question. You see, Manipur is a land of festivals where hardly a month passes without celebrations."

"Please elaborate," said Rashid.

"The state has a population comprising of Hindus, Muslims and Christians. Therefore, festivals customaries to all the religions are celebrated. In addition, there are some customary of the place which are observed by all, irrespective of their caste and creed."

"Go on," said Rashid.

"Are you really so receptive? Especially, while travelling? I am sure you have already forgotten the local terms that you learnt earlier," laughed Max.

"Bullshit. I remember all that, OK. See 'Mei okpa' means bonfire, 'Langja Taret' means tying of thread during marriage, 'Leichiba' means the main ceremony of the marriage, 'Kangshubi Lannaba' … means …"

"Well, Rashid that's very impressive. You actually have a very sharp memory. In that case, if you insist, I will tell you about some important festivals of the region," said Max.

"Go ahead we are all ears," added Rajiv who also found such things of much interest.

Max explained that in the month of May, a festival is organized for worshipping the ancestors which is called 'Lai Haraoba'. Then, there is 'Yaoshang' which is celebrated in the month of March. The celebrations of the function start five days prior the full moon day of the month. A number of folk dances are performed during this festival. 'Ratha Jatra' is celebrated in July and the festivity continues for about ten days. 'Ramadan Eid', like other places in India, is celebrated amongst the Muslim community of Manipur in the ninth month of the year. 'Kut' is observed in the month of November to primarily celebrate the harvesting. After the harvesting season 'Chumpha' festival is organized for a period of seven days to jubilate the period of good harvesting. 'Lui-Ngai-Ni' is organized once the next seed sowing period comes in the month of February. The crop harvesting holds a lot of importance in the lives of common people of the state. Then, there are festivals like 'Gang-Ngai' that is organized in the month of December. In April, the Manipuri New Year is celebrated which is called 'Cheiraoba'. 'Heikru Hidonngba' depicts the season for boating competitions which are organized in the month of September and a large number of young boys take part in the event. In addition, there is 'Naingol Chakouba' in November when the married women come to stay with their parents.

"Wow! That was a lot of interesting information," said Esha.

"Rashid how much of the local words were you able to pick up?" asked Arun playfully.

"Well, it actually was too much of data. But then, we all got to know that these guys keep celebrating something or the other across the year," said Rashid.

"Yeah. So many occasions for celebrations and drinking," added Rajiv.

"Why is liquid diet always on your mind?" said Rashid while the others laughed.

By now, they reached the outskirts of Senapati. It was a main district of Manipur. The driver parked the vehicle next to a restaurant from where the view of valley was very beautiful. Max proposed to have lunch and then accordingly proceed for Imphal. The others agreed and selection of menu was left to Rajiv and Rashid. The restaurant had a bakery shop on the ground floor and the first floor was being utilized for serving meals. Some of the tables in the dining hall were already occupied. The group took one of the tables. There were large glass windows on the three sides of the big hall and the view of mountains was still visible from their location. Their entry into the dining hall of the restaurant had drawn the curiosity of the occupants.

"I guess the locals here are not used to seeing much of people from other parts of India?" asked Arun.

"Well, in a way you are right. But then, people from other states having business interest in the state do visit this region. Although, frequency of such visitors is quite less," said Max.

"There will be people from outside Northeast working in Central departments who would be residing in Manipur?" asked Arun.

"Oh yes! But then people who are, say, posted in this state are only there for two-three years and then revert back. However, a few communities from outside have also settled in Manipur. They include the Nepalese and the Marwari community. And of course, the people from Bihar also come here for casual labour when the monsoons are over," said Max.

"What about the tourist?" asked Esha.

"The influx is low. Still, it is much better than the previous years. Interestingly, a number of foreigners who are attached with the churches frequently visit the state. They move around even in the remote areas of the state."

"That's very interesting. That means that the region is much in notice of the other countries across the globe," said Rajiv.

In the meantime, Rashid in consultation with Esha had ordered the lunch and two waiters started preparing the table to lay the food. Most of the items were rather a bit spicy, which is quite typical of the commercial cooking. The food was otherwise well prepared and reflected the fusion of Indian cooking across the entire length and width of the country. By the time they reached the Imphal city, it was almost last light. Esha wanted to purchase few things from the market before they proceeded for the hills tomorrow. Thus, it was decided to stop in the main market for some time.

"I guess it is a right call to stop for some shopping. Max says that his village is quite in the wilderness and getting even small utility items will not be easy," said Rajiv.

"OK. Then, let's make a quick list of items that will be required during this trip," added Arun.

"Max, I hope your village is a safe place to visit?" said Rashid who was reminded of his mother's warning regarding the cannibals.

"Yes. Yes. Don't worry, you are just going to be fine and will surely enjoy your stay in the village."

Arun and Rajiv made a list of items which they felt they must carry along with them. Max also added some more items which with experience he felt his friends would need. Finally, the list included items like anti-mosquito cream, some common usage medicines, rope, Maggi, knife, torch, hand towel, biscuit packets, needle with thread, packets of tea, coffee and powder milk etc. They had mutually decided to undertake this trip in the public transport. As such, Indra uncle had gone quite out of his way to ensure that good transport was provided to them throughout their trip. Max had already confirmed that the bus to his village will depart from the main city bus stand at 8.30 in the morning. His father had insisted that before they leave, they must speak to him for coordinating the finer details of their trip. Once, the shopping was over, the group decided to move for Max's house. He called his father to confirm their arrival and also informed Dhayan Singh that they will be falling back at night after the dinner. Dhayan Singh would not be accompanying the group during their trip to Max's village. Even if he wanted, he had to be part of the post-marriage ceremonies at home. Tomorrow Shilpa would be coming home for the first time after the marriage. As part of the family, Dhayan Singh had to be there to welcome his sister. Her in-laws had agreed to leave her at her parents' house for the next two three days. As such, Shilpa was primarily coming home to spent time with Dhayan Singh who was to leave for his institute shortly.

Max's mother had already taken confirmation regarding the dinner of the group at her place. Father Alison had also been invited to the house. In normal course, Father Alison would have politely refused the invitation on some pretext or the other. But today, he had readily agreed to come over for dinner, as he was also keen to meet Max and his friends. He was very proud of Max. Father Alison had been his mentor and the age difference between the two made their relation almost like that of father and son. The Lotzem family knew about this mutual feeling and had great respect for the priest. By the time the group reached Max's house it was dark. Mr Lotzem and father Alison were sitting and chatting in the front veranda. They seemed to be discussing some lively issue as both were in real good mood. After the pleasantries, Max's father enquired regarding their trip to Kohima. Rajiv took the lead and narrated to uncle and Father Alison the details of their stay at Kohima. The others also joined in to share their share of experiences.

"It's nice to hear that you all are enjoying your stay in Manipur and look keen to visit places in and around our state. In fact, just before your arrival we were both talking about you all," said Father Alison.

"Oh! Yes. I was telling the Father that you children have some stamina. From the time you all have come, there has been a lot of travelling for you. Yet, there is a will to see more places. Your high spirits remind us of our young days when nothing in life seemed inaccessible."

"Lotzem, you are now an old man. But don't you call me old. Although, you guys have been calling me Father from past twenty-five years due to my affiliation with the church, but then, I am still very young," said Father Alison almost laughing at his own joke. The others also joined in.

Hearing so much noise, the ladies of the house also came out. Mrs Lotzem and her daughter had been busy making the final preparations in the kitchen. All greeted Mrs Lotzem who once again welcomed Max's friends at her home. Max introduced his sister, Kim, to all his friends. Kim and Max had a difference of about a year plus and was almost of their age group. She was about five foot two inches and had a fair complexion like her brother. Beyond this the siblings did not have anything much in common. Kim's eyes were large and expressive; however, she reserved her smile and laughter. Her dark hair were straight and fell touching her waist. One would not call Kim beautiful but then she surely had an attractive personality which would draw interest. It seemed she already had an admirer. Through the corner of his eyes Rajiv was looking at Kim. It is universally acknowledged fact that females have a sixth sense to judge such fishy looks. This time it seemed Kim had failed. However, Rashid did not. His sixth sense or probably the seventh or further even ninth sense told him that something dubious was there in Rajiv's eyes.

"Even a cat leaves seven houses before it catches a prey. I know what's up in your mind. Even if a smallest of the virus of your head cracks out, I will press the buzzer. You understand, Press the buzzzzzzzzzzz..."

"Rashid your mind is a dump yard of shit. So, one really can't expect much from you. Kim has resemblance with someone I met in Sangai festival. That's all," said Rajiv a bit agitated.

"You should have told me before," said Rashid.

"Why do I need to tell you everything?"

"As because, the two of us are real good pals. No?" said Rashid as he put his hand around Rajiv's shoulder.

"What is the little secret you two share?" asked Max who came with a serving tray with soup glasses.

"Oh nothing really. Just the normal chit chat," said Rashid and picked up two glasses for Rajiv and himself.

Lotzem aunty and the other two girls went inside to organize things in the kitchen. Kim and Esha seemed to have clicked from the start. The girls were chatting while laying the table for dinner. Kim listened as Esha told her about her experiences in Manipur. Esha even asked Kim to join them for the trip to the village. But then, Kim had a school to take care of. Kim told Esha that as children they used to stay for quite some time in the village but she had not been there for past many years. As per Kim, there was a water stream from where the fresh water accumulated in the pond and even during summers it catered for bathing of the people who ventured out in the middle of the thick jungle. The jungle per se had dense bamboo trees which had so much fresh smell which was quite captivating. Even, the thought of the place reminded Kim of her carefree childhood. As kids, she and Max often fought on many things. However, if ever Kim was troubled by any outsider, Max rose to the occasion of being a protective brother. She found this role of her younger brother quite amusing. Over the years, the siblings had realized that they would not become best of friends, but then, they still genuinely cared for each other. In a way, Kim was proud of the way her brother has worked hard in his life. Although Max did not have an easy sail in life, still he had done well for himself.

While the girls were busy inside, Uncle Lotzem amplified the details of arrangements that he had catered for the group in the village. His real brother in the village was making all arrangements. However, during the course of their stay they will be mostly cutoff from the rest of the world. Uncle especially insisted that they must not venture out after the last light. Father Alison told them that a long time back he too had visited the village. It was a paradise. In the morning hours, one can see the white clouds moving closely through the valley. The hills on all sides were lush green and the vegetation was very thick. He advised them to move along the ridge lines to see the scenic view of the entire valley.

Soon the dinner was served and the speciality was fish. Keeping Rashid's interest in view aunty had not made pork. While they ate, aunty told them that during their stay in the village one of their niece would be preparing the meals for them.

"Well, this is going to be my first experience of staying in a village. I am really excited about this trip," said Esha.

"I really don't know as to how you guys are going to find the life there. It's a slow pace life. People there start their day much early and also sleep early," said Lotzem uncle.

"Don't you have televisions in the village?" asked Rashid.

Uncle laughed and said, "I heard that few of the families had purchased a dish but then majority of the people living there do not have such amenities. Even in our house, you will not find the television."

"That's quite all right. As such, we have Rashid with us to take care of the entertainment part during our trip," said Rajiv and Arun could not stop his laughter which was to Rashid's annoyance.

Father Alison told them that the village was at a height. In fact, from the road where the bus will leave them, the walk to the village will be for twenty odd minutes. The main road further connected other villages along the hill ranges. Off late, mobile signals were received in the area. However, the strength was good only at few dominating heights. In case, they wish to call they will have to adjust their position suitably. The good part was that the village was connected with water and electricity supplies. Although, the frequency of electricity supply to the houses was fairly restricted during the day.

"Father, can I borrow a few books from you for the trip? I guess there will be a lot of time for leisure reading available during this trip," said Rajiv.

"Why not? Right after dinner you come along with me and select the books for yourself. I am sure, you will find something worth reading in my small collection," responded Father Alison.

Aunty Lotzem had packed few pulses and vegetables which she directed Max to hand over to the girl who would be cooking for them. There was also a bundle of spices and refined oil that was part of the baggage. By the time the others continued chatting;

Father Alison and Rajiv went to get books. Their absence was for only a short while. On return Father Alison also brought along a mouth organ which he gave to Max.

"Oh thanks father. At least, now I will have something to keep them all amused," said Max.

The group finally bid their goodbye to Lotzems and Father Alison. They promised to stay in touch and then left for Dhayan Singh's house. When they reached Dhayan Singh's house, the entire family was almost waiting for them. To start with, Indra uncle turned down their proposal for commuting by bus. The route was rough and he insisted that they will go in his vehicle along with the driver.

"But uncle, we will be able to manage. Sending your vehicle all the way along with us is not right," said Arun.

"No, no. There is no representation on this issue. At least, I can't allow Esha to undergo all the discomfort of the journey," said Indra uncle.

Esha and even others were touch by the genuine concern with which Indra uncle had rejected their proposal. Dhayan Singh had today gone to the market and rented good quality of sleeping bags for them for the trip. Even aunty had made a variety of snacks for them which she felt would be consumed during the trip. It was indeed very overwhelming to see the hospitality that both the families had extended to them.

Now that they will be commuting in the vehicle, the plan was modified and the group decided to leave by 10 o'clock. As per Max, they would be in the village by lunch time. Shilpa was also expected to be home before the group left. That way, Esha would get some time to spend with the new bride. Uncle Tomba invited the group to his house for the breakfast before they left for the village the next day.

"These sleeping bags are indeed very warm and comfortable," said Rashid who had unpacked them and was squeezed inside one to just get the feel.

"Why did you open them, you jerk? Pack them up fast unless you want to go in your grave in that," said Rajiv who seemed to be really annoyed with the mess that Rashid had created in the room.

"Well, I was just trying for the correct size," said Rashid a bit defensively.

"Bhaiya, they are actually of the standard size. So you need not bother," said Gopal who came in the room to give the flask of warm water.

"Hey Gopal. So are you planning to come with us for the adventure in the hills," said Rajiv to the boy.

"No bhaiya. I guess, maybe some other time. Mom won't allow me. In all these years, I have never crossed the valley," said Gopal.

"Why so?" asked Rashid.

"That's the way things are. Maybe, we are not so adventurous. As such, we don't have anyone known in the hills and there are no hotels or resorts which cater for tourism in those areas."

"Yeah! But tell you what? Times are not too far when your state will be one of the hotspot of the tourist destination," said Arun who also came inside the room.

"Why?" said Gopal.

"Because it is an untouched land which has so much of natural beauty and above all such lovely people like you," said Rajiv who had finally completed his packing for the forthcoming trip.

The others also prepared for the trip. It was decided to go light as they would be back in two days. The sleeping bags procured by Dhayan Singh would indeed be very useful during the trip. Dhayan Singh, Max, Arun and Rajiv sat late till the night talking about the various experiences they shared during the trip. Rashid was far too tired and was sleeping with his mouth half opened. Esha too had called it a day much earlier.

"Hey! Rashid don't take so much time. Uncle Tomba and others would be waiting for us," said Max who had been banging the bathroom door for Rashid to come out. Apart from Rashid and him, all the others had got ready much earlier and were waiting for them to come for breakfast.

"There is no warm water in the geyser. Rajiv has drained even the last drop of it. So I guess you will have to wait," yelled Rashid from behind the closed door. By the time, the two of them finally came down, even Shilpa had come home. Rajiv was busy with his fresh round of photo shoot. Shilpa was looking very beautiful and above all very happy. She seemed to have matured overnight. Arun was amused by the thought as to how fast the girls are able to adapt and transform. He was hopeful that one day soon even Esha will also agree to be his wife.

Irom aunty had made a lavish breakfast. She had also packed lunch for them so that they needn't worry regarding meal once they reach the village. By about 10.30 AM, the group was ready to leave. Max and Rashid volunteered to get the baggage from the room and got the stuff loaded on to the vehicle.

"I hope you guys have loaded our stuff?" asked Rajiv and Rashid gave a thumps up sign.

"Thanks."

After saying their goodbyes to the Hashnam family the group proceeded for their journey to the hills. The drive towards the hills was gradual and en route they came across a number of water bodies which were primarily used by the locals for fish breeding. Luckily, from the time they had come to Manipur the weather had been very bright and sunny. Max told them that during night it will be a little cold. As such, in the mountains after sunset the temperature sharply declines. As per Max, after about sixty odd kilometres the road condition will not be as good. Due to constant rains it was difficult to maintain the road network in the hill regions of the state. However, they should be at the village in the next three to four hours. There was presence of security forces at various places along the road, even though; the influx of traffic on the road was not much. As they gained height, there was a bit of chill in the air. The valley looked beautiful. Especially, the Imphal River that prominently covered a large portion of the valley and its curves looked scenically beautiful. Rajiv requested to stop the vehicle, so as he could click some photographs.

After some time, the road condition was actually poor and the vehicle speed was reduced accordingly. There was barely any traffic on the road. Only few load carriers passed their way. Esha and Max had conveniently dosed off while the others were still admiring the route. In the background, old songs of Mohammad Rafi played in the car stereo. After a couple of turns, they came across the barricade of one of the security check point. Their vehicle slowed down and finally came to a halt. The driver went and showed his papers and was soon on the wheels.

"Hey guys! We are going to be at the village in the next fifteen minutes," said Max who had woken up after the check post.

"All my bones seem to be paining," declared Rashid.

"Well, then you must thank Indra uncle for providing the vehicle. Had we come by bus, you would actually have become boneless," said Rajiv.

Max told the driver that he would stay near the road head and arrangements for his stay will be made by one of the locals who owned a shop. The village was a kilometre from the road head and was connected by a narrow pathway. As soon as their vehicle stopped, it was surrounded by a number of small school going kids. It seemed that they were getting back after school. Max was reminded of his own childhood. He had started his elementary education from the same school which was about three kilometres from the village. His eldest sister had almost carried him on her back to the school on the first day. All throughout the route, he had howled and cried his heart out. Didi was ten years elder to him and was always protective. As for the school, it soon became a fun place where Max had the company of so many friends. He still remembered his first class teacher. He was a very humble old man who really loved to be with children. Some years back, father had told him that the old man had died. He had cancer. His only son had moved out of the village and worked along with some transporter.

The driver opened the bonnet, Rashid and Arun helped to take out the luggage. Esha was impressed to see that the two children who still stood next to her could converse in English quite flawlessly. Both must be in the age group of six to seven years. The little ones belonged to the village and spoke with Esha without any inhibition. By the time the luggage was being unloaded, Esha went to the shop and purchased a packet of local sweets for the children. The shopkeeper spoke his native language but the money became the common mode of understanding between them. By the time Esha came back, she could see that Rajiv and Rashid had started a fresh quarrel.

"How could you do that? I told you to keep my stuff and you had acknowledged the same," said Rajiv who seemed to be fairly annoyed.

"No. You did not. You only told me to carry the sleeping bags. See, I have kept them so properly," said Rashid indicating towards the heap of baggage which were kept out for display.

"I swear I will kill him. One thing, only one thing I asked him during the entire trip and this is what he did," said Rajiv who seemed to be quite agitated.

"Hey! You two just back off, OK. Rajiv, do not get so bothered, we will work it out," intervened Arun.

"What happened?" asked Esha with concern.

"Oh nothing much. Only that Rashid forgot to keep Rajiv's luggage and he will have no other spare clothing throughout the trip," laughed Max.

"He didn't tell me. Why are you guys blaming me?" repeated Rashid.

"Poor Rajiv. Don't worry, I am sure you will managè somehow," said Esha sounding genuinely concerned.

"He is not even left with spare underwear to change and none will be available in this place," whispered Max in Arun's ear.

"Really!," said Arun who was also finding the whole situation quite amusing.

"So what do I do now?" said Rajiv.

"Share my clothes if you like," offered Rashid without making any eye contact.

"I would rather do without clothes then to wear your ones. Max, is there some cloth shop nearby?" asked Rajiv.

"Negative. Maximum a cheap quality of towel or something may be there in this shop," said Max as he indicated towards the lone shop which Esha had just visited.

Rajiv and Max went to the shop while others waited near the vehicle. Esha chatted with the kids and Rashid explained to Arun why he was not at fault. The shop did have some cheap clothes of Chinese origin. Rajiv was encouraged by Max to purchase the undergarment, towel and one pair for the night change-overs. Finally, after much perseverance by the shop owner and Max, Rajiv did buy the bare minimum items for himself. As the track pant of his size was not available, he was forced to purchase the only pants which were of red colour.

The kids volunteered to carry their stuff till the village. Before moving, Esha distributed the packet of sweets amongst the kids. Max organized the stay of the driver with the shop owner and promised to be in touch by mobile phone.

"How far is your village?" panted Rashid.

"Oh! Well, just another five odd minutes."

"That's what you have been saying for the last ten minutes," added Rashid.

"Uncle, if you want I will carry your bag," volunteered one of the little kids whose school pants were barely holding on to his waist.

"Rashid have some shame," said Rajiv.

"I didn't tell him to carry stuff from me," said Rashid pointing towards the little one in defence.

"Shut up, you two," said Arun who was annoyed by the conduct of his friends.

It was a bright sunny day but by the time they reached the out-skirt of the village most of them were sweating. There were few houses in the way. Most of them were made of thatch roof and had a small courtyard along the house. The local hens were running from one end to the other and were being chased by a small group of boys who were half naked. The group caught their attention as they made lot of noise in their native language. The mothers of few were forced to come out to check upon their little ones. Max seemed to be quite unknown person in the village as there was no look of recognition in the eyes of the onlookers. In fact, the old man sitting near the cemented roundel of the big shady tree was the only person who seemed to know Max. Max rapidly spoke to the old man, which seemed to be like a volley of bullets to most of the others who did not understand a single word of what was being communicated between the two. But whatever was being said by Max was music to the ears of the old man as he seemed to be delighted. At least, the speed with which he smoked his local pipe matched the speed in which Max spoke. The old man made occasional nods and seemed to be happy meeting Max and his group of friends. Rajiv insisted if he could click some photographs of the old man. The elderly person obliged Rajiv when his request was interpreted by Max. In fact, he went out of his way to remove the pipe from his mouth and gave a smile which showed the few remaining teeth in his mouth. There was something more common between Rajiv and the old man which he hoped and prayed that the others in the group did not notice. The old man was wearing an identical track pant in the same red colour which Rajiv had just purchased a short while ago.

By the time they moved ahead, the news of their arrival had already been spread in the village by some of the school children who had reached their destination. Max's uncle, Andrew met them en route and the Lotzem family union took place as more and more witnesses gathered. The group was introduced to uncle and some others who were voluntarily present. Uncle seemed to be quite excited to meet his nephew who he was seeing after a very long time. Uncle Andrew was a small time contractor and resided along with his family in the village. He was also the sole custodian of the land that belonged to the Lotzem family. Max told the group that uncle had a son and daughter. The daughter was younger and had recently completed her schooling. She was pursuing her graduation by correspondence from Imphal. Max's cousin brother was working in Dimapur with the railways.

It was difficult to decide whether uncle's English was more rustic or was it his Hindi that required improvement. But, the fact of matter was that he whole-heartedly welcomed Max and his friends in the village and the house. Max's ancestral house was not far away from Andrew uncle's newly constructed house. The group was taken to the old house which Lotzem uncle had lately got renovated. The entrance was not very impressive but the rooms had been done up with proper flooring and other facilities. The doors and the windows were made of carved wood and seemed to be quite old. There were a total of three rooms which had a common passage through the dining hall. Each room had the CFL bulbs and was spacious. Max told them that the bathrooms were the biggest addition during the renovation of the house. Esha had the privilege to take up the room which had an attached toilet whereas others made space by sharing rooms. It seemed that the kitchen had been freshly cleaned. The utensils were washed and there were stock of fresh vegetables and other items of cooking in the kitchen. However, there was only one burner gas connection for use. One of the young girls from the village had been arranged to cook for them for the next two days.

Max kept the bag with pulses and other items that his mother had given him, in the kitchen. They had been smart to carry powdered milk, coffee and tea packets. Max told his uncle that they were already carrying packed lunch with them. Andrew uncle left with a promise to meet them in the evening.

"Hey! Want any assistance in the kitchen?" Arun asked Max.

"Oh no. I was just making tea for you guys," said Max.

Esha, whose room was closed, came out after freshening up and told the guys to move out of the kitchen. Till they were in the village she would look after the kitchen.

"Esha you know how to cook?" asked Rajiv.

Esha nodded with a smile and said, "Why? Shouldn't I know how to cook?"

"No. I mean yes. Arun you are lucky. Actually, never saw you cook before. So, what all can you cook?" asked Rajiv looking both at Arun and Esha.

"Well, I can cook Maggi?" said Esha who was still smiling and poured the tea in the cups.

"Only Maggi?" responded Arun quite spontaneously while the others including Esha burst into laughter.

"Man you sure are heading for trouble! You will die of constipation if she only knows how to make Maggi," said Rashid who volunteered to help Esha warm up the lunch for them.

"OK. Now that you guys doubt my cooking potential, I will cook chicken curry for you if you can manage one," said Esha.

"That shouldn't be much of a problem. Andrew uncle can manage a chicken for us. But then, it will not be the poultry one," said Max as if on loud thinking.

"Anything will do. And I will assist Esha during cooking," volunteered Rashid.

It was decided over lunch that tonight they will have an especial evening and party in their own style. They will light a bonfire near the courtyard and sit outside. Arun along with Max agreed to collect the wood for the same.

By the time they were through with their lunch, the young girl whom Andrew uncle had hired for cooking also came. Her name was Milly. Milly, was not more than thirteen or fourteen years of age. She seemed to be real fast in cleaning up the utensils. She could speak both Hindi as well as English but with a bit of difficulty. She told Esha that she would cook the basic meal for them and was pleased to hear that Esha was cooking the chicken tonight. Max planned to take them around the village before it was last light. Although, Esha wanted to hold back for the dinner preparation but then the others did not agree.

"Why do you worry? Milly has already prepared the other items. As far as chicken is concerned, I will be there to assist you. And even if you cook it bad, Arun will not dump you for that," said Rashid laughing at his own pathetic joke.

"Thanks for your support," said Esha who still held the kitchen knife in her hand and pointed it towards Rashid.

"Hey! Don't waste your effort on this chicken. I will get you a real country chicken which will be at least worth eating," said Rajiv who was almost ready to leave for village sightseeing.

The group first went to Andrew uncle's house where they were greeted by his wife. She seemed to be a simple lady who was genuinely happy to see Max and his friends. Aunty preferred to speak in her native language and Max acted as her interpreter. She welcomed them to have dinner at her place but then they conveyed that they had their own plans in place. From Andrew uncle's house they took the village passage which connected the other houses and went towards the highest point of the hill. En route, there was a small village church where the central prayers were conducted. It seemed that the priest had locked the entrance of the church at this time. The village had a mixed composition of houses made of concrete as well as of bamboos. Max explained that the life over the years had also changed in this part of the world. When he was a small kid, almost all the houses in the village were made of bamboos.

"So how did one come to know the affluence of the rich family of the village?" asked Rashid.

"The variation in the structure of the house was the only way by which the status of the family was depicted. Variation was confined to the front of the house and the decoration of the roof, however, the construction of the main structure was always the same," said Max.

"Can you indicate one such house which is presently visible?" asked Arun.

"Not really. Actually, the affluent ones have already made their houses of concrete. Wait. You see that house. Well, it reflects the classical house of a rich and affluent Kuki of the past times," said Max as he pointed towards one structure which was on the extreme end. Only a portion of the same was visible from the height but then the house did look different from the other bamboo houses.

Rajiv clicked the view of the village covering the entire layout of the houses while Max continued, "The village was made in such a manner that all the houses faced towards the top of the ridge. The roof is made of thatched grass or palm leaves. They keep the house cool during summer but new layer of thatching is to be added almost after every three years, otherwise, the roof will start leaking."

"I had read in the book that the animal's meat is also 'smoke dried' in the house," said Rajiv.

"Oh yes. When hunting was a way of life, then the meat used to be hung at the lowest tier of the house which was the kitchen for the family. A fire used to burn near the kitchen and the bed of the male member of the house was placed close to it to make him comfortable," added Max.

By now they had moved to the top of the village and the sunset behind the hills was shortly due. The deflection of the sun rays through the clouds made the whole view very beautiful. Max advised that they must now move back to the house. By the time they came near Andrew uncle's house, it was almost dark. Uncle as demanded had managed a hen for them which they carried along with them. Max volunteered to do the dressing and somehow Esha was not very comfortable to listen the details of the final fate of the hen. When they were about to reach the house a person crossed them who seemed to be in a hurry. He almost brushed pass Arun who felt a bit offended and stood close to Esha. The person turned two-three times to look at their faces and finally moved ahead.

"Who was this guy?" Arun askcd Max.

"Well, I don't know. Cannot recollect this face. As such, I am coming to the village after a very long time. Anyways don't bother," said Max.

The light in the courtyard was on and they opened the house. Rashid seemed to be really interested to help Esha in the kitchen and took the hen from Max for dressing. In the meantime, Arun and Max decided to burn the fire outside and piled up the heap of wood they had collected in the afternoon. As such, after the sunset the place had actually become cold. Rajiv whispered very slowly into Max's ear that he did have a bottle of rum along with him. Max told Rajiv to downplay the possession of his booty or else Rashid would make a human cry about it.

"What was Rajiv so excited about?" asked Arun the moment Rajiv went inside to keep his camera.

"He told me that he did have some liquor and I in turn told him to guard this information from Rashid or else he will declare him an alcoholic," smiled Max.

"Actually, yes. Rajiv seems to be getting a bit too regular with the drinks. I at times worry for him. But look at him. He forgot his entire belongings but managed to get his bottle of liquor," laughed Arun.

"Oh that! He had quietly kept the bottle in Rashid's bag," said Max.

The aroma of the non-vegetarian food came in the air. It seemed that the food preparation was in quite an advanced stage. Arun almost felt very hungry. There were butterflies in his stomach when he thought of Esha as his wife, who would cook such fabulous food. He hoped his parents will be really proud of his choice. At least for Esha's expertise in non-vegetarian cooking.

Rajiv came back to the courtyard and was wearing his red track pants. Rightly as assessed, they were a bit short but then Rajiv didn't look so bad after all. He had poured his drink in the steel glass and pulled the plastic chair near the fire. The wood had just caught fire after Max had very skilfully placed straws between the gaps. There were adequate dry logs available to keep them comfortable for a long time. By the time the bonfire was effective, even Rashid and Esha were through with their cooking. Rashid had observed the steel glass that Rajiv had tried to conceal between the rear two legs of his chair.

"Sir, you didn't order for the snacks?" Rashid almost whispered in Rajiv's ears.

"Don't act over smart. OK," Rajiv sneered.

"No. No. I was serious. After the hard day's work you must indulge yourself in some pleasure. Right?"

"Do you want to share?"

"Share what? Your alcoholic enthusiasm? No thanks. I guess I am better without one."

"Hey Rashid, you don't have to get after Rajiv even if you find him looking cool in his red pants," said Max.

"Yeah! He actually does look different in that hot pant. Good!"

"Shut up."

"Why can't the two of you stay without altercation?" said Arun who was sitting close to Esha.

"Nothing of that type. I was suggesting some snacks for the evening," said Rashid.

Rashid went inside and came back with a few packets of snacks that Indra aunty had packed for them. In addition to that he also brought some potatoes which he threw in the fire for roasting. By now, even Max had picked up his steel glass. As far as Arun was concerned, with Esha around he needed no further intoxication.

"One last question. How did you manage to get the liquor?" asked Rashid who was always fond of completing his investigation.

"He rapped the bottle in your towel and kept it inside your bag," said Max who found it very funny and laughed loudly.

"Now Mr Detective can you sit quietly. Max will sing a song for us," said Rajiv clapping for his friend.

Even Esha also joined the others demanding Max to sing a song. Max had no other choice than to relent. He took out the mouth organ from the pocket of his jacket. After all, it was worth carrying the instrument all the way to the village. Max played a melodious tune of a Manipuri song which was quite peppy. When he ended the song he told his friends that the song described the feelings of a young lover who has come back in the hills to meet his love who he has not seen for quite some time. He had been away to become rich and now had come back to fulfil his promise to marry the girl.

"It sounds so nice and simple. But then, reality is very different," said Arun who had been listening to the tune played with full attention.

"You seemed to be touched by the tune," said Max.

"Oh yes, definitely. And this time please play your English numbers," said Arun who could sense that Esha was looking at him from the corner of her eyes. Arun regretted his comments. He hoped Esha did not take them to be personal. Max played his all time favourite Bran Adam's number and the others also joined in the chorus singing. There were request for more songs and Max went ahead playing and singing as the night progressed. Finally, Max requested Esha to sing a song for them. She insisted that she had a bad voice but it seemed that the audience was in no mood to listen to her argument. Finally, Esha agreed to sing a duet along with Max. Her voice was melodious and she was able to match up the tune with Max on the English number. In fact, after the initial hitch was over her voice seemed to be so much in control. She was now enjoying singing. Even a seasoned singer like Max looked quite impressed. For Arun, it seemed as if time had come to a standstill. He could only see Esha and nobody else. Her voice pierced his heart and he longed to hold her in his arms. When they did have the eye contact, he could see so much love in those eyes. He wanted Esha so very badly in his life that off late he feared losing her. The feeling made him so lonely and sad. He could not share with anyone. All he could do was to wait for the destiny to unwrap his fate.

Rashid was enjoying himself thoroughly next to the bonfire. He was sitting on his haunches. He had dug out the potatoes from the fire and after applying some salt was busy eating it. He tossed a piece towards Rajiv who did not show much interest to eat the burning ball with the same enthusiasm. Rashid's mouth and face was black as he ate his recipe and resembled the human ape. Rajiv looked at him amused as he imagined Rashid happily tied to a tree with his tail and the kids throwing peanut through the iron bars which he caught with his mouth. Esha's song came to an end and all applauded.

"Hey Esha! You really have a great voice. Now I am convinced that you must join my rock group which I plan to launch shortly," said Max.

"I will be honoured and will look forward for the lucrative job offer," said Esha as she got up to go inside.

"Don't be so touchy. If you are overwhelmed, you need not cry in hiding. After all we are friends," said Rajiv teasing Esha.

"Easy OK! I intend to check upon the preparation of the chicken curry. Do you want me to get few pieces for you to have along with your drinks?"

"She can see through your stupid steel glasses," laughed Rashid.

Esha had now known all of them for quite some time and could catch all attempted deceptions. The moment she was out of sight Rajiv and Max refilled their glasses leaving little space to add water. Arun also went inside to assist Esha. In the kitchen, Esha was stirring the big utensil and did not notice Arun who quietly came and stood behind her. Arun hesitated for a second but could not hold himself any further as his finger rested on Esha's shoulder. She was a bit surprised as she realized that it was Arun. It seemed as if her limbs had gone numb the moment Arun touched her. She was now conscious of his fragrance. She could breathe the familiar cologne which she had got used to over the past so many months. In fact, Arun had now put both his hands over her shoulders and there was a stimulating sensation that Esha felt from her head to toe. Her heart was pounding and didn't know how to react. Slowly, Arun turned her around. Their eyes met. There was so much intensity in Arun's gaze. It was a long moment in which it seemed that nothing actually moved between the two of them. Then suddenly, Esha locked lips with Arun. He held her close as his hands slowly moved all over her. It had been a long while that they had kissed each other. When Arun finally released Esha, she seemed to be quite out of breath.

"I love you. You will be my forever, love. Very soon," said Esha who now had a smile on her face.

"I love you too. And I want you to know that whatever happens in life, I will always stand next to you. Do you understand?" said Arun while he held Esha's face in his hands. Esha smiled and nodded.

"Hey! If you keep standing so close to me, than, I may not be able to control my physical advancements. Do you understand what I mean?" said Arun playfully.

"Oh yes. Perfectly. But I am sure you will not like to create my image of a slut in front of your friends," said Esha joining in the game.

"Smart! You seemed to have already rejected my proposal of an intimate night together even before it was made."

"Shut up. Don't hallucinate. I am not that type."

"So what type am I dealing with?"

"Someone very very dangerous. I am a brown belt in Karate," said Esha as she postured herself as if actually ready to go for the prey."

"See! There are so many things about you that I still do not know," said Arun as he raised both hands in the air.

"Go slow with me and go my way and there will be much for you to find out and enjoy," said Esha with her eyes dancing notoriously.

"OK yeah!" laughed Arun and Esha also joined in.

Max placed the last pieces of logs on fire. They would keep them warm for some more time. Rashid who had eaten his share of snacks was keen to go inside to ask Esha for dinner. However, the others told him not to disturb the love birds. Barring their bonfire the surrounding was pitch dark. In the entire village there were only two lights which were lit. One was a street light and the other came from a house in vicinity. Whoever it was in that house seemed to be quite restless in the night. There were at least three rooms on the first floor of the house and the person had been alternatively switching the light from one room to the other. In fact, Rajiv had felt that someone had been peeping at them through the windows of that house.

"I hope we are not disturbing the peace of the villagers? Before someone actually decides to complain against us to Andrew uncle, we must call it a day," said Rajiv.

"No. No. Don't worry. As such it's not that late," said Max looking at his watch.

Max told them that as kids they used to sleep very early and were up before the first light. Most of the people living in the village followed this schedule. Now with dish antenna on many of the roof tops, reflecting the new prosperity in the lives of people, this precedence would have also undergone a change. After a while, Esha came out to confirm that the dinner was laid and they all moved inside. Before moving in, Max ensured that the fire was properly lit off. The chicken curry was very well prepared and Rashid seemed to be doing great justice to finish it off. During the course of meal, Max also discussed the plan for the next day. Tomorrow, they would try to leave a bit early and head for the waterfall that was about six to seven kilometres from the village location. During the rains, the waterfall looked much more beautiful. There is a large pond at the base of the fall from where the water went through the stream and further towards the valley. At present the water level would be much lower but then the place was still worth a visit. On their way back to the village, they would also visit the site of the barren village.

"For how long has that village been abandoned?" asked Arun with interest.

"Well, my father used to tell me as a child that many years ago our ancestors resided in that village. But, due to unknown reasons people had migrated from that place and settled outside. The reason for leaving that village is still a mystery. Some say that evil spirits had taken the area under its spell. The others say that there was a mass disease that had spread in that area. In fact, visiting the barren village was not too encouraged by the village people in general," said Max.

"Then why are we going there? Let's not become far too adventurous," said Rashid with his mouth full of rice and chicken. Very conveniently he had kept his spoon aside and was digging food on his plate with his bare hands. Rajiv, who had hardly touched the food, looked at him in much disapproval.

"Don't you worry? It is quite a safe place. I have myself gone to that place a number of times. And, the reason to take you there is because of its beautiful location. The entire line of the ridges is clearly visible from the place. When you stand there, the view of clouds moving in the lower side of the hill ranges is so very clear," said Max.

"Wow! It must be a breath-taking view to capture in reel," said Rajiv who seemed to be quite happy with the description of the place as Max had just given.

"Oh yes. And in that barren village there is one more thing which may interest you. During the olden times, the inter-tribal rivalry and might was reflected with the display of human bones. Also, the bones of animal were put around the houses to show the influence and power of the warriors. Such traditions are a thing of past but the reminiscence of the same is commonly found in the area," said Max.

"Now you are actually scaring us. I will rather agree with Rashid that we must not become far too adventurous," said Esha who seemed to be a bit disturbed with the last details.

After some more discussion on this issue in which everyone spoke and no one listened to the other, it was agreed to follow the schedule as planned by Max. By the time they finished dinner, Max received a call on his mobile. Today, in spite the poor signal network closer to the village, his mobile had been ringing quite frequently. Father Alison, Lotzem uncle and Dhayan Singh had called up regularly to check the general well-being and plans of the group. This time again, it was Dhayan Singh's call. Max told him that they would be tracking to some of the places near the village and the driver had been told to take the day off.

Next day morning, the first one to get up was Arun. The loud bang on the front door had alarmed him and by the time he went to open the door he realized that it was Milly. She had brought fresh milk in a plastic bottle.

"Sir, tea. I make tea for all of you?" said Milly in her little rustic English.

It took Arun a while before he understood what the girl meant. "Oh yes. Five cups of tea. Thank you," he said indicating with the five fingers of his right hand.

The dawn was yet to break and Arun checked his watch which showed that it was 5.30 in the morning. In spite the initial resentment the others too got up. Undoubtedly had Esha not been around, the delay would have been much more. By the time Andrew uncle came to meet them they were all ready to leave. Max confirmed their programme to uncle who advised them to carry adequate water for consumption en route. For uncle's satisfaction, Rashid displayed the bag containing their packed lunch, packets of Maggi, water bottle, first aid kit and a utensil in which they planned to cook enroute. The crockery comprised of disposable plates and glasses.

"Did Lunu Chuba came and meet you?" asked Andrew uncle.

"Do I know him?" asked Max as he tried to recall the name. It had been a long time since he had maintained contact with anyone in the village.

"Well, he had come from the neighbouring village. He said he knew you and wanted to meet you."

"But nobody came to meet me. When did he come to you?" asked Max with curiosity.

"He was at our house much early in the morning. Your driver near the shop had told him about you. He seemed to be rather in hurry. Maybe, he will contact you later," said Andrew uncle.

The group took the same route which they had travelled a day prior to reach the top of the village and then moved ahead. It was a steady climb and the farther they went, the entire village houses became prominently visible. They halted near a large stone which was saddle shaped and Max proudly indicated his house from there. The pause was exploited by Rashid who handed over the bag containing the utility items to Arun to carry. As they moved further ahead they left behind the paddy fields and entered the forest area from where the ridge line connected the subsequent slope. Here it was quite shadier due to the dense trees and thick undergrowth. The track they followed had narrowed a bit but was still quite prominent. This reassured that this route was in regular use by the villagers. Now, they moved along the track in the single line with Rajiv in the lead and Max at the rear end. In spite the weather being phenomenally pleasant some of them were sweating, especially Rashid. He had already removed his pullover and had tied it with a knot over his shoulders. Out of all of them he was probably the most vulnerable in terms of his stamina.

"How far is the waterfall?" asked Rashid trying to catch up with his breath.

"Well, we should be there in another hour if we maintained the same pace of move," said Max.

"I think after all, it was not a very good idea to come this far. Rather too far. Couldn't we have gone there by the vehicle?" said Rashid whose crib session had started much earlier in the day.

"I told you all, this character will keep weeping all throughout. Let's stuff the cotton gauge of the medical kit in his mouth to restore further peace en route," said Rajiv.

"Shut up. Hey Esha, would you like to halt for a while?" asked Rashid hoping that she would agree with him.

"OK. Guys let's actually take a little break," said Esha with a smile.

"Let's halt after the turn ahead of the ridge. From there the view of the valley is very clear. As such, we will reach there in another five minutes," said Max.

In next few minutes, they all reached the point from where there was a sharp slope running down towards the other hill. The way ahead would be down slope for some time. Rashid insisted that he was hungry and wanted to cook Maggi. Before starting from the house they did have their breakfast but still Rashid was hell bent to eat something more. As others had refused to eat at this junction, Rashid had to cook Maggi on his own. Although as a good friend, Max did assist him to light the fire.

"Don't keep that utensil inside the bag without cleaning it up," told Arun who seemed to be amused by Rashid's eating speed.

"Yeah. But then, there is no water available. Unless, you want me to waste the drinking water for cleaning the stuff," said Rashid as he polished the last remains of the Maggi.

The light breeze had started blowing as they finally moved ahead towards the waterfall. Arun had improvised a broken branch of the tree into a walking stick and along with Esha was the first to move ahead on the track. There was not much of movement on this route as they hardly came across anyone except the old shepherd whom they met after walking on the track for about half an hour. He had few cattles which were grazing the grass in the vicinity. The lean person must have been in the age group between forty to fifty years and was smoking a local pipe. Max tried speaking to him in the local dialect but did not get much favourable response. The man was not very happy to be intruded upon.

"Wasn't that person acting a bit funny?" said Rajiv once they reached a little further on the route.

"Well, he was not much to his senses. A number of people here are under the influence of the herbal drugs which is easily accessible within the region," said Max.

"Oh really! I should have actually guessed the way the guy was behaving," said Rajiv.

"As such you are an expert in this field," remarked Rashid who was just trailing behind.

Ignoring Rashid's comments, Max told his friends that there was a large scale of illegal drug paddling which takes place in the area. Most of such stuff finds its way through Myanmar and is moved further ahead in the International drug market. The group continued moving on the track until they heard a prominent sound.

"Do you hear that sound?" asked Max as he almost came to a halt.

"Yes," said Rashid who was moving right ahead of him.

"Well, we are closer to the water stream. The water flows between the culvert and then goes down to the valley from that gap," said Max as he indicated towards the general direction of the water channel.

"Great. How far is the waterfall from here?" asked Esha.

"We should be there in another few minutes," said Max.

"He is typically behaving like a highlander. For the last one hour, he has toed the same line that the waterfall is just few more minutes away," said Rashid.

As they started descending on the other side of the hill, Max got a message beep on his phone. This was for the first time since they had left the village area that the mobile signals were actually available. This was in spite the fact that in the entire line of mountain ridges there was not a single mobile tower that was installed. Still surprisingly, at this side of the hill on the height the mobile seemed to be working. Father Alison had sent the message.

"Hey, Father writes 'Learning sleeps and snores in libraries but wisdom is everywhere, wide awake, on tiptoe. Never does nature say one thing and wisdom another. Hope you all are enjoying the nature which teaches us so much. Regards,'" said Max.

"I must say, Father Alison is so full of life. His positivity seems to be infectious," said Rajiv.

"Yeah! I would have quit my studies years back had it not been Father's constant support which inspired me to fight against all odds. He truly has been my mentor."

By the time they came to the foothill, once again the mobile signals were lost. Esha regretted of not making a call. It had been more than a day she had not called home. She made a mental note to call her parents when they reach back home. As such, her mother had been quite apprehensive about their plan of visiting such a remote village. By now, the sound of flowing water became quite evident and Max yet again indicated the general direction of the fall. Due to the heavy undergrowth, even at this distance the fall was not visible. When they almost reached the destination they saw the pond and the waterfall. It was a huge waterfall through a rocky mountain which was cut in the crystal shape and looked quite green and brown in colour due to the growth of thick moss. There was heavy undergrowth all over and especially the two large trees on the either side of the fall provided the perfect shade. The temperature seemed a bit lower and the wind had a chill. There was also a natural fragrance of moss and moist mud in the air. It must be a real delight to be here during the peak summers. Although, the quantum of water of the stream had reduced during this time of the year, still it looked very beautiful. The pond was near full and in the green background even the small pebbles at the bottom of the pond were clearly visible. It was naturally shaped in such a manner that only once it was filled to its optimum capacity, the water would flow down from the sides further into the stream. Arun was the first one to reach the pond and splashed the water. His instant expression reflected that the water was pretty cold. When he extended his wet hand to Esha for support she found it freezing cold. Max told them to be cautious, as the stone on which they stood was looking quite slippery.

There were a few rocks on the either side of the pond and the dry area next to it had sunlight falling through the shades. Rajiv spread the bed-sheet that they had brought along with them and stretched his legs. The sunbathing seemed to be pleasurable. The only irritant in this peaceful world of Rajiv was Rashid. He was trying to pull the bag which Rajiv had improvised to be used as the pillow. Rajiv would have opened his third eye, if possibly it was there. As of now, he stared at Rashid through the socket of the available pair.

"What! Don't you glare at me like that? You are crushing the packed lunch," said Rashid who still held the straps of the bag.

"One day I will kill you rat. Take out your lunch and let me rest in peace," said Rajiv as he got up to release the bag.

Rashid was quick to release the bag back to Rajiv the moment he took out the lunch packets and the disposable crockery. He decided to leave Arun and Esha to themselves and joined Max who was sitting at a distance away from the shade. He was cutting a piece of wood with his small knife and shaping it into a spoon.

"Wow! You can do that? What all can you make with the bamboo wood?" asked Rashid.

"Well, a few things. Actually, bamboo is best used to shape up a number of utility items and decoration pieces," said Max.

"I see the bamboo trees all over. Why don't you show me how to make some items with it? Please?" asked Rashid.

"All right, let's first get a log and see what best we can make out of it," said Max as he got up and moved towards the undergrowth where there were a few bamboo trees. Rashid followed him.

Within few minutes, Max very skilfully cut a bamboo log. He had checked the piece for its flexibility before selecting it. Although, the knife that Max used was small in size but was equally sharp and cut through the wood with ease. Max told Rashid that as a kid he had learnt the art of cutting the bamboo and making various items from it. His knife was at work as he simultaneously spoke with Rashid. In the olden times, things like glass plate, comb, chair, table, stool, spoon, etc were made with bamboo wood. Even the soft outer layer was used to make bags and containers. Max had cut four pieces of bamboo and joined them with the weed strips in a zigzag manner to make a lamp shade. The end product looked beautiful and Max gifted it to his friend.

"After you are through with your management programme, you must actually think of opening up a cottage industry which will promote bamboo products," said Rashid who was happy with his gift.

"Thanks for the suggestion."

As they were moving back towards the waterfall, Max stopped en route. He observed something on ground. There were fresh marks of footprints. It seemed that more than one person had been present. The marks indicated that they had been formed a short while ago and the heavy imprints of the front sole suggested that the trail setter were on a run. Normally, during this time of the year not many people come to this place. In addition, the locals did not wear such sports shoes as the imprints indicated. The marks were positively of good quality of shoes. Max preferred to stay quiet on the issue rather than confiding with Rashid as greater assumption on the whole thing would have scared the others.

By the time they were back at the waterfall, Rajiv had made tea for everybody. It was decided that after lunch they would move towards the deserted village. From that village there was a direct route that will take them back to their village. For lunch, Milly had made mixed vegetable with potatoes and local beans. The beans had hard peel, which required to be chewed properly. Max told them that this vegetable was considered to be a delicacy in the area and was sold at a reasonably higher rate in the local market. The girl had also tried her hand at making the parathas which were of various shapes and sizes. Rashid ate like never before and post lunch reflected his inability to march any further.

"You know quite well that if we don't move now then it will be difficult to reach back home on time," said Arun.

"Then let's drop the idea to visit the haunted village and head straight back to home," said Rashid.

"Well, there will not be much of difference even if we go through the barren village. On the other hand, on this route it is more of down slope. So decide which route to follow," said Max.

After some discussion it was finally agreed to go through the barren village as was originally planned. Max en route told them that his great grandfather belonged to the barren village. As a child, he had gone to the place a number of times. Although, the village was in shambles but the place has scenic beauty. From the direction they would approach the village, there was dense vegetation. However, on the other side there was a steep drop of the hill and the entire view of far off valley was clearly visible. There was also a water stream which went much closer to the place between the culverts.

This time Max led the route. It seemed that the track was not in much common use. In fact, the undergrowth from the sides overlapped over the track. Max marched ahead clearing all such obstructions. The sound of some of the insects was so prominent. Usually, such sounds are heard during the night. The group quietly moved ahead. Once again, Max observed general disturbance in the foliage which was still fresh. Maybe, some other group of enthusiasts was moving ahead of them on the same route.

After about an hour they took their first break. Esha although a bit tired was coping well. Rashid seemed to be the worst hit. He had taken the bag from Max and was fiddling with it to find some eatables. To his respite, he was able to dig out few apples and packets of biscuit. He offered some to Esha and left the others to volunteer. In another hour, they were able to see the barren village. It was located on the gradual slope and the grass around the place was quite green as if it was a faraway of a golf course. It was indeed a beautiful sight and each member of the group felt that it was worth the trouble to come this far. Once they reached the barren village the view of the valley was breathtaking. Rajiv clicked a number of photographs while Arun and Esha were happy to be left alone to themselves in such a beautiful place.

"It's almost like a dream to be with you in such a scenic place," said Esha who sat next to Arun and faced the valley.

"Tell me. Are you fond of mountains or the sea?" asked Arun.

"Ah. Both. But why did you ask that all of a sudden?"

"You may not like to hear it but my mind was moving much ahead in time. If we two; you and me … travel again then it will be towards the mountain. And maybe, sea at close vicinity," said Arun holding Esha's hand.

"Why maybe? Of course, you and I will travel to many of such places. Oh Arun! Even I long and hope for such days ahead," said Esha as she rested her head on Arun's shoulder.

Arun took out a packet of salted cashew nuts from his pocket and offered it to Esha. Esha laughed. "How did you manage to hide this packet from Rashid?"

"At times you need to learn how to survive," laughed Arun and turned around to see his friends who too were enjoying themselves.

Rajiv was clicking photographs of Max and Rashid. Rashid had taken the famous pose of Marilyn Monroe. The only difference was that she did not have a bag, neither a partner like Max to ogle her with big round eyes. Marilyn Monroe would have again died vomiting had she seen the way Rashid posed. Max and Rashid obliged the camera by giving some more stupid poses. After some more fooling around, Max took Rajiv and Rashid to a place in the corner of the barren village. Here the ground was undulated at some places. Max told them that these were the graves in which the spirits of his ancestors resided. There he murmured a small prayer which only he understood.

Once the ritual was over, Rajiv asked Max regarding the remittances of bones that was littered in the area. Max took them to one of the broken huts. The actual occupants of the hut must have been dead a long time ago. But even now, evidence that once life existed in this place was clearly visible. One of the partially broken walls had a painting made on it. The painting depicted the local hunters trying to kill their prey with the long spears. It was made in grey and maroon colours and the work was so exquisite that the fear in the eyes of the prey and anxiety in the eyes of the hunters was clearly visible. The wooden frame next to the wall indicated that once there was a door in existence. In spite of the damage to the wood by termites, the original blue colour on the frame was prominent. On one of the corners, a small piece of white and brown colour was hanging. It in all probability looked like a piece of bone of some wild animal. Max explained to his friends that in the olden days, the bones of ferocious animals were hung around the house.

"How far is the water stream from this place?" asked Rashid the moment they stepped out again in the open.

"Well, it will be about five minutes walking from here. But, we will follow the opposite route towards the village," said Max as he indicated towards the general direction leading to his village.

"I guess, I need to clear up my stomach before we advance any further. The stream seems to be the ideal place. I will be back soon," said Rashid as he advanced towards the culvert.

"Disgusting! Why does he have to eat so much if he has no control?" said Rajiv but Rashid was far away from the hearing distance as he almost ran towards the water stream.

The evening winds were picking up speed and it was decided that they must soon start their return journey. The village route from here onwards was generally down slope and they would comfortably reach in time. Milly would have prepared the dinner for the night. Before moving out of the house, Esha had given her their requirements.

"Isn't Rashid taking a bit too much of time?" said Arun.

"Oh yeah! He has been off for quite some time," said Rajiv who checked his watch for the time.

"I better go and check for him," said Max with concern.

"OK. I'll also come along with you," added Rajiv.

There was dense undergrowth in the route towards the stream. Max selected the narrow trail which seemed to be much in the state of disuse but was the shortest access to the stream. The visibility due to the dense undergrowth was restricted in the area. Both of them wondered as to which route Rashid would have taken. Soon, the sound of water became evident after some distance and they called for Rashid. There was no response. Both Max and Rajiv were more alert and even the slightest of sound seemed so clear.

"He couldn't have crossed across the stream. Where the hell did he go?" said Rajiv with rising concern in his voice.

"This doesn't make sense."

"Are there any wild animals in the area?" asked Rajiv.

"No. I never really heard the threat of wild animals before. But then who knows."

"Let's spread out and cover a larger stretch," said Rajiv.

"No. We must stick together. Wandering alone especially after we had no response from Rashid will not be a good idea."

"Don't you worry? I have adequate experience to handle such situations," responded Rajiv who felt that Max had doubt regarding his capability to manage on his own in such crisis.

"Oh shut up. This is not the time to show your machoism," said Max with a bit of agitation in his voice. Rajiv had never seen this side of Max. He felt offended and wanted to respond but something inside told him to wait and watch. Another thing that he now observed was that Max moved through the terrain very skilfully. It was like a fish back again in its water. Max skid downwards towards the base of the stream in a sideways posture. This added more speed and stability during descend. His arms were well spread to maintain a balance and also assist to clear obstacles en route. Rajiv tried to match pace with Max as they moved further down into the culvert.

At the river base there were round stones, some of which were partially submerged under water and others were dry with a bit of sand quoting on them. Max and Rajiv leaped over these obstacles and crossed the stream. During the rainy season, the width of the stream must be much wider and the crossing over would not have been so easy. The other side of the stream had a levelled area although it too had dense undergrowth. There was more than one trail that was available. These must be used by local villagers who routinely came to cut the bamboo trees to meet up their supplies. However, there were no signs of fresh encroachment. Max selected one of the trails which he was sure connected a broader path. Walking on the trail they soon came out in the open area from where the visibility of the area increased. Still, there was no sign of Rashid. Rajiv yet again called for Rashid on top of his voice but then there was no response. Rajiv had been calling Rashid's name periodically and by now his throat had also gone sour. His voice would have travelled further ahead in the hills but then failed to generate any response.

"What is it? Why did you stop? And what is there in your hand?" asked Rajiv as he saw Max sit on his knees to examine something.

"Someone has thrown this and the smell of the tobacco leaves is still fresh," said Max as he examined the silver quoted packet.

"You mean to say … is it abduction? Has someone abducted Rashid?" asked Rajiv.

"I don't know. But yes, definitely someone else was here. Maybe, there was more than one person. Let's go back," said Max as he got up.

"What do you mean, let's go back. Where is Rashid?"

"I said I don't know. There are no signs of struggle; however, he would have not ventured so far just to ease his stomach."

"You brought us here. You got to know more than this. Why will someone abduct Rashid? Who is involved? Max, you swear give me a weird feeling," said Rajiv who seemed to be very angry.

"Look, Rashid is also my friend. So you need not react like this. We will find a way out. But as of now, you and I in the middle of this jungle can't do much to help Rashid. We need to be back in the village and look for some clue and possible help. Do you understand?" said Max.

Although, Rajiv was angry but he knew that what Max was saying was right. They will have to return back. Arun and Esha would also be waiting for them. If required they would have to take help of police. By the time they crossed the stream both could hear Arun who was calling for their names. It seemed that he too had moved down towards the culvert area. They almost met in mid route. Esha was also along with Arun. Both had a worried look and many queries for which none of them had any answers. They all climbed back through the hill and once again reached the haunted village. There was no sign of life there. On Max's recommendation, they decided to move back to the village.

Esha was the worse effected with the way events had coursed themselves. She had cried and even as they reached the outskirts of the village she was not able to control her sobbing. Arun held her hand and didn't know any other way to console her. Like others, he was equally shocked and could not bring himself to terms regarding the possible abduction of their friend. There was nothing much to talk en route. Rajiv kept checking his mobile for any possible signals. There were none. He planned to get in touch with the outside world to get help to save Rashid. A part of his anger was on Max. He somehow felt that Max had got them all in this trouble.

Max's body language had been stern and Rajiv believed that there was more to Max then they all possibly knew. Even Max understood what Rajiv felt but then Rashid's safety was the first priority in his mind. What Rajiv felt about him could be dealt later. As they came closer to the village, they all heard a bird call. It was a weird sound and was repeated several more times. Max tension was evident on hearing the bird call as he paced faster towards the village.

"Max, what do you recommend that we should do?" asked Arun the moment they reached the house.

"Why ask him? I will call the police and let them investigate the matter. He cannot be behaving like Sherlock Holmes at the cost of Rashid's life," said Rajiv who still could not locate the mobile signals on his set.

"I really don't know what makes you turn the guns at Max and behave as the leader of the firing squad. Look, this is not the way the situation can be handled. Let's all stay composed and work out the options that are there for us," said Arun.

"I think, now I know who is involved in this. You all need not worry. I will do everything under my powers to get back Rashid safe and sound," said Max.

"Great! First he says he doesn't know who could have abducted Rashid. Now he seems to know everything. He will get back Rashid and in the meantime we all can go off to sleep after a hearty meal," mimicked Rajiv.

"Rajiv! Go fuck yourself. I need not listen to your bullshit. If you feel that police can resolve this, then you better go and contact them. And by the way, the nearest police station is just about four hours drive from here. In case, you do find the men you look for, you may still not really find them motivated enough to act. Do you understand?" said Max who also seemed to be quite agitated.

"Stop it both of you. We already had enough on our hands. Rashid is gone missing and Esha doesn't seem to be too well. Now, you two have opened up a new front. For God sake, we must just focus on saving Rashid," said Arun.

"Where is Esha?" asked Rajiv with concern in his voice.

"I gave her a pill to get down her anxiety. She is resting in her room. Hopefully, she will be fine after sometime," said Arun.

It was almost last light and being the first day of first quarter of the moon, it would be pitch dark after sometime. Their options now seemed restricted. Max once again tried to convince Arun and Rajiv that they must keep quiet and let him resolve the issue. He told them that in all possibilities Rashid had been abducted by a local militant outfit that was aiming to make some quick money from this abduction. During the day, at times he did get some signals which indicated that they were being followed. But then, he did not correlate the events and never thought that such a thing would happen. The militants would have probably taken Rashid to their nearest camp. Max will take assistance of Andrew uncle and try to locate the camp tonight itself. Once the location of the camp is clear, they would decide their next course of action. They will also take assistance of some of the reliable persons of the village to gain information which would help in Rashid's safe return.

"How will you reach to the camp?" asked Rajiv who seemed to be a bit receptive this time to Max's suggestions.

"I will take assistance from Andrew uncle. It has to be a militant outfit whose members are frequent visitors in this area. They will have some level of public support also. We will get some lead from this," said Max.

"I will also come along with you. When do we leave?" asked Rajiv.

"Rajiv, I appreciate your concern but then I can't risk taking you along. You are not from this area. In case, the situation goes against us then your presence can prove to be real dangerous for all of us. I don't want any bloodshed over this issue," said Max.

Before Rajiv could air his view, Arun said, "Well Rajiv, I would agree with Max. Let him try to resolve the issue at the local level. If it doesn't work then we can fall back to the police and the local administration for help."

Finally, even Rajiv relented and it was agreed that after taking Andrew uncle in confidence, Max will try to locate the militant camp and Rashid. Max went to meet his uncle to discuss the entire plan in detail and came back after an hour. By the time the uncle and nephew returned, they seemed to have made up their mind regarding the approach they would take. Max and Andrew uncle will leave in another one hour. Uncle had arranged for two boys who would act as their guide. As per the information available, there was a militant camp which was located some ten kilometres from the village. Rashid's abduction by this camp was quite likely. In the recent past, the outfit had carried out similar activities. The good news was that there was a rift within the group due to the changing ideological beliefs and therefore most of the activities of their own cadre were contested from within.

There was a gravelled track that connected the militant camp from the road head which was three kilometres away. However, to avoid any alarming moves they planned to cover the entire distance by foot. As per the plan, tonight they will reach the outskirts of the camp and confirm if Rashid has been made captive. If the same is confirmed, then they will negotiate with the group the next day. The plan seemed to be logical and Arun and Rajiv had no other options than to agree. Max and Andrew uncle left after sometime and promised to stay in touch through mobile or fall back the next morning.

Rajiv once again checked his mobile and there were still no signals available. Yesterday, they did receive some calls but today the status of mobile network looked hopeless. Arun and Rajiv were both anxious for Rashid but then they had nothing further to say. They will have to wait till the morning for Max to return with some news.

"Any news of Rashid?" asked Esha who just came out of her room. From the time they had come home she had been in her bed.

"So how are you feeling?" asked Arun with concern.

Ignoring Arun's query, Esha once again repeated her question. He told her that although Rashid had not returned, still attempts to track him were underway. Arun then narrated to Esha the entire happenings of the evening.

"Poor Rashid. I never thought such a thing will happen to him. He is the only son of his mother. His mother will die without him. He is the only hope of the family," said Esha whose emotions once again overpowered her and she could not control her tears.

"Esha let's not lose hope. Let's pray that Rashid comes back safe," said Arun holding her closely.

Rajiv felt equally helpless as they were restrained by the circumstances. He decided to walk till the road head and check for improvement in the mobile connectivity. He took Arun's jacket as it was a bit nippy outside. It was indeed a very pitch dark night and he actually wondered about the plight of Max and his uncle in the difficult terrain of the mountains. However, his greater worry was Rashid. He hoped that the militant do not carry any atrocity on Rashid. As such, Rashid was a loud mouth and was prone to get into trouble with people. He just couldn't think of leaving Manipur without Rashid. In spite of their constant arguments, he was fond of his friend. Like him, Rashid had also been a fighter. He had fought against all odds in his life and made efforts to be a winner. His mind pondered over what Esha had just said. His mother and sisters will find it so difficult to survive without him. The whole game of destiny at times seems to be so unfair. Maybe it would have been more just had he been abducted in place of Rashid. Unlike him, Rashid still had a mother and two sisters to care for. Much later did Rajiv realize that his eyes were wet and that the tears flowed dropping down the cheeks.

"Why did you not stop him? Where has he gone?" asked Esha the moment she realized that even Rajiv had left.

"We all are going through much difficult times. Rajiv is equally disturbed. I saw it in his eyes. He seemed to be so frustrated with the situation that he almost accused Max for being involved in Rashid's abduction. It's good for him to spend some time with himself. I am sure, he will be more composed when he returns," said Arun.

"I hope Rashid comes back safe. Arun, why will someone abduct Rashid? He does not represent any ideology of any segment of the local people. He is just a simple citizen of the country who is moving around in his own country with his friends. What has the world actually come down to? There is so much of hate and ill.

At times, the world around us looks so bad. Will Rashid survive all this Arun?"

"Yes he will. He is a good man and deserves better in life. To me it looks like a case of extortion. The youth in this region are mostly jobless. So, for them this is one way of making quick money," said Arun.

"Where does Rashid have money to give them? Or for that matter his family?"

"He may not have money but he has friends. If need be, we all will pitch in our bit," said Arun, meaning every word of it from his heart. Esha hugged Arun. She had not seen this aspect of Arun's personality before.

Max continued his march. Andrew uncle was right behind him and in spite of his old age was fit enough to match his strides with him. The two local boys were leading them in the darkness. Before starting, Max had refused to eat anything. Andrew uncle knew that his nephew was tired due to the day's exertion which had been more mental than physical. His wife had packed some eatables which he would give to Max at the appropriate time. It would take them about three to four hours to reach the camp site of the militant outfit. They had planned to observe the location during the night and make further communication only in the morning.

"How much did you tell your friends regarding this abduction?" asked Andrew uncle.

"They have not put all the pieces together? Hopefully, that won't be required if we are able to accomplish the task successfully."

"Your friend had many questions to ask. Will you allow him to probe further? What's his name?"

"Rajiv."

"Oh yes. Rajiv. Will you tell them now?"

"I hate to discuss those details. You all know about it, then, why bring up the issue?"

"OK. OK. No more questions regarding that aspect. Do you think you will find some acquaintance?"

"Let's see. Dad once told me that a few of my times are still there. They are pretty senior and have reasonable influence and say. They will treat us fairly."

"How about your friend? Will he be OK?"

"Yes. Through their message they had confirmed it to me. They know, I am here and the abduction is a way to reach out to me. Only thing is that I need to find out the actual motive behind the whole deal."

The moment Rashid opened his eyes he realized that he had survived the assault. Although, there was still pain in his head and the upper temple seemed to be slightly swollen. He checked for any other possible damage. Luckily, for him there was none. It had happened so fast that he was not able to react and even raise an alarm. The person who hit him had used the bamboo stick for the blow. Were they two persons? Yes. Now, he remembered more clearly. The one who hit him was wearing a green shirt and blue jeans. The other one was dressed in black shirt and trouser. They both had short hair and then it was blackout...

"He has gained consciousness. He is moving. Tell Mark, he has gained consciousness," shouted the little man who was peeping through the bars of the locked room. To restore his authority he held a stick which was compatible to his own size.

"Who are you? And why am I here?" said Rashid.

"Hey! I am the one who carried you all along the route on my back," said the small man with a sense of pride on his face.

"Why did you get me here?"

"How do I know? Only Mark will know. He knows everything. You want to meet him? I have already called for him," said the little man with a sense of satisfaction.

Mark seemed to be someone important amongst them. They had locked him in this room with a guard to keep a watch. Rashid realized that he had been abducted and was a captive. However, to his own surprise he did not feel any panic. The fear and all logical conclusions could wait for a while. As of now, he wanted to drink water. He felt very thirsty.

The little man promptly handed over a bottle of water which Rashid gratefully accepted. He almost emptied the entire bottle and when he finally pulled it away from his mouth; he realized that it had a strong pungent smell.

"Hey, why is there a smell in the water?" asked Rashid as he tried to sniff.

"Oh that! Don't worry it is the same bottle in which I had my country liquor. Didn't clean it before filling it up with water," said the little man as a matter of fact.

"You said that Mark has got me here. I want to meet Mark. Call him," this time Rashid sounded more authoritative.

"Welcome to our camp, Mr … sorry I …," said the person in the centre of the group which had just opened the other side of the iron gate.

"My name is Rashid," said Rashid who could barely see the faces of men who now stood so close. The only light available was in his room which exposed him more than those outside the room.

"Of course, Mr Rashid Khan. I believe you hail from Muzaffarnagar and are presently a student of a management institute. However, your mother and sisters are still residing in your home town. You have come with your friends to our lovely state for a holiday trip. So how did you find our state? Is it beautiful, ha?" said the person who seemed to be the important leader of the outfit.

"How do you know so much about me?" whispered Rashid as a chill went through his spine. For the first time he actually looked scared.

"Why, you thought that the tribals like us can only dance around the fire to entertain you?" laughed the leader at his joke. The others also joined him with the roar that went in the air for some time.

The leader introduced himself as Mark. He was the divisional commander of his outfit which was fighting for the liberation of a new state for its people. Their struggle had been on for many years and now they wanted to reach to the final outcome. For this they had realized that only the arms struggle will not be much of a help. They had to look for more advance modes. For this their own people, especially the educated lot, had to contribute and make greater sacrifices to fulfil the aim of free country for its people.

"That sounds great. My best wishes are with you. But, in all this how am I involved?" asked Rashid.

"Mr Rashid, we are almost same age. Hope you will not mind if I call you Rashid?" said Mark who indicated others around him to break off. Before others peeled off, Mark instructed dinner to be sent. He would have food with Rashid who he said was their esteemed guest and must be looked after well. Only the little man and one more person who was carrying a rifle stood guard as Mark opened the lock of Rashid's room and entered inside.

Mark sat on the chair next to Rashid. The room was not a classical prison. Rather Mark told Rashid that it was a type of guest room that they had created for friends who came to the camp sometimes. The room had a bed, table, chair, water camper, table lamp, radio and an attached bathroom. Only thing was that the room was at times locked from outside so as the guest may not leave the place on his own. Rashid understood what Mark meant. The bottom line was that he was not here on his own free will and neither did he have any rights to walk away from the place by choice. Mark offered him a smoke which he politely refused. Mark lit a cigarette and took a long drag. During this time there was complete silence where nobody moved and Mark kept staring at Rashid. Although, Rashid was scared to death but he was trying to keep a brave front. Suddenly, Mark burst out in a loud laughter.

"You know what? Many in my outfit feel that I have abducted you for a ransom?" said Mark.

"If not for money, than, am I brought here to bestow good luck upon you?" asked Rashid trying hard to sound acidic.

"You are really funny. Indeed, it will be fun to have you here," said Mark as if he was pleased over his choice of abduction.

"Till how long will I have to stay here?" asked Rashid who was finding Mark to be cynical man.

"Not very long Rashid. I hope so," said Mark and once again burst out laughing as if it was some kind of a joke. He removed his leather jacket to make himself more comfortable and Rashid noticed that his arms had a number of tattoos made over them. Mark saw Rashid staring at his arms. He started shaking his arms in the air as if he was dancing on some fast number. His potbelly also moved along with the rhythm of his arms as he shook his hips while his eyes remained close. His two guards also could not avoid looking at their boss. With a little bit of encouragement, even they would have also joined in this non-musical show. Suddenly, his mad dance stopped and he opened his eyes to yet again stare at Rashid.

"Do you like my tattoos?"

"Yes," said Rashid trying to be polite with him. He still wasn't sure if Mark was a dangerous person or a comical guy.

"In case, you too want to get a tattoo I can arrange for the right type of artist," offered Mark.

"No. No. I mean although they look good but I really can't have them displayed over my body," said Rashid who was finding it difficult to continue talking to this guy.

"Don't worry. You can get the tattoos made on your big fat ass and that way you can keep them as well as hide them," said Mark and once again busted in a loud laughter. His two guards also joined him. The trio stopped laughing only when dinner was brought in the room.

"Come, have your dinner," said Mark.

Rashid was little apprehensive. For the first time in so many days, his appetite had actually gone missing. He told Mark that he was really not hungry and would prefer to skip the meal.

"You liar. I know, you can eat mountains in minutes. You hungry dog," said Mark as he pulled one of Rashid's cheeks reflecting his affection.

After a bit of hesitation, Rashid took some rice. He still could not bring himself to taste the curry and the other items.

"Not comfortable eating our stuff, Ha?" asked Mark.

Rashid could only nod his head in denial. But then, Mark told him that he could try the vegetable curry and pulses which had been especially made for him. With food in mouth Rashid felt a bit relaxed.

"So, what all do they teach you in the management institute?" asked Mark.

Rashid was completely taken by surprise. He actually did not expect such a query from the leader of a militant outfit. His surprise was evident on his face.

Mark took a pause from eating and asked, "Why, can't I ask you such questions? You know what; I was a very bright student in my student days. I stopped attending school after my eighth standard. Who knows if I had continued my education, even I would be in one of the institutes like yours. What do you say, ha?"

Rashid decided to agree with Mark over most of his comments. However, he still had to elaborate his life in the institute, as Mark was quite persistent about it. In spite his remote background and life in the wilderness, Mark indeed was a sharp person. At times, to check the correctness of the information passed on by Rashid, he asked the same question in some other form and confronted him to the best of his satisfaction. It had been a long day for Rashid, but still, rather than being alone he was happy to chat with his abductor. Mark seemed to be more acceptable to Rashid as they shared more things about each other. Mark told him that he was fond of cricket and football. During free time in the camp, he played both these games with his boys. As frankness between them increased, Rashid complained to Mark regarding the manner he was abducted. At least, his boys should have avoided the physical assault. The dinner plates were removed but they still continued with their talks as the night progressed.

"You are a good guy. Why don't you join my group? We two can really have a lot of fun," said Mark and waited for Rashid's reaction.

"I think I will be better off closer to my people. However, we can meet sometime," said Rashid who could not think of a better answer.

Mark seemed to be seriously considering the option and he was quite for some time. Then he laughed and Rashid was yet again nervous. However, he mustered his courage and asked, "Why are you laughing?"

"Well Rashid, I will also love to meet you again but then who knows. Our shelf life is very less. When I joined the outfit, I was just fourteen years old. We were ten of us. One ran away and the rest eight died over the years. So who knows whether I will be there to meet you again? Even my luck may also run out."

Rashid was touched by what Mark just said. It is the situations which decide the person that we shape up to be in life. Mark was just like any of them, only his situation was a bit different.

"Why don't you surrender to the authorities? Try a fresh start all over again," said Rashid.

"Some of the people who were part of militant outfits in our state did surrender. A few were able to join the mainstream but a majority of others still are aimless. I do not fall in any of these categories. You know why? Well, I believe in the cause of my people. We have not been represented properly in the past. Our poor background led to more exploitation without any long term dividends. We now are aware of our weakness and also our strength. We need to get together and work on our strength and then we will win."

"Win? Win against whom? Is India not your country? It seems to me that your ideas are noble. You want to serve your people by providing them a better life. However, the means that you are using are not right. They will only lead to further losses."

Again Mark started laughing loudly. When Rashid gave him a questioning look he said, "Oh well! I was thinking that you give such nice speeches that we can use you as our permanent spokesman. What do you say, ha?

Rashid too laughed along with Mark. The sentry on duty also seemed to be relaxed as they felt that the captive had become friend of their leader. After some more chat, finally Mark got up to leave. He told Rashid to sleep well. Rashid could not hold himself and asked again, "Hey, Mark why did you get me abducted?"

Mark laughed as he moved ahead and then turned around and said, "You have a sexy fat ass and that's why we abducted you."

"When will you leave me?" asked Rashid without any fear in his voice. He felt from the heart that after all Mark was not a bad person.

Mark was no more seem through the iron bar of his room but still he heard him say, "Very soon. My friend, very soon you will be a free man."

Rashid's room was once again locked and the little man on duty was replaced by another older man who started snoring the moment the light in the room and the alley were switched off. He was no more scared and hoped that all this will end soon. With these thoughts Rashid went off to sleep least realizing that tonight a number of people will have sleepless night because of him.

In the meantime, Rajiv had reached the road head where he found the vehicle parked. In the dark, it was difficult to locate the shop. Luckily, he had brought along a torch which he now used to find his way till the shop. Max had arranged for the driver to sleep in the shop itself. Rajiv thought he would at least put the driver on alert to move at short notice, if required. On reaching the shop he banged the front door which was opened only after some period of waiting. The people inside including the driver wanted to verify Rajiv's credential before letting him inside. Along the shop there was a large room where the driver and the shop owner had made space for themselves. They were naturally surprised to see Rajiv at this hour of the night. They fired a volley of questions. Rajiv couldn't keep the secret any longer and told them about Rashid's abduction. The driver panicked and started murmuring his regrets to come so far along with them. He took out his mobile to dial a number.

"Hey! Is your mobile working?" asked Rajiv and immediately got the response as the driver nodded his head. He again checked his mobile but found no signals. Maybe, the signals of his service provider were weak here. The driver was speaking to someone in his native language. He seemed to be agitated during the course of the conversation. Rajiv in the meantime requested him to give him the mobile to make a call which the driver ignored. Finally, after few minutes of listening on to his caller, the driver handed over the phone to Rajiv.

"Sahib wants to speak to you," he said.

Rajiv took the phone and realized that it was Indra uncle on the other side. He told uncle about the way the incidents had happened. Initially, even uncle was taken aback. But soon uncle composed himself and assured Rajiv that he would personally come there to ensure that Rashid is brought back safely. He confirmed to call back soon. Rajiv did not have to wait for very long. This time when he picked up the call, it was Dhayan Singh on the line. His father had told him about the entire episode and he confirmed that soon he along with his father and uncle will reach the village. They would start in the early hours before the dawn breaks and reach the village.

"Max, should not have proposed the visit to his village if the damn area was so unsafe," said Rajiv.

"Well, Rajiv I am sure Max never meant to cause trouble for Rashid or for that matter to any of you guys," said Dhayan Singh.

"I know. But then, at times you feel frustrated seeing the situation beyond control," added Rajiv and kept down the phone with hopefulness of soon seeing Dhayan Singh. He contemplated the rationality of contacting the police but thought it would be wiser to follow that course with the consent of others. Then, it struck him to make one more call. He sorted the permission of the driver to use his phone and then called Father Alison whose number was stored in his mobile.

Father Alison received the call on the very first ring. Rajiv repeated the entire events to the Father. He seemed to be equally disturbed. He told Rajiv that his repeated efforts to contact them during the day proved to be futile due to the poor network. When Rajiv informed him that Dhayan Singh and others were coming over tomorrow, Father asked for the contact number of Dhayan Singh. He too intended to come along with them to the village. The words of Father Alison consoled Rajiv who felt that together they would be able to rescue Rashid.

Rajiv narrated the entire developments to the driver and told him to wait for the arrival of Indra uncle. The driver too felt a little better on hearing that his employer would be reaching shortly. Through the shop owner, Rajiv came to know that such abduction were not very uncommon in the area. Such activities were undertaken with the motive of extortion and he hoped that in the end the entire thing will get resolved peacefully.

By the time Rajiv returned, he found Esha and Arun sitting in the main hall. Rajiv narrated his entire conversation with Dhayan Singh, Indra uncle and Father Alison. He also told them that in all possibility the abduction was aimed to earn money and hopefully Rashid will soon be freed.

"Rajiv, there is something that I wish to share with you. After you left, even Esha and I went out. We went to Andrew uncle's house hoping to get some more information. There we met Max's cousin and she revealed an astonishing fact," said Arun.

There was a silence and Rajiv waited for Arun to say something further. But then Esha spoke, "I still can't believe what that girl had said. Maybe, she was wrong in her allegations. There is a possibility that as Max had involved his uncle, therefore, the girl was agitated knowing the risks involved and lied to us."

"It may or may not be so. Don't forget that Max is her first cousin and such allegations are not framed on own family members unless they are true," said Arun.

"Will you guys please tell me what exactly that girl revealed?" asked Rajiv who was completely clueless on the whole issue.

"Max's cousin said that Max was a militant and was caught some years earlier by the security forces with a weapon. At that time he was under eighteen years of age, therefore, he did not get a term in the prison. However, he was tried under the juvenile justice and served one year in the remand house. After his release, Max's whereabouts remained unknown to others for all these years. Now, that he had resurfaced his cousin feels that he will only bring trouble for their family," said Arun.

"And where do we all fit in his plan?" asked Rajiv.

"Come on guys! You really can't be suspecting Max like this. He is a friend and will mean no harm. Above all, I see no reasons for him to get us all here to create trouble, as his cousin suspects," said Esha.

"Yeah. What will he achieve by getting Rashid kidnapped?" asked Arun.

"Wait a second. Maybe, Rashid's abduction was under a plan which got somewhere misconstrued. What if they had planned to abduct all of us but failed in the attempt? Maybe, Max's absence is to prepare to round off the remaining of us," said Rajiv.

"That's ridiculous. What's gone wrong with the two of you? What will he achieve by getting all of us kidnapped, even if for a second, I go along with your theory," said Esha with the sense of disgust.

"Esha, that's the catch. Max has much to gain. The militancy in the region has almost wiped out. They know they cannot fight the government with guns. Therefore, if they abduct common people from other parts of the country, then they will once again draw the limelight and be in a better position to negotiate with the government. Such things are not uncommon and keep happening at so many places. Max looks like a clean person from outside and his present links with the outside world will help him to fulfil the aim of his organization. That way, he becomes a hero and nobody gets to question him. Don't forget, he was caught with a gun. You never know how many innocents he had killed during those days," said Rajiv.

"I can't believe that I am actually listening to you Rajiv! And you Arun, how can you possibly listen to all this crap?"

"Look Esha. Please understand. We are in a situation where even if we want help, it will not be forthcoming. We all are worried about Rashid's safety. And under such circumstances, we are just evaluating all options. And you believe me; I am the last person to suspect the integrity of a friend," said Arun who seemed to be hurt with the way Esha had accused him.

"In case, you guys are correct in your thinking then what should we do?" asked Esha who did not know what better to say.

"Well, we must stay alert till the time Hashnam and the others arrive. Also, we must inform the police. After all, Rashid's safety cannot be compromised," said Rajiv.

Arun and Rajiv decided to stay vigilant for rest of the night. Even Esha refused to go off to sleep.

Rashid suddenly woke up. He was profoundly sweating in spite that the night was cold. He dreamt of being tied to a pole as Mark stood next to him. Mark was telling him that if Rashid refused to serve his organization, he will shoot him. Before shooting him, Mark as a saviour wanted to tattoo his....

Mark had been rather too friendly with him last night. Rashid could not figure out the reason for this friendliness. He was sure that such hospitality was not extended to the captives. On the offset, he was not able to figure out the reason for his abduction. Had money been the motive, then, by now the aim would have been revealed. Though Mark seemed to be cynical but not to the extent to abducted people for meaningless chit-chats. Above all and most importantly, he knew about him and his background. Such information is obtained if one has some serious business in mind.

"Is anyone around? Hello! Is someone there," called Rashid.

"You weeping whore. Why can't you let me sleep in peace? What is it that you want?" the sentry guarding his door replied.

"Can I make a call?"

"At this time? Are you crazy? Who will take your call at this hour?" demanded the sentry who seemed to be getting irritated with Rashid.

"You let me make a cali and I will give you my watch," offered Rashid and hoped that the man will fall for the offer.

"If someone comes to know about this, they will kill me," replied the sentry from the dark alley but this time his voice was much softer.

"Promise. This stays between the two of us."

There was a long silence. Finally, he extended the phone through the iron bar and said, "Hand me the watch and only one call. OK?"

Although Rashid hated to part with his possession but then he had limited options. Once he got the phone he tried to recall the phone numbers of his friends. Arun had four zeros in his number and hence Rashid remembered it. He dialled Arun's number. A recorded voice told him that the number was out of reach. He felt that his luck was yet again betraying him. He typed a message hoping that the same would be received by Arun. He wrote that Mark had abducted him and he didn't know anything about his location or demands. The only other number he could recall was of Max and tried the same. After a few rings Max replied.

"Hello."

"Max," whispered Rashid.

"Yes."

"Hey! Rashid this side. They have brought me to some place and locked me in a room. Please help me."

"Rashid! So good to hear your voice. Did they hurt you?"

"No."

"Did they ask for any money?"

"No."

"Where are you? Can you describe the location?"

"No. I gained consciousness some time back and found myself in this room. Sometime later, their leader came and strangely had dinner with me. His name was Mark..."

It was so sudden that Rashid was taken by surprise. The mobile was snatched from his hand. He did not realize that the sentry had opened the door and entered the room. He disconnected the call and put the mobile on silent before placing it in his pocket.

"No more calls. You will get me in trouble."

"But, I couldn't even....."

"Shut up. I said no more calls. Now, quietly go to bed or else I will slit your throat."

Rashid realized that it was just futile to request this man. He had panicked. After five minutes another sentry came and replaced him. Maybe, the changeover of duty was the reason for his panic. Rashid hoped that his friends had contacted the authorities to get him released from this place.

None of them could sleep properly during the night. As the dawn broke, they decided to yet again to go and meet Andrew uncle's wife and daughter. The family was equally disturbed when they met Max's friends. The girl still seemed to be agitated and felt that her cousin had deliberately got her father in trouble. She had tried to call her father from their neighbour's house but his phone seemed to be switched off. She did not have Max's number or for that matter the number of his parents. In spite of her young age, she was boldly and maturely exploiting all options for the safety of her father.

"Are mobiles working here? We don't have signals on our phones," said Rajiv.

"Signals are only accessible if you go towards the road head or climb up towards that hill," said the girl as she indicated the direction.

They decided to go for the road head. That way, they will also meet the driver. The moment they reached the road head the mobiles were working. Arun saw a fresh message on his mobile.

"The message is from Rashid. He says that some Mark has abducted him and he is not clear of his present location," said Arun with excitement in his voice.

"That means Rashid is fine till now," said Esha.

"Let's try to call him. But, this doesn't seem to be his number," said Arun.

"Oh! He didn't carry his mobile. I found it lying in the room. He had placed it for charging. As such, Rashid hardly used his phone. Try to call on the number from which the message had been sent," said Rajiv.

Arun tried calling the number but in spite of the repeated rings nobody picked up the phone. Next, they tried calling up Max. A service provider's recorded voice confirmed that the phone was switched off. Now, it seemed that there was hardly any possibility to access either Rashid or Max. Rajiv decided to make a few more calls on the number from which the message had been sent. However, the status remained unchanged. Arun now called up Dhayan Singh.

Dhayan Singh confirmed that he along with his father, Father Alison and uncle Tomba had started from Imphal. They will be reaching the village in next two hours. Arun updated them about the latest developments. After a pause, during which he seemed to be talking to his father, Dhayan Singh told Arun to forward the number from which the message had been sent.

Now, there was not much they could do than to wait for Dhayan Singh and the others to arrive. They told the driver to be ready in case they have to move at a short notice. In the meantime, they went to the shop for a cup of tea. None of them actually had eaten anything since the last night. Just the thought that help was coming their way to locate Rashid seemed to make them feel a little better. They ordered for tea. The tea stall owner confided to them that he was also aware of Max's past. Rather, the whole village was aware. That was the reason that Max and his family had left the village. Apart from Max's father who sometime came, nobody else in his family visited the village anymore. There were rumours that Max had killed a number of people when he was part of the outfit. Some others say that Max had never really committed any crime during the course of eight months when he worked for the militant outfit. Max himself was never around to confirm or deny such statements.

"Once you join such outfits, then it is very difficult to stay out of their loop. Some way or the other they track you down," said the shop owner.

"But, I still don't think that Max has anything to do with Rashid's abduction," said Esha.

"Hope so. But what worries me is that he has still not contacted us. Both Max and his uncle should have come back or else called us," said Arun.

"You remember, he said that he knew who had picked up Rashid. He seemed to be sure of it. But I am wondering as to why he has taken uncle Andrew and the guides along if he has a role to play in all this," said Rajiv analyzing the situation.

"There are so many questions which seem to be unanswered," said Arun.

The guides had brought Max and Andrew uncle to the vantage point from where the camp was visible. It surely seemed to be a camp of an outfit. Apparently, it was another half an hour walk due to the undulating ground ahead till the camp. There was adequate vegetation in the area to provide them cover from the view. The camp appeared to be temporary in nature. Still, it catered for the accommodation and training of at least fifty cadres of the outfit. The inside of the perimeter had a ground which must be in use for training. Then, there were some thatched roof accommodations that seemed to be the living areas of the cadres. A few of the structures were of concrete and looked reasonably well concealed. There was no fencing to mark the boundary of the camp and neither were there any watch towers. Established camps usually had such security measures in place. As these things were not there, therefore, it was obvious that lookout men will be ahead of the camp location. They must stay vigilant and avoid the trails leading to the camp. Only one track connected the camp site and it too seemed to be in a state of disuse.

"Do you think this camp is the one we are looking for?" asked Max to his uncle.

"There is no other camp in the radius of fifty kilometres. The guides are both very sure of that," said Andrew uncle.

“Rashid said, Mark was the leader.”

“Do you know him?”

“Yes.”

“Should we risk going inside?”

“No. In case, the assessment of the guides is not correct then we will land up in more trouble.

Max knew that if they had come to the correct location of the militant camp, he will get the response. He moved further towards the camp under the cover of the dense vegetation to conceal himself. He made the perfect bird call as they had been taught. During those times, that was the mode of passing the signals amongst themselves. Probably these days, the cadres will be relying more on technological backups to communicate. There was no response, as he saw no movement in the camp site.

Max waited and yet again made the bird call. Eventually, this time he saw someone acknowledging his call from the camp. He was wearing black trousers and a combat shirt that was generally preferred. He had a crew cut and a slight paunch. The suspect made deliberate movements around the camp to clear initial identification. Max smiled as he could recognize the person. He had surely put on a few extra kilos. Last they met was some fourteen years ago. It was amazing that he had survived so far. Memories of all those years came back as a flash to Max. It seemed like yesterday when he too had wandered in these jungles. He had mastered to quickly prepare the weapon for fire at short notice. Max was good with his rifle. A small dagger was always tied near the right hip pocket for use, in case of some unforeseen eventuality. He loved playing with the dagger. While honing his skills, the frequent dagger marks on the tree bark often annoyed the senior cadres within the camp. But, he would still practice. He had mastered himself so skilfully that he could take anyone even blindfolded. Both he and Mark were considered to be the best amongst their lot. They were the quick learners and volunteers to undertake any task in spite of their young age.

Mark was now waving to indicate that all was well and they could approach the camp site. Max went back to the point where Andrew uncle was waiting along with the guides. Max insisted to approach the camp alone but then his request was turned down by Andrew uncle. However, Max took a commitment from Andrew uncle that while he would negotiate with Mark, uncle will not interrupt. The guides were told to revert back and uncle instructed them to tell everyone that they would be returning shortly along with Rashid. Once the guides left, Max and Andrew uncle also moved towards the camp. The sentries guarding the camp premises were instructed to let them enter. Still, as a matter of routine they both were checked. None of them had weapon and their mobile phones also seemed to be switched off due to poor battery charge. Mark stood along with his three guards and watched them enter his domain.

"So, you are again back?" said Mark and laughed at Max.

"Did you leave me with any choice?"

"Welcome. Max welcome to the camp. But, you should have come alone. Why get someone along? This basic was taught to you much earlier."

Max stayed silent for a while and then asked, "Where is Rashid?"

"Oh! He is comfortably sleeping in the room, I guess," said Mark as he indicated towards the place where Rashid had been locked.

"I want to meet him," said Max.

"Let's first talk."

"No. First I want to meet Rashid," said Max with sternness in his voice.

Mark signalled one of his guards to get Rashid as he sensed that Max will not discuss anything further until he sees his friend. Soon Rashid was brought to the place where others were waiting. The moment he saw Max, there was a sense of relief prominently visible on his face. He ran and hugged his friend while the others closely observed them.

"Thank god! You came. I was really scared," said Rashid and he meant every word. He had been thinking about his family and the pain they would go through in case he died.

Dhayan Singh called and confirmed that they were just about to reach the village. Arun, Rajiv and Esha had been at the tea stall since morning. By now, some villagers also came to know about Rashid's abduction. A few of them came to the shop and in their local dialect tried to extract further information from the shop owner. At present, the group could just be patient and wait. There was still no news from Max and Andrew uncle.

"How much money do they ask for if it is a case of extortion?" Rajiv asked the shopkeeper the moment he was over talking to the last person at the counter.

"Well, depends. In this case, the price must be pretty high. After all, the person is an outsider. And then, they would have done their share of homework to track their target. Who knows, what will they ask for?"

"See, I told you! There has to be a fire for all this smoke. This kidnapping is not a fluke chance. There is definitely more to it. You both heard what Max's cousin had to say. Now, even this guy confirms that the abduction has to be under a plan," whispered Rajiv so as only Arun and Esha get to hear.

"I am still confused and shocked," said Esha who had hardly spoken throughout the morning. Something within her still did not let her believe that they all were wrong to judge Max, as a friend.

Dhayan Singh parked his vehicle next to the shop as the driver of their other vehicle stood to guide them. Even before they could got down of the vehicle, the driver rapidly spoke in Manipuri and narrated the incident from his prospective. Father Alison was also along with them. The presence of all these people was an assurance to Arun, Esha and Rajiv that things will finally be resolved. They all sat at the tea shop. Rajiv narrated the entire incident all over again. One thing that he avoided to speak was about his own qualms on Max's integrity. However, he lowered his voice when he revealed what Max's own cousin had verified about his past. There was a long silence as the information was a shock to all of them, except Father Alison.

"Father, you were aware of Max's past? Weren't you?" asked Rajiv.

"Oh yes. I was aware. But then, you can't be suspecting your own friend. He was just a child when he got involved in this. They were hard times for that boy and he fought his way to come out of it. His past cannot be connected to the present problem at hand," said Father Alison sounding a little defensive. He was the one who had helped Max in those days to move ahead in life.

"Father, I am not pointing fingers. But then, Rashid is missing. Possibly by now chopped into pieces by some people who lack clarity. He has a family which is totally dependent on him for survival. All this worries us," said Rajiv.

"I know son. And yes, have faith in god. HE will restore peace and get back Rashid for us," said Father Alison.

"Let's go towards the location of the camp and see what best can be done. In case it is extortion, than by paying we may negotiate the situation. That's how it happens all the time," said Dhayan Singh.

"But, we don't know the location of the camp," said Arun.

"Oh! We do know the location. It is four to five kilometres from milestone twenty-five on the main road. That means we need to keep moving on this road for about ten odd kilometres to reach milestone twenty five. From there, we may have to walk in case there is no further connectivity till the camp," said Irom uncle who sat next to his brother.

"Let's not waste time and head for the location," reiterated Indra uncle.

"But then, how are you so sure about the location of the camp?" said Arun who seemed to be as confused as Rajiv and Esha.

"Well, the moment you forwarded the mobile number from which Rashid had sent the message, uncle Irom got its location tracked through the authorities at Imphal. In case, we are not able to resolve the issue by ourselves then more help will be forthcoming. So relax, we will surely get Rashid rescued," said Dhayan Singh.

Father Alison asked if Max's parents were informed regarding the entire episode. Arun told him that they had not. Father seemed a bit relaxed and said he was sure that Max will come out clean on this issue.

"Father, don't take me otherwise. But then, why are you so sure? Your judgement can go wrong," said Rajiv.

"No. I cannot be wrong. I have full faith in Max. He has fought against his circumstances to build a future for himself."

Indra uncle told his brother Irom to stay with Arun and Esha while they would head for the camp. In spite of Esha's arguments for being included in the group moving to the camp, Indra uncle did not agree. He said his stand would have been the same even for Shilpa. He instructed his brother that in case they did not return in the next four hours, then, he must get help as they had discussed. Arun was also left with no other option than to accompany Esha and in some way he did find rationality in Indra uncle's decision. The three of them decided to wait at the tea shop till the others returned. Then others started for the camp and hoped that Rashid will be safely rescued. Dhayan Singh again took on to the wheels as Rajiv sat next to him while the elders took the rear seat. Father Alison knew that there was much that Max's friends wanted to know about him. So he decided to disclose Max's past.

Max was a bright student in his childhood. His parents lived in their native village and his father taught in a school which was far away in the hills. Father Alison had known the family for many years and whenever he visited the hills, he would always come over to meet the Lotzem family. Max as a child deeply felt that his people in the hills were deprived of the facilities which others were extended in the plains of Manipur. Such disparity was evident during his few visits to the plain areas along with his father. Max grew up with the feeling to contribute for the poor people of his region.

Then, a turning point came in his life. That time, Max was just thirteen years of age. There were clashes between two sects of communities in the village from where his mother belonged. Almost the entire village was wiped out. This included a number of close members of Max's maternal side. He had grown seeing many of them and was very disturbed when he came to know about the incident. His mother used to cry a lot missing her dear ones. All this was tough for Max. He wanted to fight back the bad guys who had caused so much pain to them, especially his own mother.

Lotzem was not aware as to the impact this incident had left on his son. Whenever, he came home during weekends he did find his son quiet and a bit disturbed. He assured himself that it was a change which children undergo during adolescence. But then, it was not as simple as that. Max and few of his school friends one day went missing from the village. They did not go to the school which was about three odd kilometres from the village. No one heard where they had gone. Lotzem tried to search his son. He contacted the authorities but then nobody was able to trace these boys. Sometime later, unconfirmed news came that the boys had joined a militant outfit. There was no way by which the families could come to know the whereabouts of these boys. Soon, they came to terms with life that they would never ever see their children again. Then, after six months Max came home to meet his mother. Mother tried to convince him to leave the outfit. Max said that it was not possible now. He left his mother and sisters. Before he left, his elder sister warned him that his sinful acts would not only haunt him but will bring bad name to the entire family. They fought and the sisters said that he was a curse to all of them. Max vowed never to return home.

After three months, Max's elder sister lost both her legs in a blast while she was boarding the bus from Imphal back to her village. She had gone to the city to fill her forms for higher education in the City College. She almost died in this accident. Ironically, her recovery was far too expensive for the family to bear. Mr Lotzem had to take heavy debt to get treatment for his first child and the family was almost bankrupt. When Max came to know about the accident he felt very helpless. He had abandoned his family at a time when they needed him the most.

Due to the medical assistance constantly required by Max's elder sister, the family shifted to Imphal. In addition, in Imphal, Father Alison became a big moral support to the family, especially because Lotzem had to still work in the school in the remote hills. Max tried contacting his mother again. But this time, she also stood her ground that she will only meet him if he leaves militancy. Max contemplated the idea for another two months. Finally, he wrote to his father that although he wanted to return but did not have the courage to change the course of his life. He also informed him that out of the ten of them who had joined the outfit two had died while planting an explosive device. He was himself no more convinced with the cause for which they had picked up the weapon. He missed his family and wanted to be a helping hand to his father and others at home. Mr Lotzem discussed the entire thing with Father Alison who agreed to travel to the hills and meet the boy.

Father Alison met Max in the hills and convinced him to surrender. After a month, in a ceremony in which a top government minister was present, Max surrendered. He was just fifteen years of age. No major charges were framed against him as he was not involved in any serious crime. Considering his age, he was tried under juvenile justice and was kept in the remand house for a period of one year. After completing his term at the remand house, Max came back home. Father Alison recommended that Max be sent to a boarding school where he would be far away from his previous life. He also agreed to bear the entire cost of Max's education. Max was sent to Nainital for his schooling and later did his engineering from Surat before joining the management institute.

Max always lived with the guilt that due to his deeds, in some form god had punished his elder sister. She had soon learnt to walk with her pastorate legs and became a nurse. However, Max could not muster enough courage to ever meet her. He just hoped that one day god will give him strength to face her. Although, she had never correlated Max's acts with her tragic accident and still loved her little brother. One person who was still angry with Max was his second sister, Kim. She felt that the Pandora of family miseries was to the credit of her brother who himself had walked away while the others had to face the blunt.

"Now you understand why I am so sure that Max cannot commit any sins? In spite of the pain, he always laughs. All throughout his schooling and college days, he would not come back home. Rather he would pick up some job, however menial in nature, so as he could earn some extra money to support his family. Till the time he did not clear his management exams and took study loan, the boy just managed with two pairs of clothes. Had it not been his hard work, the Lotzem's would still be under heavy loan."

"I hope Father your instincts about Max are correct," said Rajiv while Dhayan Singh and his father quietly listened.

Rashid was overjoyed seeing Max, so much that his rationale mind did not even question the sudden presence of his friend along with his uncle. He was made to sit at some distance while the others spoke in their native language. He actually could not understand what was possibly been spoken between Max and Mark; however, he did gather that he was not the main topic of discussion. He had thought initially that Max will explain to his abductor that Rashid's abduction was a mistake and Max's intervention would set him free. But, nothing of this type seemed to have happened. He felt like a scapegoat. Mark and Max seemed to be discussing something quite different. However, what was been discussed was not very clear to Rashid. He still thought it better to quietly listen to these two. Maybe, some clues may actually come to light. Rashid was also no fool. He had made following observations about the situation at hand. Firstly, Max and Mark had past affiliation and they saw each other as equals. Next, Max did not seem to be in agreement with what Mark had to say, although, Mark was excited as he spoke. They did not allow others involvement in their talks. Even, Andrew uncle was sitting at some distance.

"Now that you have seen for yourself that your friend is fine, can we talk?" asked Mark.

"Mark, what is there to talk? Our choices are different unless one of us wants to imitate the life of other."

"But once we shared common choices. Remember, how we wanted to help our people and fight for their liberation," said Mark.

"Have you really been able to get any of them liberated? You know it is not true. All that you are is a leader of a group which extorts money and only lives for his survival. I have seen enough of it. This life can only leave behind regrets. Till date, I regret my past. Anyway, tell me what you want to talk to me about?" said Max overcoming his initial reluctance.

Mark seemed to be working over a plan. He was the regional commander of the outfit which was dying in terms of its spirit. The new cadres didn't seem to be well motivated. A large number of them joined because they are almost useless to the society. They have their selfish interests and do not care for any betterment of the society. This state had made Mark pretty unhappy. In addition, within the outfit his position had become stagnant without any further changes in status. He was still young and could manage the present status for some more years. But then, he cannot continue with this stature all throughout his life. As far as the sincerity for the cause was concerned, there was hardly any left in the outfit. Amongst the senior lot, the focus was on personal development and growth. Some had moved ahead and had established themselves in businesses or were meeting their political aspirations. They were alienated with their ground cadres who they were just using for their larger aim. Over the last few years, the security forces had increased their domination within the area and the scope for the outfit activities was getting further restricted. The number of surrenders had also increased over the years and the whole idea of having cadres was becoming meaningless. At times, people like Mark felt that they were being used like puppets.

Mark wanted to change all this. In last ten years, he has been the key person who had collected revenue from the area. The seniors within their group had not even bothered to check the details regarding how funds were being raised. They were just happy as long as Mark worked on ground to generate funds for them. It had been a tedious job for Mark to generate such huge amounts for the outfit. Today, many relented to contribute for the cadre, not because of the ethos of the cadre but because of the reputation of Mark. He was known to be a ruthless person. The outfit was having a free ride over his hard work. He had raised this issue amongst the seniors within the outfit, but they had not taken Mark seriously. They gave him a feeling that he was only good to carry out the ground work and could not be involved into the strategic thinking of the outfit. This had badly hurt Mark.

Very few within the cadre had come so far. He was amongst the few who had survived fourteen years of continuous ground operations for the outfit. But then, his efforts had not been appreciated. Now, Mark had decided to delink himself from the outfit and to start his own group. His group will actually work for the cause of the people. Mark felt that such a thing was possible as he knew the insight regarding the fund generation without which none can survive. He hoped to start his own recruitment and then expand in all areas wherever their people were living within the state. Even the main cities of the state could be influenced by him.

"Great! That's quite a lot of planning. But, I still don't understand as to how I fit into all this? And why abducted Rashid?"

asked Max and even Rashid looked at Mark as he was being spoken about. He had just no clue as to what was being discussed between Max and Mark.

"Well, if I have to start on my own, then, logically I need someone to assist me manage my financial world? And yes, as equal partner. Therefore, the moment I came to know that you are coming to the village, I thought I must contact you. But then, your schedule was too short and I could not risk moving out in open, so I decided to abduct one of the soft targets. And knowing you well, I was confident that you will reach out to get back Rashid."

"Look Mark, I have left this world a long time ago. In no circumstances will I ever get back to this. So, let's leave it at that and I will move out with Rashid. As far as my coming to the camp is concerned, the information is erased from our memory."

Mark tried further to convince Max that his proposal was worth considering. As such, according to him no man could run away from his reality. As far as Max was concerned, his reality according to Mark was a future for his people. He will have to do something for the poor people of his region and could not walk away from these obligations. Together both of them could achieve anything for their people. He had the power and Max had the intelligence which was a deadly combination. Max's education could be utilized to automate the financial handling of the large scale of money that their outfit would collect. They could even invest their money in international market through hawala. They will, this way, find means to convert the black money into white and also ensure that the supply of finance could be regulated in long term.

"Firstly, Mark let's get this straight that all this is your plan, so don't you address it as 'we'. And next, it is a stupid one. I will never get in this hell ever again."

Max now told Mark, who at some point in life was a good friend that he must rather surrender to the security forces. There was no future of all these things. Mark had survived all these years due to share luck which he must not try any further. The world around them was changing and there were so many opportunities for people which had never been there before. Under such circumstances, rather than staying isolated from the real world, an attempt to reconnect with normal life must be made. Even if, he makes a fresh outfit the end result will be the same. They will cause meaningless bloodshed and then once again someone like Mark will be born who will also aspire to have independent leadership.

As far as the cause of freedom was concerned for their people, the true liberation would only come with education, health, job, financial stability and such related issues. That is the only route to prosperity and well-being of people irrespective of their caste and creed. Nobody in the entire world can generate public support for any cause which leads to exploitation of their own people. Periodic financial collection from people in the name of cause is also a form of exploitation. Regarding the difference in views with the government, the only way to resolve the issue is through proper dialogues. Many of the outfits functioning in Manipur had already come under agreement with the State and the Central government. These cadres are being encouraged to join back the mainstream and over the years the response is improving. If the status of militancy is compared with other states of Northeast, they have made rapid advancement. Today, most of these states are free of militant activities and are progressively developing. The days are not very far when Manipur will also make equal progress. Therefore, the fight for the cause with weapon in hand and exploitation of own people will no more take people any further. Even our neighbouring countries that had been supporting such activities in the recent past to destabilize India, have come to terms that such orchestrated arms struggle will just be a futile attempt.

Max went on to further give rationale of the ills of such arms struggle within the state. For some reason, even Mark did not interrupt him. He had a smirk on his face as he nodded a few times during the course of this monologue. Max occasionally spoke in English and Rashid tried to patch up the pieces to understand as to what was conspiring between the two. He did make out that Max was not in agreement with Mark and was lecturing him better than Prof P K Das of their institute. Max's uncle, although far away from this controversial discussion was also in attendance to witness him speak. He had lit his local cigar and was puffing through his nostrils at the same rapid speed in which his nephew was speaking to the militant leader. Overall, both uncle and Rashid were impressed with Max.

Rashid was now confident that Max will get him out of here so he asked, "Hey guys! You have been talking for quite some time. Can we have some refreshments? I am feeling rather hungry.

At this junction when Rashid could be at risk, asking for food seemed to be a bit weird for Max. But before he could respond, Mark laughed and said, "you're right my friend. Let's have something to eat."

Mark ordered for the breakfast. He seemed to be brooding. Max had nothing further to say or explain. He told Mark that he will like to move out of there at the earliest along with Rashid. Mark insisted that he must have one last meal before he left. Max actually wanted to refuse and felt Rashid was stupid to ask for food at a time his life was being negotiated upon. Max again politely requested Mark to let them leave.

"Why, you think I would have poisoned your food? We were friends. In fact, even after so many years, I still take you to be my friend. Don't worry none of you will be harmed. That Mark promises to you."

"Mark leave all this and surrender" said Max almost feeling sorry for him. Mark had always been good to him and they were close friends in the past.

"You know what? I thought I will be able to convince you to join me. But look at you. You rascal! You are now more educated and a wiser man. Possibly can't be convinced by a man like me, who has spent the best years of his life in the jungles. Hah!"

"It's never late Mark. Even you can leave all this and see the world from the other side," said Max.

"Can't. It's not so simple. You were just a child when you left. I have worked for fourteen years with weapon in my hand. I did lot of good and bad things in this time. They cannot be wiped out. Especially, the bad ones. Even if I want to change the course of my life, it is next to impossible," smiled Mark.

"So what are your options?" asked Max.

Mark explained that he could no longer stay in this camp. He along with his five confidants will be moving out of this location shortly. Some of the moles within the camp were suspicious of his activities. He would not be surprised that a few of the men here in the camp have already alerted the senior cadre. He will move to a safe place. If required, cross over to the other side for assistance where he had some friends. He had kept enough money to back him up for quite some time. Once he stabilizes he will find new cadres for his outfit and then expand. Had Max joined, it would have been a bonus. But then, for Mark there was no turning back and no regrets. He did add that in some lifetime he too will also like to live a clean life.

They were quietly having their breakfast when one of Mark's boys came to inform him that a vehicle was trying to move on the track towards the camp. The track was almost in the state of disuse and had hardly seen much traffic over the years. That was one of the reasons for selecting this location for the camp site. Even if, attempt was made to drive the vehicle till the camp the possibility was low. The route ahead was really bad. However, the present issue was to find out about the intruders. Mark instructed his boy to send a team to get the occupants of the vehicle. There was a sense of hesitation as the boy had been taught not to get any trails back to the camp? Still, he went to get Mark's orders executed. Nobody knew this better than Mark, who had survived fourteen years of such a life that it was a risk for the security of the camp to get the intruders. But this time he decided to break the rules.

"They must be your people? Sharp enough to locate us. Hah? Let's meet them. Even I want to meet people of your clean world who hold priority over me," laughed Mark.

Mark had spoken in English this time to make it convenient even for Rashid to understand. Max and Rashid were puzzled as to how their friends had been able to locate them. Still, there was genuine happiness on Rashid's face. Max knew from experience that Mark was taking a risk and probably someone from within the group would question this judgement of having unrestricted entry in the camp. Therefore, they must soon make their exit from the camp. Mark did not seem to be much bothered about the whole issue. He narrated to Max as to how their friends who had joined the outfit with them fell in the hands of destiny. Out of the ten of them, only he and Max were the ones who still survived.

The guards at the main entrance of the camp indicated the arrival of the group that was being escorted. Yet again as per the drill, all of them were physically checked and their mobiles were confiscated. Prominent amongst them was the tall man who claded as a priest. Max was surprised to see Father Alison leading the others, which included Indra uncle, Rajiv and Dhayan Singh. They were brought to the place where Mark and others were present. There was silence for sometime till Mark laughed loudly.

"I must compliment you Max. It seems, you too have made quite a little gang of your own," said Mark in English so as everyone could understand.

"Mark, these are all very fine people and must not be held. At least, that is the minimum I can expect out of you," said Max as the guards in the vicinity started drawing closer. Even Mark noticed this and yelled at his men to fall back. Finally, there was only one man who stood guard with Mark and the others moved away. Mark signalled Father Alison and the others to be seated.

"So, you do not wish to take my offer?" asked Mark as he closely observed Max. However, Max preferred to stay silent this time. Mark again laughed. This time the laughter was for a longer duration.

Mark told his guard that the entire group be safely escorted till the road end. There was no point in further holding on to these people in the camp. Max would never join him and abduction of Rashid was only to contact Max. It was not aimed for the extortion. He quietly confided to Max that he too planned to leave the camp shortly before the things got dangerously out of hand. He felt that Max was lucky to have such support system of friends who could get him out of militancy. He almost envied Max for this as he knew his own situation was entirely different.

"Son, why don't you leave all this? This life that you have chosen for yourself cannot be for good. If Max can fight back, so can you," said Father Alison who had been sitting next to Max.

"Father, I am not as lucky as Max. There is no point of return for me," said Mark with a smile. There was a look of deep loss on his face.

To fill up the silence Mark spoke. He was also thirteen years of age when he had joined the outfit. There was nobody who stopped him to take such a bold step. His mother and father were killed in a tribal clash. The people who carried out those atrocities did not even spare his two younger siblings. Their house was burnt and he never could gather the courage to go back to the village again. He tried to seek help from his so-called remaining family. But, Mark's distant relatives failed to be of any assistance. When he tried to contact one of his paternal uncles, he was told that he was grown enough and must know how to take care of himself. After that he never looked for any family. He slept mostly in the open and ate whatever was offered in charity. Most of the times, he cried and prayed to god to end his life. He missed his parents very much and felt so lonely.

A shopkeeper gave him a menial job but in exchange he was just offered meals twice a day. Life continued for Mark where he waited from one meal to the other, which was never ever sufficient. At times, when he could not focus on his work he was beaten and locked in the small room that had as such become his home. He felt very angry with himself, the world and the god who had created him. Under such circumstances, he even cursed his own parents to have left him alone in such a miserable state. He did not like this life and desperately wanted to have a control over it.

Once some firing incident took place in the area near the shop. The police rounded up all the young boys who were found in the vicinity of the accident site. Mark was also one of them. He was beaten and locked in the police station and was released the next day. He decided never to return back to the shop and went along with one of the boys who had been locked up along with him. Both these boys had something common between them. They were homeless and were very angry with the way life had treated them. Soon, both of them found their way to the outfit where there were others like them.

All these aimless boys got fresh meaning of life at the militant outfit. The gun at hand gave them the feel of power and respect that had always been denied to them. Max was also one of them. His objective was to work for the people of the region and at that point of time believed that the power of gun will bring about this change. He still had some, idealism so to say. But the others had no space left for idealism. They were the ones who had been driven by hunger, humiliation and anger. The leaders in the outfit were also clever to understand this primary difference. Therefore, Max was assigned tasks which did not contradict the rightful ethics. He worked with seniors within the cadre for planning issues, especially the administrative ones. As far as the others like Mark were concerned, they were allotted more ruthless jobs. Most of them died early while executing such risky tasks.

Mark's conscience had stopped troubling him for a long time. He did not question the orders that were given to him and executed them with utmost exuberance. He did come to know when Max surrendered. He had always found Max to be a level headed and sharp boy. They had shared a good relation and discussed a large number of issues together. Still, Mark never realized that one day

Max will surrender. Almost all of them didn't regret joining the outfit. Although, Max was largely alienated from ground reality, still he too was passionate to fight for his people. His surrender was not taken in a good light by the outfit and a strike back to haunt him down was also planned. However, with time the idea was dropped and slowly all forgot about Max.

As time passed, Mark's name was dreaded and his credibility within the group increased. He was given independent responsibilities and he further became ruthless. Because of increased involvement in militancy his name also became famous with the security forces. Two years prior, the government kept a huge prize on his name. He was believed to have executed a number of massacres. As for Mark, he just laughed. He did not owe anyone any explanation but he only knew that he would never ever carry out such atrocities which had changed his own life. Irrespective of the charges on him, he definitely had committed a number of unpardonable crimes. Even god cannot pardon him for his deeds. He will have to live with all that till his last. However, there were no regrets. Only way he could counter balance his action was by doing something fruitful for his people. For this only, he wanted Max to join him. Together they would have collected all the black money from the bad guys and used it to help the poor. Now that Max had decided not to join him, he would single-handedly carry out this task. That was what he had decided to do and no one could change his mind.

Mark felt the firm hand over his shoulder, and it didn't take him long to realize that it was Max. It was not often that Mark had such outpour of emotions. Very few in the cadre would have seen him so vulnerable. But today, he did feel sad and had recalled his past life after a very long time. He was taught all along that this path was non-reversible. Max was an exception who had fought his way through and defied this unwritten code.

"You all must leave now before I have a change of heart," smiled Mark.

"Wish you luck," said Max who didn't know what else to say to Mark. They hugged and then Mark passed final instructions for their departure. Mark also apologized to Rashid for the inconvenience that was caused to him. As the group proceeded towards the exit of the camp, Mark too went inside his room. Nobody really observed that Mark kept looking at them through the small window of his room till the time they were finally out of sight. Once they left, he laughed loudly as he realized that his eyes were moist. He had not felt this way for a very long time.

Four armed men accompanied the group up till the road head. They were taken through a different route which was well conceded due to the dense undergrowth. To most of them, this time, the distance seemed to be longer, although on ground it was a shorter route. Their single line column finally reached the road head and the vehicle was visible which was parked at the road bend. As they all mounted the vehicle the armed guard retreated back to the camp.

"Is it paining?" asked Rajiv as he indicated towards the blue mark on Rashid's forehead.

"Not really. Hopefully, this mark by Mark should fade out after sometime," said Rashid. Others laughed as they realized that Rashid's funny bone was intact in spite the event of the last few hours. However, Max seemed to be in his own thoughts. He had not imagined that one day he will meet Mark and wondered what his friends must be thinking about him after all the revelation of his past life. They would have lost all respect for him and his family and must be regretting their friendship with him. During the remaining part of the journey, Dhayan Singh interpreted his side of story to Rajiv regarding the way they all had moved from Imphal. Soon they reached the location of the village.

None of them was prepared for what was about to unfold. There was a large gathering of people next to the shop. The crowd included men, women and even children. Some of the children were quite young to even find admission in the school. By the time their vehicle halted it was surrounded by the crowd from all sides. A young girl came near the vehicle tearing through the crowd. She looked very agitated and the moment she saw Andrew uncle in the vehicle through the glass window she started crying. Her tears were of relief. Rajiv whispered and told others that she was Max's first cousin.

When the occupants of the vehicle got down they saw Irom, Arun and Esha also standing on one side. They were relieved to see that Rashid and others had come back safely.

"What happened? Why are you crying? And this entire crowd? What is this all about?" asked Andrew uncle as he held his daughter with both his hands.

"I was scared for you. I didn't know what else to do. We were all so worried for you," said the girl who still was sobbing and tried to hold on to her father.

"What really happened? Why have so many people gathered?" asked Andrew uncle. This time he looked towards Arun who was standing in the vicinity.

After a slight silence during which nobody spoke, Arun narrated the whole thing. After Indra uncle and others left for the camp, a large crowd of villagers came to the shop. Andrew uncle's daughter led this crowd. They accused Max of getting Andrew uncle into trouble. The guides who had taken them towards the suspected militant camp had returned to inform that Max had taken Andrew uncle to the camp. The guides had also informed that Max knew the leader of the camp very well. They shared past friendship.

The guides felt that Max may have a role to play in his friend's abduction and he may also get Andrew uncle in trouble. A few others from the village also supported this logic. They accused Max of conspiring along with the militant outfit for his personal gains. His return to the village after so many years was also linked to his dishonest intentions. The villagers wanted to confirm these doubts from them the moment they came to know that Max's friends were waiting at the shop. That is how so many people had gathered near the shop.

"And you also thought that your friend was involved in this abduction business?" asked Andrew uncle looking at Arun with anger.

Arun kept quiet. He did not know how to answer this one. The fact of the matter was that all of them had their doubt on Max's integrity. Irom uncle had also discussed the issue of getting police help in case the others did not return in next few hours with Rashid.

"These villagers are uneducated and maybe stupid but how could you suspect Max? He takes you all to be his close friends. From the time Rashid had gone missing he has not even taken a glass of water," said Andrew uncle.

In the silence which fell, Father Alison was the first to hear the sobbing. His heart came out for the boy. He was reminded of the young Max who he had counselled some years ago. It seemed that the time clock had taken a full cycle.

"Max. Don't you feel like that! Everything will be just fine. You're god's special child who he loves the most. You just follow his path of goodness and don't bother as to what others have to say. The world had been unkind to even our holy father the Jesus Christ," said Father Alison.

"No Father. It's not as simple as you make it sound. I feel hurt. Look at all these people gathered here. All of them believe that I was involved with the activities of the outfit. Mark was right. You cannot delink from your past, no matter what you try," said Max.

The entire gathering did not expect such a harangues statement. They wanted to see a rugged militant and not a human being just like them who was hurt over such allegations. So they all quietly watched as Max poured his heart out. He said that he had joined the militant outfit as a child because he was made to believe that the power of the gun was always unchallenged and could bring about changes in the lives of people. He continued with this belief till the time he met Father Alison. Father told him that god will account him of his acts one day and if he wanted to bring changes in his life and the lives of others then he must change his course. He did follow what the Father had taught him and thought all along that he had made his life better. He aspired to be someone whom his family and friends could be proud of. But then, the reality was different. In spite of all his efforts, his past will always track him and ensure that people will always suspect him. So it didn't really matter that he had educated himself or holds any amount of goodness for others. Errors of life just cannot be erased.

Max felt that the same was true regarding so many others like him who had left arms to return back to normal life. The society will not let them return to normal life. They will always be reminded of their past and will be all along looked upon with mistrust. He now saw that his life was no different than that of Mark. Rather, at least Mark was clear that he has no scope to revert. Today, for the first time Max felt that he has rather failed in his life.

"Max, let me tell you that this time you are wrong. Yes, we suspected you, especially me. But Max, do you know why we suspected you? I will tell you. We suspected you because men like you who have the courage to change the course of their lives are rather so few. We read about them in books but we do not find them around us. And when they are actually around us we not only fail to recognize them but also suspect them. We have studied together in the institute for almost about two years but see how little we knew about you. We all assumed you to be a happy go lucky type of a guy. Your laughter could cover everything, your pain, sadness and fear so well that we never got to see the real Max. Many a times, Rashid used to tell me that you are lucky because you seemed to have no problems in life. He as well as all of us got fooled by your smile. Yes Max, you actually fooled us," said Rajiv as others also nodded in agreement.

"You are trying to boost my fallen moral? Right?" asked Max.

"Wrong. It's true that none of us were aware of your past background. But now that we know about it, we all are proud of you. And not only your friends but I am sure your entire village will be proud of you," added Rashid whose eyes were also filled with tears.

Esha came and held Max's hand and reassured him that the incident had generated more respect for him. Each one including Dhayan Singh, Arun, Indra uncle and Irom uncle also expressed their admiration for Max, which composed him further. His cousin apologized for suspecting his intent.

"I guess I spoiled your trip to Manipur. God knows what impression you all will carry of this place and its people," said Max.

Rajiv on behalf of all others assured Max that the trip would have been rather incomplete had they not undergone this experience. Max had stood out as an icon for the youth of this place whose footsteps others will like to emulate. He definitely inspired not only his own people but a large majority of people who think that it's difficult to change their circumstances. They all will go with very fond memories of this place and cherish the days that they spent together in Manipur.

By now, more people had joined the crowd that had gathered around to witness the entire thing. Their aggression had converted to respect for the young man from their village. It was time for the group to leave. Indra uncle instilled the urgency of moving back to Imphal as the group was to catch the flight next day. They bid farewell to Andrew uncle and others present and started their return journey. En route they came across the school children who were returning back home. Max was once again reminded of his own childhood and hoped that these children also get the same opportunity to outshine in their lives.

It was a bit warm outside as the temperature had suddenly gone up in the last couple of days. A few showers would again moderate the temperature as has been the trend. However, most of them would be gone from here by then. Inside the hall, the temperature was much better due to the wall air-conditioners that had been installed under Ramchander's personal supervision. The auditorium in the south block was almost full and the ceremony was to start anytime. Today, a renowned economist of the country was the chief guest. A few media persons were also present to cover the event.

Indra uncle with aunty were sitting along with Mr and Mrs Deshpande, Esha's parents. They seemed to have got along pretty well. Arun's parents were also suppose to come for the convocation ceremony but due to the ill health of his grandmother had to cancel their programme at the last minute. They would have to wait for some other opportunity to meet Esha and her parents. The young couple will soon have to work it out. Mr Deshpande had instantly liked Arun in their first meeting yesterday and had conceded to her daughter's choice. His wife who had spoken with Arun a number of times on the phone was more than happy for her daughter. Luckily, they both had got the job appointments in Bengluru and would be joining their respective companies by next month.

Rajiv had got the job offer from a company in Singapore and had been given two months time to join. Mr Deshpande volunteered to extend all possible help to Rajiv on his arrival. It would indeed be helpful for Rajiv to have some acquaintance in a completely unknown place. Before moving to Singapore, Rajiv planned to visit his brother in the States, who had recently got married to an Indian girl from Gujarat. For the first time, in last few months the interaction between the two brothers had become more frequent. Dhayan Singh Hashnam was moving to Mumbai to work with one of the largest company in the finance world. He had stood first in the entire course, out beating Ankit and Arun. Shilpa was excited to know that her brother will be moving to Mumbai. She had always longed to visit the beautiful city of dreams.

Rashid will be heading for Hyderabad and would start his career in the marketing line. He had presented quite an impressive module for market analysis as his final project which his company had found to be practical and wanted Rashid to assist them to incorporate the same for their products. He loved his very first recognition in the marketing world. Ammi and his sisters had agreed to move along with him to Hyderabad. He had already started planning in this regard. Today, he considered himself to be fortunate to reach such privileged pedestal in life.

Max was moving to Delhi for his new assignment. His initial job required a lot of travelling and he was looking forward to visit various places in North India. Ironically, there were no job offers towards the Northeast. Maybe someday, he would return to work in his own region. At times, he pondered about the idea to work in some NGO, but then, felt it was far too early to take this call.

The ceremony began with the welcome address of Mr R R Vankatash, the Dean of the institute. He then called upon the stage the chief guest to address the young professionals. The speaker gave them a few valuable tips for their fresh assignments and wished them luck. The top ten including Dhayan Singh and Arun where honoured by academic medals and a lot of adulation by the audience. Subsequently, there was ceremonial photograph of the entire course along with their faculty in the lawn outside the auditorium. There was indeed excitement in the air as a new phase of life was about to start for all these students who had passed through this premium institute.

"Hey guys! I hope we all stay in touch," said Rajiv.

"Definitely. In fact, we must get together once a year. What do you say guys?" added Arun.

"Get married soon and we all will have a good get-together," said Rashid and everyone laughed.

"Hey! We can meet without me and Arun tying the knot so soon. Marriage is not on cards before next year," replied Esha.

"Really! Then I must walk up and convince uncle to get rid of you as early as possible. As such, he is getting the best poster boy of the institute as his son-in-law," said Rashid indicated in the direction of Mr Deshpande who was busy talking to the Hashnams.

They all promised to stay in contact and Dhayan Singh proposed to open up a blog on the net to stay in regular touch. Tonight, a party was planned in which the parents of Esha and Dhayan Singh were also invited.

Max's phone was in the vibratory mode due to the ceremony but he was alerted enough to take the call. It was Father Alison's number. He had spoken to him last week and told him about this big day of his life. Father must be calling him to wish luck as always. The initial laughter died down soon and then Max seemed to be a bit serious. The others also noticed this change and hoped that all was well at Max's family front. Max mostly listened and had occasional questions. After sometime the call was disconnected. They waited for Max to say something as they could make out that the call had possibly disturbed him. There was a long silence and then avoiding the eye contact of his friends Max told them what Father Alison had to say.

Father Alison had read the local newspaper in which there was news about Mark. Yesterday night, the security forces had encountered a group which was crossing into our side from Myanmar. The group was led by Mark and was armed. They resisted arrest and all fourteen were killed after a pitch battle. A large sum of cash and electronic equipments were also confiscated by the security forces. They say this was one of the biggest catch of the recent times.

There was silence and all of them could feel the turmoil that Max felt. Finally, Rajiv put an arm around Max and said, "My friend you left that world a long time ago. The ghost of your past had to rest in peace at some point of time. You move on, as it inspires many like us."

They all knew that Max needed some time for himself. But he was a fighter as always and would move ahead. Max sat on the bench with little mixed feelings of his past and the present while the others left with the promise to meet in the evening.

INDEX